"ALL THE ENDS OF THE EARTH"

"ALL THE ENDS OF THE EARTH"

Challenge and Celebration of Global Catholicism

Jane E. Linahan and
Cyril Orji
Editors

**THE ANNUAL PUBLICATION
OF THE COLLEGE THEOLOGY SOCIETY
2019
VOLUME 65**

ORBIS BOOKS
Maryknoll, New York 10545

The publishing arm of the Maryknoll Fathers and Brothers, Orbis seeks to explore the global dimensions of the Christian faith and mission, to invite dialogue with diverse cultures and religious traditions, and to serve the cause of reconciliation and peace. The books reflect the views of their authors and do not represent the official position of the Maryknoll Society. To learn more about Orbis Books, please visit our website at www.orbisbooks.com.

Published by Orbis Books, Maryknoll, New York 10545-0302.
Manufactured in the United States of America.

"Mystical yet Political: A Liberative Encounter with God through Popular Piety," by Wilson Angelo Espiritu, is a reworking of a previously published paper, "Popular Piety as a Locus of Salvation: Towards a Mystical-Political Hermeneutic of Liberation," in *Pamisulu: An Interdisciplinary Journal of Theology and Philosophy of the Mother of Good Counsel Seminary*, 6, no. 1 (November 2018): 56–96. Used with permission.

"Decolonizing Ourselves: Looking toward the Gospel and the Margins," by Linda Land-Closson, contains portions of a previously published paper, "The Paradox of Privilege: Fr. Gregory Boyle, S.J., Relational-Cultural Theory, and the Expansion of the Margins," in *Jesuit Higher Education: A Journal* 6, no. 2 (2017): Art. 21. Used with permission.

Queries regarding rights and permissions should be addressed to: Orbis Books, P.O. Box 302, Maryknoll, New York 10545-0302.

Library of Congress Cataloging-in-Publication Data

Names: Linahan, Jane E., editor. | Orji, Cyril, editor.
Title: All the ends of the earth : challenge and celebration of global catholicism / Jane E. Linahan, Cyril Orji, editors.
Description: Maryknoll, New York : Orbis Books, 2020. | Series: The annual publication of the College Theology Society 2019 ; volume 65 | Includes bibliographical references.
Identifiers: LCCN 2019052517 (print) | LCCN 2019052518 (ebook) | ISBN 9781626983717 (trade paperback) | ISBN 9781608338351 (ebook)
Subjects: LCSH: Globalization—Religious aspects—Catholic Church. | Catholic Church—Doctrines—History—21st century.
Classification: LCC BX1795.G66 A45 2020 (print) | LCC BX1795.G66 (ebook) | DDC 230/.2—dc23
LC record available at https://lccn.loc.gov/2019052517
LC ebook record available at https://lccn.loc.gov/2019052518

A Tribute to Professor Lamin Sanneh

Before his death in January 2019, Lamin Sanneh was the D. Willis James Professor of Missions and World Christianity at Yale Divinity School. His work centered on the cultural and religious encounters between the North and South Atlantic. More than anyone else who wrote in the field, Sanneh understood the importance of the cultural repositioning of African (and Asian) Christianity and wrote massively, not on global Christianity, but on the birth of world Christianity. His project put the theme of culture at the center of world Christianity, which led to an increasing interest in this subject as a new field of theological investigation. In the years leading up to our conference, when we had decided on the theme of global Catholicism, Lamin Sanneh was very much on our minds. He graciously agreed to present one of our plenary addresses. In late December 2018, when we contacted him to finalize his topic, and he provided a summary of what he would present, little did we know that our phone conversation would be the best plenary that he never had the chance to give—he died a few days later, on January 6, 2019. He is now our new African ancestor in the faith. We remember him with fond memories and dedicate this volume to him.

Contents

Part I
Building Justice and Peace

Part II
Negotiating Borders and Barriers

Part III
Following the Footprints of God

Introduction

Jane E. Linahan and Cyril Orji

Catholicism is, in its essential nature, a global faith. The very word "catholic" implies a faith all-inclusive in its outreach to the peoples of the world. The belief that God's salvific intentions encompass every human person is based not only on the biblical texts that explicitly state this, but also on the very meaning of the gospel message, that is, that an all-inclusive, communion-creating love wells up from the depths of the Triune God and flows out to the very ends of the earth.

What this means becomes more vividly impressed on our minds, hearts, and imaginations as globalization increases our connections with the peoples and cultures of our world. An honest encounter with cultures other than our own also brings a heightened awareness, not only of how the Christian faith has spread and embodied itself in myriad cultures, but also of how that expansion has at times come at the cost of the violation of peoples and cultures, and of the earth itself. It is to be hoped that the past can teach lessons for building a more positive future. We are at a historic crossroads, a potential moment of grace: How will we chart our course going forward, in living out a faith that is truly global—in a world that is powerfully connected, yet deeply divided—in fidelity to the authentic meaning of "catholic"?

The intention of this volume and the convention on which it is based is to explore, not only implications of and needed responses to that very broad question, but also what "global Catholicism" means, in the concrete ways in which it exists in the twenty-first century. This exploration is necessarily open-ended and will not be concluded here, but possible directions for the future will be considered.

The themes of "challenge" and "celebration" were deliberately chosen, to highlight significant elements to attend to, with
regard to global Catholicism. "Challenge" and "celebration" are
in tension, yet complement each other, and both are rooted in
the gospel. The definite article was, also deliberately, left out of
the subtitle of the volume, to emphasize the openness: there is
no one-and-only that constitutes either "the" challenge or "the"
celebration of global Catholicism. The possibilities are endless.

"Challenge" may be taken in at least two broad senses, summed
up under the headings of "challenge to" and "challenge by." What
are the challenges presented *to* Catholicism by the world of the
twenty-first century? These include the call to acknowledge the
tragic legacies of a Christianity imposed by force under colonial
expansion, with the insistence that its Western European form
was normative for all times and places—to the devastation of
non-European cultures and traditions. These include, as well, the
call to learn what it means to be a faith that is inculturated among
all the peoples of the world, to learn from, and be enriched by,
myriad cultures, and to find new ways going forward that are truly
inclusive of all. And, not least, "all the ends of the earth" evokes
the reminder that being truly "catholic" implies responsibilities,
not only toward all the peoples of the globe, but also toward the
precious gift of the earth itself.

What are the challenges to be presented *by* the Catholic faith
to the world at this juncture in its history? This question concerns
the imperative to witness to the values of the gospel and to stand
against the violation of all of God's creatures, wherever this occurs around the globe. But it is also a challenge to be offered in
humility, love, and companionship, acknowledging that we are
fellow-pilgrims on a journey toward all that God's creation was
meant to be.

"Celebration," as well, is intended here in at least two broad
senses. Exploring the global dimensions of Catholicism ought
to lead to a profound appreciation of the many ways the beauty
of the faith has been embodied throughout history in peoples,
places, and cultures. The inexhaustible richness of their perspectives and lived experiences is to be treasured, shared, celebrated,
and welcomed into the mission of building up the Reign of God.

But what is perhaps most to be celebrated is the divine graciousness that grounds this richness and this history, including its present challenges. We are graced to be participants in the unfolding of God's plans of love for the human race and to be called to work in hope toward the culminating celebration of that love.

Our convention on global Catholicism was planned in the hope of raising up challenges facing twenty-first century Catholicism, as well as the vast richness to be celebrated. An intentional decision was made to invite theologians from the Global South as our plenary speakers, in the hope of affording our Society's theologians—most of whom are from the Global North—the opportunity to listen to, and to dialogue with, voices from other sectors of the Catholic world. We invited them to speak from the perspective of their own experiences of Catholicism in their own lived contexts. This provided the opportunity to learn from our sisters and brothers around the globe and to celebrate our one faith together.

This volume is organized according to the themes emphasized by our plenary speakers. Maria Clara Lucchetti Bingemer opened our convention by a reminder of what is central to the gospel, the "nonnegotiables" of Christian theology, justice and peace. Her lecture brings a Latin American perspective to the crises facing our times, and particularly the crisis of the identity and credibility of Christianity itself. Responding to these and finding God in the midst of their challenges is to be done by walking with the "little ones," just as the Incarnate One did, and as the Latin American bishops called the church to do at Medellín. Impelled by the "urgency of love," Bingemer writes, Christianity offers the mystery of "solidarity and communion," if the followers of Jesus "refuse to give up on investing in bold initiatives to build justice and peace."

The essays in Part I explore various dimensions of this imperative of justice and peace. Perhaps no symptoms of injustice today are more massive and portentous than the migration crisis and environmental destruction. In "A Green Church on the Move," James Dechant demonstrates that the two are closely linked, since destruction of land, resources, and food supplies has forced migration on vulnerable populations. He notes that "place" is essential to shaping our embodied being, and that loss of place threatens personal and cultural identity—as happens under colonization and forced dislocation. The church is called to acknowledge this loss and its cost, and to "listen to the voices of ecological refugees," because the places of the earth, and those who live in them, *matter*.

Continuing the theme of the intertwining of ecological and social justice, John Sniegocki's article places the work of Vandana Shiva, an ecofeminist activist and scholar, in dialogue with Catholic social teaching, particularly Pope Francis's *Laudato Si'*. Though there are convergences in their thought, especially in faulting the mind-set that reduces the earth to a resource to be exploited and that undermines the interdependence of living beings, there are also significant ways that Shiva's more detailed analysis of critical issues and attention to the lived experiences of women extends and deepens Francis's teachings.

Daniel Rober brings the thought of Argentine scholar Walter Mignolo into dialogue with that of Pope Francis. The former argues that the modern West has left a legacy of "dark deeds" that victimize the darker peoples of the world, as attested by the slave trade and the extermination of native peoples in the name of colonial projects of "progress." Mignolo's concept of "cosmopolitan localism," entailing "communal nodes" that cooperate from the local level—rather than the center-periphery model—has both important convergences with and divergences from Francis's ideal of synodality. Both offer needed correctives aimed toward subverting an (ecclesial) paradigm that maintains the distinction between the center and the periphery, with its attendant privileging of the former.

Tracey Lamont's essay titled "Postmodern Theological Curriculum Theory" follows this up by calling attention to the vulnerable "other" to be found in our very classrooms. It raises the important question about the assumptions that underlie even the way we teach Christian theology. Every teacher—indeed, every person of faith—needs to be aware of our built-in biases and to make a hospitable place for difference to be honored and respected.

Sister Shalini Mulackal offers a view of the state of Catholicism in India and sets the tone for Part II's theme of negotiating borders and barriers. Her survey reminds us that Christianity was already an ancient religion in India, prior to the arrival of Western Europeans. Over the centuries, Indian Catholics have found ways to coexist with other denominations and other faiths. Today, as a religious minority, their situation is tenuous, and, as with Christians throughout the world, they are called to address situations of injustice, sometimes even within the church itself. Their experiences shed light on pathways toward negotiating borders with the "other" and surmounting barriers to communion.

The other essays in Part II reflect on the theme of negotiating borders and barriers in various ways. Michael Hahn's essay points toward some hopeful possibilities for global Catholicism. He sheds light on how to negotiate the tension between safeguarding ecclesial communion and expanding and deepening that communion through authentic synodality. His explanation of key characteristics of such synodality suggests hopeful pointers going forward that can complement the ecclesiological vision of Pope Francis and "reshape ecclesial communion."

Stewart Heatwole takes up the important matter of inculturation as another avenue of possibilities for the global church. But he cautions against confusing inculturation with "cultural appropriation." Using examples from Saint Paul's dialogue with the Athenians, Heatwole lays bare the dialectic between "cultural appropriation" and inculturation, providing guidelines for recognizing and avoiding the former and supporting the latter.

In her research that resulted in the essay "West African Catechists," Maureen O'Brien investigated the real-life experiences of those who carry out an essential ministry. Her report includes segments of interviews that tell a story of the liminal nature of their status in the church and the challenges they face in navigating the borders between lay and ordained ministry, between their communities and the clergy—challenges, we might note, that play out in many settings across the world church.

Paul Schutz draws from the work of the Jesuit astronomer and philosopher of science William Stoeger to shed light on the vision of "splendid universal communion" described in *Laudato Si'*. In light of Christianity's historical links with colonialism and environmental degradation, Schutz goes beyond Stoeger to locate in Buddhism a "hierarchy of compassion" that can be a resource for addressing Christian relations with native peoples and the natural world. He concludes by reflecting on how a Christian appropriation of these pristine Buddhist ideas might become an act of atonement for the sins against native peoples and the environment.

The heading of Part III, "Following the Footprints of God," is drawn from Stan Ilo's plenary lecture titled "Reform from the Margins." Although they overlap with themes from the other sections, the essays in this section also bring our attention to the on-the-ground ways that Christianity is lived in the margins, on the borders, and in the everyday lives of ordinary Christians throughout the world. They underline the call to be attuned to what voices that are not at the ecclesial center have to tell us, as we explore anew what it means to be a world church.

Stan Chu Ilo argues against a static form of Christianity. He cautions against maintaining the old brand of Christianity, that is, a European-dominated Christianity overly concerned with ecclesiastical power and domination. Contemporary church reform will come to naught if its priorities continue to be shaped by this mentality. But Ilo thinks there is a way forward. To this end, he draws attention to signs of reform taking place outside the West and particularly in the Global South. He highlights the need for a "liberation historiography" that reverences the voices in the margins and calls us to a conversion from Western Christianity's "cultural hubris." Ilo argues for a reform that begins at the grassroots, that is open to the complexities presented by sincere listening to and presence to the lived experiences and sufferings of those outside the centers of power, and, especially, that is ready to "follow the footprints of God" among the peoples in the margins of the world.

Popular piety is of great significance in the lives of many of the world's Catholics, especially of those on the margins. Wilson Angelo Espiritu deals with a number of the misunderstandings and criticisms that have been leveled against popular piety, and argues that its practices can embody an authentic, lived relationship with God as well as provide fertile ground for movements of liberation.

Gregory Aabaa's essay returns to the theme of ecological crisis and how to ameliorate it. He argues that the Catholic faith must be open to a polyphony of voices, particularly the voices of indigenous peoples, such as the Akan of Ghana, who have a well-developed spirituality that guides their relationship with the environment. Catholicism, he argues, has a lot to learn from this native African wisdom with respect to eco-cultic practices.

In "Decolonizing Ourselves," Linda Land-Closson reminds us that "Northern Hemisphere Catholics" tend to forget that we are shaped by our dominant Western anthropology, with its values of colonization: independence, autonomy, dominance, and invulnerability. She raises the question of how well that anthropology coheres with the gospel, in addition to reminding us that it is not shared by everyone (or even the majority) in the global church. We would do well to learn from alternative models that underscore our essential relatedness—even with its attendant, and necessary, openness to suffering.

The final set of essays are from a panel on the work of the late ethnographer and anthropologist of South Asian religion Selva J. Raj. Although one of the themes of the panel participants is "transgressing boundaries and crossing borders," also emphasized in Part II, they have been placed here as a way of gathering up many of the strands of this volume and of leaving us with the call to attend to and honor the myriad voices and cultures of global Catholicism, and particularly, those at the margins. Reid Locklin introduces the panel by noting the significance of Raj's work and its attention to the popular practices of Indian Catholics. Raj was critical of favoring expressions of faith and forms of inculturation that are imposed from the top down over those that arise from the grassroots of lived faith.

The other panel essays attempt to develop implications of Raj's work for "a theology of the world church." Annie Selak describes how Raj is a faithful exemplar of the theological vocation, precisely because his "being present" to lived experience and to the reality of liminality was a faithful witness to the mystery of God in the diversity and complexities of the human situation. Susan Bigelow Reynolds examines Raj's analysis of shared ritual, especially as practiced at the grassroots level by Catholic and Hindu worshippers, for its potential as "embodied dialogue" that builds relationships, more than dissolving differences. Finally, Mary Beth Yount highlights Raj's critique of prioritizing the concerns of the ecclesial center over those of the faithful at the margins of power and privilege. She extends his ideas to argue for an ethics of "radical particularity" that requires actual presence among those in the margins and empowering the organic development of faith initiatives and "decision making at the most local level possible."

All of these are valued voices in a conversation that continues to unfold. It has no conclusion now; that is yet to come. We wait together in hope. May we be good listeners, faithfully heeding the promptings of the Spirit to be heard in *every* voice.

Acknowledgments

We wish to express our gratitude to everyone who contributed to this volume and to the success of our 2019 annual convention on global Catholicism. Thank you to all who attended and who presented papers, and especially to all who submitted their work for this volume. A great debt is owed, as well, to those who served as peer reviewers: their help was essential to this project and is deeply appreciated. We are grateful for the invaluable help, advice, and support offered by editors of past annual volumes, especially Elena Procario-Foley and Phil Rossi. Very special thanks is owed to Bill Collinge, director of publications for the College Theology Society, and to Jill O'Brien, our editor at Orbis Books, for their editorial expertise, without which this volume would not have made it to publication. Our convention was so blessed by the presence and words of our plenary speakers, who literally did come from "the ends of the earth" to be with us. And our deepest gratitude goes to David Gentry-Akin, past executive director of CTS National Conventions, for supporting our vision from the beginning and encouraging us to "think big" in realizing it.

PART I

BUILDING JUSTICE AND PEACE

Justice and Peace, the Nonnegotiables of Christian Theology

A Latin American Perspective

Maria Clara Lucchetti Bingemer

The times we live in are undergoing several crises. One is a profound *ethical* crisis. References to ethics are ubiquitous today, and we can find ethical committees in all sorts of public and private institutions. But in general, ethics no longer refers to a system of values that configures life, as was the case in ancient and premodern times.

In premodernity, "morality" was theological, which means that "morality" was God, and faith was the reason for practicing virtue. Thus, human beings were first of all at the service of God. Service to other human beings went together with service to God, but following as a second order. The world was theocentric and "full of gods," as the Greeks said.[1] With the arrival of modernity, a process of separating morality from religion began. Humanity, no longer religion, constitutes the touchstone for secularized human development. Morality, understood as being an extremely individual matter, consists in duties to oneself—it aims at personal improvement, thus enhancing individual autonomy.

The second is a *cultural* crisis. Our time is characterized by uncertainty and insecurity, with a dearth of stable and solid positions in society and a lack of clear identities as individuals and communities. Because of the possibility of different moral codes and belief systems, there are no longer any certainties or absolute truths. We are in the midst of a plurality in which nothing is categorically affirmed, and we sometimes feel we are on unstable ground when it comes to reflection and knowledge.

One of the great challenges of the postmodernity in which we live, perhaps unprecedented, is the relativization of this whole state of affairs. We are immersed in diversity and plurality, situated within a weak, negligent, and impotent institutionalization of differences, with their resulting fugacity, malleability, and short life-spans. The problem of lacking a clear identity mostly emerges from the difficulty of sustaining any kind of long-term identity. Everything is fleeting; nothing is forever.

The third is a *religious* crisis. The thirst for transcendence and spirituality is widespread today. The crisis of modernity and the advent of so-called—properly or improperly—postmodernity rescued the absolute that modernity intended to banish and extinguish, according to the prophecies of the masters of suspicion: Freud, Marx, and Nietzsche.[2] But it is, however, a faceless absolute without definite and precise contours or the thickness of an institution.

Human beings who lived through the crisis of modernity, or who were born at its climax, and now swim in postmodern waters are—according to Danièle Hervieu-Leger[3]—like "pilgrims" who walk through the intricacies of all the different religious proposals, having no problem moving from one to the other, or at times making their own religious creation with elements of several or even many existing religions. A great number would even declare themselves without religion, but not without faith, as says recent research on the new ways of believing, such as the Brazilian census of 2010.[4]

Within this religious crisis, and linked to the previous two, I would point to a fourth one, speaking now from within Christianity: an *ecclesial* crisis. This statement has to do particularly with the Catholic Church, but also with the historic Christian churches and even with some trends of the Pentecostal world. The Catholic Church is living through moments of deep crisis, with myriad sexual abuse scandals and financial woes.

For the first time, this church has a pope from the south of the world, with a different style of governing and communication. His steadiness in reforming the church is undoubtedly something that produces hope, at least for many people in the church, and many more outside the church. But we cannot ignore or deny that the sexual abuse crisis is deep and very serious.

There is no region in today's church that is protected from that scandal. Although most cases that have appeared in the media are related to abuses that took place in the North, we have in Latin America the case of the Chilean Church, a well-respected institution that had struggled against dictatorship with courage and prophetic attitudes.

The church's sexual abuse scandal is no longer episodic, something that happens only here and there, once in a while. It is something structural, which allows us to question if institutional Christianity today, the way it is organized and configured, truly has a future. Or if, on the contrary, it is time now to rethink and reinvent the community of those who follow Jesus Christ, in order to help people overcome desolation and again experience hope and joy in being Christians and belonging to the church. The future of the Christian church is the issue I want to address in this text.

Christianity in Today's Crisis

Christianity's crisis apparently goes together with the crisis of institutionalized religion in general. And Christianity has been not only a religion but also a culture and the civilizational matrix of half of the world. It is not unconnected with the political systems with which it has been identified throughout time. Christianity shaped the West as culture and worldview. And we cannot evaluate this fact as negative, but we also cannot fail to see it critically.

According to the French Dominican theologian Christian Duquoc, Christianity today must overcome obstacles that are due not so much to its failures as to its successes.[5] Among them, perhaps the most important is the transition from persecuted faith, hidden in the catacombs, to the official religion of the Roman Empire. The Constantinian shift, which happened in the fourth century, changed the destiny of the Christian faith. Many authors have reflected on that, albeit never with enough emphasis.

While primitive Christianity had withdrawn from all desire for social and political domination, the conversion of the Roman Empire was understood by the official church as an achievement destined to transform the whole world. The evangelical mandate to announce the gospel to every creature was interpreted as a socio-political-religious task, which resulted in the colonial project in other continents (Latin America, Asia, and Africa), erecting Europe, its culture, and its inhabitants as the paradigm for all humanity. The model resulting from this movement was Christendom, which came to be almost the terrestrial form of an institutional messianism.

The evangelical movement truly seemed to build a "global" Christianity. But was it truly global? What about the local and particular cultures affected by the violence of the colonizers, together with the annulment of their divinities and religions? The Christianity brought by the Europeans to *América*—for instance—appeared to the indigenous peoples' eyes as a war between people and gods, due to a henotheist mentality in relation to the Aztec world, as Octavio Paz and other thinkers have noted.[6]

The general perception of the indigenous peoples was that they were being confronted by an invader and an enemy world protected by strange, foreign gods who were also enemies.[7] In this context, the cross, the Virgin Mary, the saints—all that constituted Catholicism, the religion of the colonizer—appeared to the Amerindian world as the symbol of the strength of their enemies and the cause of their defeats and losses in an obviously unjust war.[8]

The Second Vatican Council and the period that followed it addressed the great temptation that lay in that model of Christendom. The council opened the possibility of a new era, "a breath of unexpected spring"[9] for the church, as John XXIII said. The council documents show that it is only possible to recover the credibility of the Christian proposal if the nostalgia of a glorious past is overcome and Christians commit to rededicating themselves to the original project of Jesus, with his Jewish origin, his humble and loving service, his frail community—at the same time vulnerable but faithful—and his luminous hope for the world in which he lived.

The early Christian community had to live in painful disappointment stemming from the failure of the Master, crucified as an evildoer. This initial desolation was overcome with the hope brought by faith in the resurrection of Jesus. In the beginning it took the form of the expectation of an immediate future: the second coming of the Crucified One, risen and exalted in glory, who would renew all things.

Christianity lived this way for four centuries, evolving from a hope of an immediate Parousia to an expansion of this same Parousia, delayed in time, but remaining on the horizon as a driving inspiration. The persecutions generated thousands of martyrs who shed their blood and witnessed before diverse authorities their faith in Jesus.

The Second Vatican Council intended to rescue these origins, these sources. This could have raised the suspicion of there being an intention of simply repeating the past. In Jon Sobrino's words, we hear a valid warning not to remain attached to the past, since there are no absolutizations. For "yesterday and today and tomorrow imply temporality and are essential for human being. . . . But if one of these moments is absolutized, or if one of them is presented with exclusion of others, temporality is not humanized."[10]

In fact, we learn from history that "there are pasts which bury history and are like chains that imprison. And there are pasts that are history-triggers, like springs that propel forward."[11]

So it is with the past of Jesus of Nazareth and his early followers. It is a source of living water that delivers and feeds. It is also the constitutive element of any future that may or should have a Christianity still worthy of that identity and name. For this we must return to the faith tradition's sources and recover hope. In this, the Hebrew source helps us. Messianic hope must be recovered, not in a merely political or intellectual sense, but in a sense that integrates the mystical elements of faithfulness and love.

Marc-Alain Ouaknin, in his book *The Ten Commandments,*[12] says that the Ten Commandments are not just injunctions or prohibitions. On the contrary, they are the bearers of a dynamic ethic of the future: to be more, to live better, to give substance to the word, to open to unprecedented fecundities. They carry a whole conception of the biblical person and his or her relations with others: another man or woman; a parent or child; another person, my neighbor, known or unknown; another who is God; and also relations with nature, work, and Scripture. Commenting on the Fourth Commandment, Ouaknin says: "Remember your future."[13] By that, he would mean—as I interpret it—that it is not impossible for a faith tradition to recover its credibility, if it overcomes nostalgia and any other obstacle that represses its original project. Perhaps this is how it recovers its breath of hope: by making memory of the future, of what is coming and is the content of our hope.[14]

The genius of the messianic hope is not to separate the elaboration and the proclamation of the concept of humanity from the representation of the future, nor to separate the latter from a critique of the conditions of experience. The proclamation and representation of Christianity have a proper name: Jesus of Nazareth. His mystery affirms that it is possible to meet God in humanity. The possibility of living transcendence and the primacy of the Holy Spirit is human flesh, inserted into time and space. This is what humanity aspires to, and the Christian faith affirms that it took place in Jesus of Nazareth. Therefore, his past is our future.

It is therefore possible, despite all appearances to the contrary, for the Christian faith to regain its credibility, under the condition of overcoming the nostalgia of a hegemony of Christendom that only distorted and harmed it. Perhaps in this way it will recover the breath of provocative and fresh hope that says that remembering the past is an inescapable part of living the present and building the future responsibly.[15]

This is our challenge today. In the midst of this crisis, what is the way to rescue the purity and freshness of Christianity—that is, its identity? What can we see as a future for Christianity in today's world? What are the nonnegotiable elements that can make Christianity still worth living and proclaiming today?

Christian Faith: God in History and in Human Flesh

What is the imprescriptible core of Christianity, the nucleus of the gospel of Jesus of Nazareth and the corresponding image of God? The indispensable and nonnegotiable of Christianity is the care of the other: The Other, with a capital letter, who is God and also any human being. But also the other besides us, and mostly the vulnerable other: the poor, the widow, the orphan, the stranger. God-in-Godself is ineffable, unspeakable, but God in Jesus Christ wanted to show God's closeness to the human being, in all its ambiguity, and therefore through God's revelation, we can discover God in the little ones (Mt 25:40). We can discover God, not from a metaphysical and ontological a priori, or from a simply moral, legal, or liturgical a posteriori, but fundamentally from an ethical perspective. The incarnated Word is that a priori. Jesus Christ, with his Incarnation, has desacralized the sacred and has sacralized human beings.

We are facing a process of losing the words for speaking about the God of the Western Judeo-Christian tradition. We often think that God is present only in what is explicit in our religion, but God is present in the implicit. Because God's ways are not our ways, God is always present incognito. In our concrete time and space, the approach to, and recognition of, the other are the great opportunity God offers us, in the same movement in which we remember God and make memory of our neighbor. However, the estrangement from or denial of the other are indisputable signs of our forgetfulness of God and neighbor.

God is experienced by the grammars of all times, but the grammar of universal brotherhood and sisterhood is the only one that can be expressed in human language, which speaks in one single movement of God the Father and all human beings. The grammar of love—unlike all others, which are usually exclusive and self-referential—is inclusive and defends equality and justice in difference. The true knowledge of God consists then in the daily practice of mercy, which is, in reality, knowledge of God through the recognition of the neighbor.[16]

Judeo-Christian revelation can confirm this. In portraying God as vindicator of the poor and the oppressed, the Old Testament makes it clear that a close connection exists between justice and the revelation of God. The New Testament expands this revelation not only in the person of Christ, "who became poor for our sake so that by his poverty we might become rich" (2 Cor 8:9), but also in that song of Christian identity containing the longest definition of God in the Bible, sung by a woman's lips: he is the "mercy that . . . brings down the powerful from their thrones and lifts up the lowly; that fills the hungry with good things and sends the rich away empty" (Lk 1:50–53). This revelation is incompatible with the cult of the god of wealth (Mt 6:24) because the true owners of the Kingdom of God are the poor (Lk 6:20).

Thus we find, near the end of the New Testament, the only

biblical phrase that speaks not of what God does but of who God is: "God is Love" (1 Jn 4:16). We know the reality of love and goodness not by speculating about them but by seeing them at work. We understand their meaning when they touch us and move us. That is what a "narrative theology" attempts to explain.[17] And that is the reason why this way of doing theology is more and more considered a good alternative to the speculative way.[18]

Both *agape* and charity are at odds with our most frequent experience of love, which the Greeks called *eros*. Almost all of the *agape* that we humans possess springs from our *eros,* which it then transforms. That can often be seen in the love of couples for one another or in the love of parents for their children. Nevertheless, the ambiguity of our erotic desires has led many thinkers (from Aristotle on) to claim that the most complete experience of disinterested love is to be found in friendship—*philia*—or at least in some forms of friendship.

Claiming that "God is love" de-authorizes any instrumentalization of cultic worship. As human beings, we are incapable of giving God anything that is worthy of God. The only thing God asks of us is a little trust and a firm resolve to love one another as equals. This is a theme that evolves marvelously in the Old Testament, reaching its apex in Isaiah 58:

> Is not this the kind of fasting I have chosen: to loose the chains of injustice and untie the cords of the yoke, to set the oppressed free and break every yoke? Is it not to share your food with the hungry and to provide the poor wanderer with shelter—when you see the naked, to clothe them, and not to turn away from your own flesh and blood? Then your light will break forth like the dawn, and your healing will quickly appear; then your righteousness will go before you, and the glory of the LORD will be your rear guard. Then you will call, and the LORD will answer; you will cry for help, and he will say: Here am I. (Is 58:6–9)

Therefore, the human attitude that is both a consequence of that encounter with God and a preparation for it in fullness consists in the willingness to fight for justice, fraternity, and equality among all human beings. If people are involved in this struggle, then they need not worry about whether they believe they can find God or not. According to the New Testament, they have already found God even if they do not realize it (Mt 25:31–46; 1 Jn 4). When God gives Godself to humankind as Father, the first result (and best proof) of that donation is full equality among human beings as among sisters and brothers. It is as if God were telling us: "I have come down to you, but now you must bend down toward those who are below you or far from you." Equality is the most religious, the most theological, and the most Christian of all human longings because reason is incapable of justifying it. Nature is full of examples of inequalities, so we must recognize that a qualitative leap is taken in human beings. Since humans are "transcendent" with respect to nature, inequalities in the natural world cannot be used as arguments to justify human inequalities.[19]

According to the theological-anthropological perspective, which states that human flesh is forever dwelling in God's being and life with the Incarnation of the Word in Jesus of Nazareth, the Christian indispensable must be found in that human flesh and not elsewhere. That makes the Christian indispensable something structural that is shared by all human beings, founded on the Holy Spirit, who makes all creatures capable of God as creatures of the same Father in heaven. This structural condition and capacity, despite being universal, must be incarnated in time and space, although the use of images is always ambiguous and can build idols instead of icons. Regardless, it is imperative to run the risk.

The Latin American Proposal: A Starting Point for a Global Project

In Latin America, in the year 1968, there was a local proposal for a new way of conceiving Christian life and church belonging. It happened in Medellín, Colombia, at the Second General Meeting of the Conference of Latin American Bishops (CELAM). It was a local project. The church of the continent desired to no longer be a projection of the European church, but wanted to live according to its own features and characteristics, discovering and projecting a new and more authentic face.

That meant following Vatican II's orientations. On September

11, 1962, one month before the beginning of Vatican II, Pope John XXIII broadcast a radio message that surprised both the church and the wider world. He affirmed: "Where the underdeveloped countries are concerned, the Church presents herself as she is. She wishes to be the Church of all, and especially the Church of the poor."[20]

Thanks to the pope's words, the idea of the church of the poor broke through. The council opened up new paths for that. The legacy of Vatican II, found especially in the pastoral constitution *Gaudium et Spes*, calls attention to the duty of being attentive to the human as the heart of the church's vocation and mission. According to the opening words of that document, "The joys and the hopes, the griefs and the anxieties of the men of this age, *especially those who are poor or in any way afflicted*, these are the joys and hopes, the griefs and anxieties of the followers of Christ. Indeed, nothing genuinely human fails to raise an echo in their hearts. For theirs is a community composed of men."[21]

Gaudium et Spes also speaks about the conditions that make a human life truly human:

> There is a growing awareness of the exalted dignity proper to the human person, since he stands above all things, and his rights and duties are universal and inviolable. Therefore, there must be made available to all men everything necessary for leading a life truly human, such as food, clothing, and shelter; the right to choose a state of life freely and to found a family, the right to education, to employment, to a good reputation, to respect, to appropriate information, to activity in accord with the upright norm of one's own conscience, to protection of privacy and rightful freedom even in matters religious. Hence, the social order and its development must invariably work to the benefit of the human person if the disposition of affairs is to be subordinate to the personal realm and not contrariwise, as the Lord indicated when He said that the Sabbath was made for man, and not man for the Sabbath. This social order requires constant improvement. It must be founded on truth, built on justice and animated by love; in freedom it should grow every day toward a more humane balance. An

improvement in attitudes and abundant changes in society will have to take place if these objectives are to be gained.[22]

That was the direction indicated by the reception of the 1968 council in Medellín. It led to a structural critique of an evangelization conducted by and for the elites.[23] The new proposal for the continental church in the following years supposed a new way of conceiving the whole church, which would now turn preferentially toward the victims of inequality, injustice, oppression, and institutionalized violence.

The bishops took as the starting point for their conference the question: "What does it mean to be a Christian in a continent of poor and oppressed people?"

> The Latin American bishops cannot remain indifferent in the face of the tremendous social injustices existent in Latin America, which keep the majority of our peoples in dismal poverty, which in many cases becomes inhuman wretchedness. A deafening cry pours from the throats of millions of men, asking their pastors for a liberation that reaches them from nowhere else. "Now you are listening to us in silence, but we hear the shout which arises from your suffering," the Pope [Paul VI] told the "campesinos" in Colombia.[24]

Following the pope's invitation and inspired by the spirit of the council, the church in Latin America assumed its vocation and destiny to be the source of a new ecclesial model based on the biblical binomial: faith and justice. "There are in existence many studies of the Latin American people. The misery that besets large masses of human beings in all of our countries is described in all of these studies. That misery, as a collective fact, expresses itself as injustice which cries to the heavens."[25]

In the "Presentation of the Conclusions" document, the bishops gathered in Medellín stated that "the Latin American Church has a message for all the men who in this continent have 'hunger and thirst for justice.'" Recognizing the situation of injustice under which the Latin American peoples lived, the document pointed out the causes of that injustice, rooted in the exhaustion of the transforming potential of both capitalism and Marxism.

The option for the poor was then inaugurated; at the same time, the continent was in a situation of institutionalized violence. The bishops declared:

> We ought to sharpen our awareness of our duty of solidarity with the poor, to which charity leads us. This solidarity means that we make ours their problems and their struggles, that we know how to speak with them. This has to be concretized in criticism of injustice and oppression, in the struggle against the intolerable situation which a poor person often has to tolerate, in the willingness to dialogue with the groups responsible for that situation in order to make them understand their obligations.[26]

Earlier in the same chapter, they wrote:

> We wish the Latin American Church to be the evangelizer of the poor and one with them, a witness of the value of the riches of the Kingdom, and the humble servant of all our people. His pastors and other members of the People of God will give their life, their words, their attitudes and their action, the necessary coherence with the evangelical demands and the needs of Latin American men.[27]

The subtitle, "Preference and Solidarity," points to the roots of what will be called the preferential option for the poor:

> The Lord's distinct commandment to "evangelize the poor" ought to bring us to a distribution of resources and apostolic personnel that effectively gives preference to the poorest and most needy sectors and to those segregated for any cause whatsoever, animating and accelerating the initiatives and studies that are already being made with that goal in mind. We, the bishops, wish to come closer to the poor in sincerity and brotherhood, making ourselves accessible to them.[28]

This was also a church that wished to speak the language of the indigenous and native cultures and to validate and respect their traditions, their rituals, and their modes of worship. Where those traditions and cultures lived together with a Christian culture brought by colonial evangelization, the effort had to be made to integrate them as a constitutive part of church discourse and praxis.

This church saw the challenge of injustice as inseparable from the challenge of violence. The state of the injustice and poverty of the continent was called by the bishops gathered in Medellín "institutionalized violence."[29] The question of conflict and violence was and continues to be treated as a major challenge on the continent. Liberation theology has devoted much attention to this subject.[30] Violence is far from being overcome on the continent, but its face has changed. Now, instead of the army and the soldiers who persecuted and tortured people who struggled for justice and against poverty, the agents of violence are often the drug dealers.[31] An entire generation of young men is steadily being killed every year.

Indeed, the whole world is suffering—as Pope Francis often describes it—a kind of Third World War. As just one example, radical jihadist groups in the Middle East are making entire cities disappear. Children suffer violence, along with women and the elderly. Panic dominates the region and forces many people, even more than before, to flee to the richer countries of the United States and Europe.

Christian theology and ethics must speak to these challenges. Faithful to reality, it is imperative to revisit the gospel, searching out new and creative paths toward making peace a concrete reality in our world. The challenge for Latin American theology is to persevere in accomplishing the priorities set over the past fifty years. This requires rescuing the memory and testimony of those who built these priorities and worked on them even at the risk of their own security and lives. We need a theology of witnesses, of spiritual masters, more than erudite and abstract texts. In this sense, the biographies of the mystics, the martyrs, and the saints are powerful "living texts" that can be revisited and whose reserves of light and wisdom will never be exhausted. Latin American theology is born from the vital experience and the martyrdom of a "cloud of witnesses,"[32] men and women who devoted themselves to make possible a different future for the continent.

The option for the poor on economic, political, social, and cultural levels generated a new theology, which is now well-known worldwide: liberation theology. According to Jon Sobrino, the first awakening for humankind in modern times was the awakening from dogmatic slumber, thanks to thinkers like Kant and Hegel. The consequence of this first awakening is the *intellectus fidei*.[33] The second awakening, this time from the slumber of inhumanity, helps us to understand the need for theology to be preferentially *intellectus amoris*. This is a theology concerned with "taking the crucified peoples down from the cross." Liberation theology has always tried to be this *intellectus amoris,* understanding itself as a theology at the service of God's infinite mercy.[34] It is a theology whose point of departure is the need for justice as a need basic to all humanity.

In recent years, liberation theology has not given up this calling to be *intellectus amoris*. Now this intelligence of love is richer than before, for it has enlarged its scope and recognized other anthropological poverties—besides the socioeconomic and political kind—as challenges for its discourse: the ecological crisis; the injustices of gender, race, and ethnicity; the need to overcome interreligious prejudice, and so on. All these are also anthropological poverties afflicting human beings, and liberation theology continues to give very close attention to all of them.

With this visit to a local church (i.e., the church in Latin America), which tries to propose a local experience to the universal church, we can approach what is the imprescriptible and the non-negotiable of Christianity today, in this time of crisis and doubts.

Justice and Peace: The Nonnegotiables

Concerns about injustice and the need for transformation of social structures—which the church had begun to address directly in 1891 with Leo XIII's encyclical *Rerum Novarum*, further developed in the 1960s by the Second Vatican Council and reshaped by the Latin American Church with the documents of Medellín and Puebla—were always present to Christianity and constitute the nonnegotiable elements of its identity.

Poverty is an evil that has to be excised, and for that, society has to be transformed at its root. We can recall here the prophetic words of Dorothy Day:

> What right has any one of us to security when God's poor are suffering? What right have I to sleep in a comfortable bed when so many are sleeping in the shadows of buildings here in this neighborhood of the Catholic Worker office? What right have we to food when so many are hungry or to liberty when . . . so many labor organizers are in jail?[35]

Day's fervent words tell us that in making justice a first priority, Christians are not making just a sociological or political choice. They are making a *theological* choice, backed up by serious theological reflection and by the whole history of the church. They affirm once more that it is necessary to opt preferentially for the poor because God did so. God is revealed as God of the poor, the one who comes having heard the cries of the people in distress; the one who speaks and gives voice to the poor, the widow, the orphan, and the foreigner; the one who leaves divine privileges and assumes our vulnerable and mortal flesh, being obedient until death on a cross. The primary motivation for a Christian to struggle for justice is not to create concrete political structures, but rather to do God's will and build God's kingdom. The changing of structures and the transformation of reality are a consequence of that primordial option.

Choosing justice will bring together the option for nonviolence and for peacebuilding. Justice and peace, according to biblical texts, not only are inseparable, but even kiss each other as loving sisters or passionate lovers, as in Psalm 85:

> I will hear what God the LORD will speak: for he will speak peace unto his people, and to his saints: but let them not turn again to folly. Surely his salvation is nigh them that fear him; that glory may dwell in our land. Mercy and truth are met together; righteousness and peace have kissed each other. Truth shall spring out of the earth; and righteousness shall look down from heaven. (Ps 85:8–11)

Statements by the magisterium of the church have acknowledged these two priorities. Paul VI, in his letter *Populorum Progressio* of 1967, stated:

> Even more recently, We sought to fulfill the wishes of the Council and to demonstrate the Holy See's concern for the developing nations. To do this, We felt it was necessary to add another pontifical commission to the Church's central administration. The purpose of this commission is "to awaken in the People of God full awareness of their mission today. In this way they can further the progress of poorer nations and international social justice, as well as help less developed nations to contribute to their own development." The name of this commission, Justice and Peace, aptly describes its program and its goal. We are sure that all men of good will want to join Our fellow Catholics and fellow Christians in carrying out this program. So today We earnestly urge all men to pool their ideas and their activities for man's complete development and the development of all mankind.[36]

Pope Francis, also, who has been shaping his pontificate according to an untiring concern for justice and peace, has made some important pronouncements about these two nonnegotiable elements of Christianity. It would take too long to quote all his declarations in favor of the poor or to recall all of his gestures, attitudes, and initiatives in that direction. We could mention among these latter: all the concrete things Cardinal Krajewski (made a cardinal by Francis in 2018) is doing in his name for the poor of Rome; or Francis's initiative to combine three dicasteries into one, the Dicastery for Integral Human Development, where he personally is responsible for everything that has to do with migrations, one of the clear priorities of his pontificate.

In February 2019 in an interreligious meeting in Abu Dhabi, Francis declared: "Justice is the second wing of peace. No one, therefore, can believe in God and not seek to live in justice with everyone, according to the Golden Rule. So whatever you wish that men would do to you, do so to them; for this is the law and the prophets." He proclaimed, "Peace and justice are inseparable!"

and stated that "human fraternity" also comes with the duty of rejecting and condemning war, citing its "miserable crudeness" and "fateful consequences."[37] He also issued a call to the religions of the world, urging that they "should keep watch as sentinels of fraternity in the night of conflict. They should be vigilant warnings to humanity not to close our eyes in the face of injustice and never to resign ourselves to the many tragedies in the world."[38]

The Future Is Communion

In this reflection on the nonnegotiables of Christianity, the urgency that drives us forward is evident. Paul said in the beginnings of Christianity: "For Christ's love compels us" (2 Cor 5:14). The reality of our time is that we have no more time. And this urgency is due to the fact that "the old has gone, the new is here!" (2 Cor 5:17).

In fact, everything is urgent when it comes to the future that gives meaning to our life. This was already understood by Jesus of Nazareth in his time and also by his first witnesses. The future is a time of waiting, yes, but also an end of waiting. Everything is new, and the old human being has passed. But we have not yet fully realized what we hope for and we must continue to fight and rediscover new ways of saying what is at the heart of the mystery of life.

The future is as real as, or perhaps even more real than, the past and the present. It is this future that allows us to continue to believe that life has a meaning, that it is worth losing our life to find it, that what comes to us is not a nebulous threat, but a luminous horizon of meaning that shapes our whole life.

Our times, sometimes as dark as Hannah Arendt and many others have claimed, can be lived with hope. This is how Etty Hillesum, Simone Weil, Óscar Romero, Ignacio Ellacuría, Christian de Chergé, Dorothy Day, Thomas Merton, Martin Luther King Jr., and so many others have kept fighting and waiting and so are for us today witnesses of the future. That is why they are our contemporaries. They did not cease to question history and institutions. Those who among them are Christian also questioned the church, but they did so in order to protect a horizon further away than the immediate sufferings they were enduring.[39]

Christianity has a future, and this is an invitation to live the present looking forward, impelled by the urgency of love that can no longer repeat worn-out narratives, which cannot communicate anymore; impelled also by the creativity that obliges us not to dwell only in texts and formulations subject to becoming outdated, but to let the narrative of the witnesses emerge fresh and new; and impelled by the audacity that allows us to find amid the profanity of the world and secularity of times the Word that resonates where least expected.

Above all, Christianity has a future because it is a mystery of communion. The genius of Christianity is its grounding in solidarity and communion, not in solitude. The future must be made of communion to overcome the pain of loneliness and evil. The future tells us that in the adventure of faith, God alone is God. Everything else, including the church, is only a sign, a "sacrament." Neither is the church the kingdom, nor the hierarchy the church.

The dynamic mystery Christianity has to offer is solidarity and communion. This is the greatest contribution that the Christian proposal can make today, in a world thirsty for listening, truth, and deep relationships. But this world can only be built if Christianity comes back once and again to its nonnegotiable elements—that is, if the people of God who follow Jesus Christ refuse to give up on investing in bold initiatives to build justice and peace.

Notes

[1] I am referring here to Thales of Miletus. "Some think that the soul pervades the whole universe, whence perhaps came Thales's view that everything is full of gods" (Aristotle, *De An.* 411 a7–8).

[2] See Paul Ricoeur, *Freud and Philosophy: An Essay on Interpretation* (New Haven, CT: Yale University Press, 2008), 32.

[3] Danièle Hervieu-Leger, *Le pelerin et le converti: La religion en mouvement* (Paris: Flammarion, 2001).

[4] 2010 Brazil census: Número de católicos e espíritas cai e cresce o dos sem religião, https://censo2010.ibge.gov.br.

[5] Christian Duquoc, *Cristianismo memória para o futuro* (São Paulo: Loyola, 2000), back cover.

[6] Jorge Muñoz Batista, "Octavio Paz: Nuestras raíces culturales," in *Iglesia y cultura latinoamericana* (Bogotá, 1984), 27–46, apud José Gonzalez Dorado, *De Maria Conquistadora a Maria Liberadora* (Santander: Sal Terrae, 1987), chap. 3: "La ambigüedad de la Conquistadora ante el mundo amerindio."

[7]Bartolomeu Melià made this clear, referring to the Guaraní world and the pacts of the Spanish. See Bartolomeu Melià, "O Guaraní reduzido," in AA. VV., *Das reduções latinoamericanas as lutas indigenas atuais* (São Paulo, 1982), 228–41. See also Enrique Dussel, "La historia de la Iglesia en América Latina," *PUEBLA* 18 (1982): 165–92; and Gonzalez Dorado, *De Maria Conquistadora a Maria Liberadora* (Santander: Sal Terrae, 1988), 30.

[8]Dorado, *De Maria Conquistadora a Maria Liberadora*, chap. 3.

[9]John XXIII to the leaders of the Azione Cattolica Italiana, in *Acta et Documenta Concilio oecumenico Vaticano II apparando*, Series 1 (Antepreparatoria), vol. 1, *Typis Polyglottis Vaticanis* (Vatican, 1960), 5; cf. *Documentation Catholique* 56.1300 (March 29, 1959): 388.

[10]Jon Sobrino, *Concilium: Revista internacional de teología* 364 (2016): 75–91 (issue titled *Ways of Liberation: Joys and Hopes for the Future*, celebrating the fiftieth anniversary of the journal).

[11]Ibid.

[12]Marc-Alain Ouaknin, *Les dix commandements* (Paris: Points, 2009).

[13]Ibid., my translation.

[14]See Duquoc, *Cristianismo memória*, back cover text.

[15]Ibid., 9: "It is not impossible that Faith recovers its credibility, if it overcomes this homesickness and this obstacle, reediting under another form its original Project. Perhaps then it can recover the blow of hope so provoking for the sociopolitical *status quo*. 'Remember your future,' says the fourth commandment, according to Jean Marc Ouaknin" (free translation into English).

[16]See Luis Duch, *El exilio de Dios* (Madrid: Fragmenta, 2017).

[17]José Ignacio Gonzalez Faus, "God?" *Cristianisme i Justícia*, booklet 157 (2015).

[18]See ibid., n. 24: "It is curious that the word 'love' suffers the same fate as the word 'God' suffers, as described by Buber at the beginning of this booklet. 'Love' is the most noble word in our language, but it also the most prostituted; it has served all too often to justify dastardly deeds."

[19]See Albert Comin, *Unity of God, Multiplicity of Mysticisms*, *Cristianisme i Justícia*, booklet 92 (Barcelona, 1999).

[20]Pope John XXIII, September 11, 1962, radio message, http://w2.vatican.va.

[21]*Gaudium et Spes*, 1.

[22]Ibid., 26.

[23]See Pe. Henrique de Lima Vaz, *Igreja Reflexo/Igreja Fonte, Cadernos Brasileiros* [Rio de Janeiro] 46 (March–April 1968): 17–22.

[24]Second General Conference of Latin American Bishops, Medellín Documents 14, "Poverty of the Church" (nos. 1–2). The statement by Pope Paul VI quoted in this passage is from his Address to the Peasants, Mosquera, Colombia, August 23, 1968. Quotations from the Medellín Documents in this article are taken from Second General Conference of Latin American Bishops, *The Church in the Present-Day Transformation of Latin America in the Light of the Council*, II: *Conclusions*, 2nd ed. (Washington, DC: Division for Latin America—USCC, 1973).

[25]Medellín Documents 1, "Justice," sec. 1, "Pertinent Facts," no. 1, "Facts."

[26]Medellín Documents 14, "Poverty of the Church," sec. 3, "Pastoral Orientations," no. 10.

[27]Ibid., no. 8.

[28]Ibid., no. 9.

[29]Medellín Documents 2, "Peace," no. 16.

[30]See, for instance, Jon Sobrino's and Ignacio Ellacuría's works about the military violence in El Salvador. See also Monseñor Romero's homilies protesting against the civil war entrenched in the country. And see all the reflections by Latin American theologians in the context of military dictatorships during the 1970s and the '80s.

[31]Penny Lernoux, *Cry of the People: The Struggle for Human Rights in Latin America: The Catholic Church in Conflict with U.S. Policy* (New York: Penguin, 1982); Enrique Dussel, *De Medellín a Puebla: Una década de sangre y esperanza 1968–1979* (México: Edicol, 1979); Carlos Mendoza Alvarez and Hector Conde Rubio, *Arqueologia de la violencia: Nuevos paradigmas en el pensamiento y el lenguaje para la praxis no violenta* (Mexico City: Universidad Iberoamericana, 2017).

[32]See Hebrews 12:1.

[33]Jon Sobrino, "Awakening from the Sleep of Inhumanity," in *The Principle of Mercy: Taking the Crucified People from the Cross* (Maryknoll, NY: Orbis Books, 1994), 1–11.

[34]Ibid.

[35]Dorothy Day, *Selected Writings,* edited and with an introduction by Robert Ellsberg (Maryknoll, NY: Orbis Books, 2005), 69–70.

[36]*Populorum Progressio*, no. 5.

[37]*Catholic World Report*, February 4, 2019, https://www.catholicworldreport.com.

[38]Ibid.

[39]Pierre Bouretz, *Testigos del futuro* (Madrid: Trotta, 2012), 20.

A Green Church on the Move

Migration, Ecology, and Ecclesial Mission

James Dechant

In early 2016, the United States federal government, through its Department of Housing and Urban Development, announced around a billion dollars in grant money to help communities deal with the effects of climate change. One such grant, worth $48 million, went to the native residents of Isle de Jean Charles, a small Louisiana island some eighty miles southwest of New Orleans. As reported by the *New York Times* in May of that year, the grant represented "the first allocation of federal tax dollars to move an entire community struggling with the impacts of climate change."[1] The island's residents, most of whom belong to the Biloxi-Chitimacha-Choctaw tribe, face the loss of their heritage and culture. They face involuntary migration as their homeland disappears under the rising sea. Their "climate resilience" grant is meant to alleviate the burden of the tribe's impending member-ship in a club that no one wants to join: the growing population of displaced peoples known as ecological refugees.

The case of Isle de Jean Charles captures the twin calamities facing our twenty-first-century world: the environmental crisis and the global plight of refugees. In this essay, I discuss these issues together and think about how the church (both Catholic and the wider community of Christians) might respond to them. In light of this convention's theme, we might consider "all the ends of the earth" as not just colorful language to describe a worldwide religion, but as an invitation to consider the relationship of global Catholicism to the earth itself. A twenty-first-century ecclesiology must rethink the identity and mission of the church in light of this new phase in our pilgrimage through history, and it must mobilize to address the loss of human habitat.

In his 2015 encyclical *Laudato Si': On Care for Our Common Home*,[2] Pope Francis speaks about "a tragic rise in the number of migrants seeking to flee from the growing poverty caused by environmental degradation" (*LS* 25). By 2050, climate change could displace between fifty million and two hundred million people.[3] Implicated in causing either poverty or physically unbearable conditions, ecological degradation lies at the heart of many modern migrations. Attending to these ecological refugees will be one of the most pressing tasks for the global church in the twenty-first century.

In this essay I will first establish the link between ecological degradation and forced migration by drawing on several contemporary examples. *Laudato Si'* will help situate these examples in a theological framework. Second, I lay out the harms of these forced displacements by exploring how place is formative for identity, drawing on the work of Mary McClintock Fulkerson and Willie James Jennings. Third, I argue that migration is a significant "sign of the times" that the church must engage, building on Peter Phan's "migration theology" and incorporating the new reality of ecological refugees. Fourth and finally, I offer some suggestions for how the church might respond to the twin calamities of climate change and the refugee crisis. Only by becoming a green church on the move might we aspire to fulfill our current ecclesial mission.

Establishing the Connection

Migrations are rarely attributable to one factor alone. Still, whether directly (through the destruction of local habitat) or indirectly (via conflicts over diminishing resources), ecological degradation plays a key role in many refugee movements. I want to give some texture to this understanding by presenting three examples of forced migrations attributable, at least in large part, to anthropogenic ecocide (that is, severe environmental harm inflicted by humans).

Consider first the example already mentioned: Louisiana's Isle de Jean Charles. Unsurprisingly, a nexus of contextual factors describes the tribal residents of this island: they are indigenous, poor, southern, and few in number. Their community is, essentially, peripheral to the concerns of our society. These islanders represent the demographic identified by Francis in *Laudato Si'* as most affected by climate change. They are "largely dependent on natural reserves" with few "other financial activities or resources which can enable them to adapt to climate change or to face natural disasters, and their access to social services and protection is very limited" (*LS* 25). When a vulnerable population such as this faces the threat of rising sea levels, which scientific consensus pins on human activity, we stand condemned of denying that population's very existence (*LS* 95), no matter how much grant money we belatedly offer.

Many migrants and ecological refugees, however, lack even the support our government gives to Isle de Jean Charles. Consider, as a second example, the situation in the western highlands of Guatemala. This region belongs to an area of Central America called the "dry corridor" for its drought-prone climate. More than half the residents are subsistence farmers. This indigenous, agrarian, and historically poor region has suffered even more in recent years as the changing climate has wiped out crops of maize and potatoes. Extreme weather events, increasingly wide fluctuations in temperature, unpredictable and irregular rainfall—all these factors contribute to reduced grain and vegetable harvests and increased malnutrition. For many, the only option is to emigrate. As one resident says, "These crops are for survival. If there aren't crops, people leave."[4] They abandon their lands and head north, hoping to find work that can support their families. In 2018, nearly fifty thousand immigrants from this region were deported back to Guatemala from the United States and Mexico. For a few years, American foreign aid supported agricultural programs for vulnerable regions such as Guatemala, programs that showed promising results. Since then, however, the United States cut such funding, an action that has only exacerbated the border crisis. This illustrates Francis's point that "the human environment and the natural environment deteriorate together" (*LS* 48). If we are to address the root of the problem, we must understand how "a true ecological approach always becomes a social approach," especially by taking into account the rights of the poor and underprivileged (*LS* 49; cf. 93).

The ecological crisis poses risks not only to livelihoods but to entire cultures. Consider, as a third and final example, the Carteret Islanders, a community of a few thousand living on an atoll off the coast of Papua New Guinea in the South Pacific. Their home is sinking into the sea. While the precise cause of the islands' gradual submersion is complex—a sea-level rise due to global warming, natural volcanic activity, or some combination of the two—their path forward remains as troubled as that of the residents of Isle de Jean Charles or western Guatemala. A 2010 documentary called *Sun Come Up* captures this community's plight as it faces an existential struggle over whether and how to relocate from its ancestral home. As one resident states in the film, if they relocate to safer areas, "We will not be the Carterets people anymore." Another resident recognizes the fact that "most of our culture will have to live in memory. That part of our life will be washed away. How do we keep this attachment to our home?"[5]

In *Laudato Si'*, Francis says that our identities are formed by special relationships to local context. "The history of our friendship with God," he writes, "is always linked to particular places which take on an intensely personal meaning. . . . Going back to these places is a chance to recover something of [our] true selves" (*LS* 84). What, then, can the church do in light of the loss of such places? How can it speak of ecclesial identity when physical, geographic identity has been so fundamentally compromised?

Place-Formed Identity

In this section I discuss how place shapes human identity, engaging two contemporary theologians who offer critical insights for an ecclesiology that aims to respond to the ecological crisis: Mary McClintock Fulkerson and Willie James Jennings. Both thinkers paint rich portraits of how theological thinking gets embodied and experienced. I will highlight a few of their contributions to thinking about place and identity.

In her 2007 book *Places of Redemption*, Fulkerson describes her work as one of practical theology, the first task of which is to describe a situation. The particular situation she describes is the now-defunct Good Samaritan United Methodist Church in North Carolina. Fulkerson illuminates the concrete context that shapes the religious lives of the congregation, a congregation committed to providing a place of welcome. Using postmodern theory, Fulkerson develops a thick conception of "place" to account for this community. Within this conceptual framework, place is "a structure of lived, corporate, and *bodied* experience." Place is not just a set of coordinates; it is always a lived experience, the contours of which are shaped by our own particular circumstances. "The world," writes Fulkerson, "*takes shape* through our bodies."[6] Two aspects relate this category to ecological refugees.

First, place "is truly fundamental in generating knowledge" (Fulkerson, *Places of Redemption*, 25). We live in worlds of meaning, not in the abstract geometric planes of Google Earth. The members of Fulkerson's church would have different knowledge of the gospel if they moved to a different place. Ecological refugees, therefore, suffer when their embodied knowledge becomes untethered to a persistent environment. Second, the members of Fulkerson's church find unity, as a corporate body, in *what they do*. Place is "a gathering of meaning that endures through practices" (36). Place, as much as it shapes individuals, is in turn *shaped by* the people who participate in shared practices there. When a home becomes uninhabitable, knowledge and practices suffer, if they are not erased entirely. In this context, we ought to hear the cry of the Israelites in exile, when they ask, "How could we sing the Lord's song in a foreign land?" (Ps 137:4).

Fulkerson's understanding of place as generative of knowledge and sustained by practices "contests the view from nowhere" (26). That view from nowhere is not a philosophical strawman but a very real attitude characteristic of the colonialist mentality. Such is the subject of Willie James Jennings's historical and constructive project in *The Christian Imagination*, from 2010. Where Fulkerson charts what happens to place as it comes to be, Jennings takes a retrospective look at what happens when place is lost.

The theft of place that Jennings focuses on is intimately tied to the history of colonialism. The tragic legacy of the early modern epoch is one of forced dislocation and upended identities. "The age of discovery and conquest," he writes, "began a process of transformation of land and identity. . . . The deepest theological distortion taking place is that the earth, the ground, spaces, and places are being removed as living organizers of identity and as facilitators of identity."[7] Racialized hierarchies came to take the place of the land's signifying power as "whiteness replaced the earth as the signifier of identities" (Jennings, *Christian Imagination*, 58).

Why is the disruption of such geographic formation so threatening and so traumatic? Recall Fulkerson's argument: place is fundamental in generating knowledge. Jennings extends this insight by describing how one's moral vision is shaped by the land: he writes that "moral sensibilities [are] space-textured," tied to the stories of particular places and events that occurred there and nowhere else (54). When we lose familiar spatial anchors and concrete references to local landscapes, our moral vision can become abstract and community can break down.

What Jennings finds in this colonialist story is a "disruption, even mutilation of the paths to the wisdom necessary to live in the world" (58). Here we should be reminded of the words of Francis: "The history of our friendship with God is always linked to particular places." Jennings urges us to rehabilitate the doctrine of creation so that it becomes grounded in our lived experience of place. "A Christian doctrine of creation," he writes, "is first a way of seeing place in its fullest sense. Christianity is in need of place to be fully Christian" (248).

Both Fulkerson and Jennings, then, teach us how place shapes our identity—moral, communal, and spiritual. They sound the alarm about what happens when our bonds with place are disrupted or severed. I find their work refreshing, even though it *should* be old news to Christianity. After all, movement has always been a central feature of the church, and it will only become more so in the age of ecological refugees.

Migration Theology

In his article "*Deus Migrator*—God the Migrant," Peter Phan claims that migration is "a pressing and perennial concern for the church as *church*." Today more than ever, Phan points out, migration is a "seismic phenomenon." In 2013, over 3 percent of the world's population lived outside their countries of origin; in

2015, about twenty-four persons were displaced every minute; about half these refugees were children.[8] Phan says that the Catholic Church must understand itself as an "institutional migrant," an identity he illustrates by tracing a series of historical migrations that shaped Christianity and made it into the world religion it is today (Phan, *"Deus Migrator,"* 847, 850–53). Migration, Phan submits, is a critical sign of the times that must shape our theology.

From here, Phan outlines how a migration theology might look, including a dialectical methodology in three steps: first, socio-analytic mediation (gathering data from social sciences and the stories of migrants); second, hermeneutical mediation (giving theological meaning to such data); third, practical mediation (moving toward concrete actions that embody an "option for the migrant") (855–57). Phan says that this option for the migrant requires respect for human rights and eschatological hope. Such hope is embodied in actions that are rooted in the past yet look toward the coming future. We express this anticipation communally through liturgical word and sacrament (864–67). (I return to this aspect below.) Phan concludes his article by examining traditional theological loci in light of migration; in Christology, for example, we can understand Jesus as the archetypal migrant, journeying beyond his home both in his earthly life and via his Incarnation into the flesh (857–67, esp. 862–63).

If migration is a clear "sign of the times," then ecological migration constitutes a paradigmatic case of this reality. Phan's migration theology speaks to the conception of place articulated above to help us understand the age of ecological refugees. If we agree with Fulkerson's claim that place generates knowledge, then Phan's option for the migrant calls us to understand the loss of place not simply as a social problem but as a theological problem. The church as a transnational institution cannot *re-place* the lands left behind by ecological refugees. The church as a human and divine institution, however, must recognize the pain and suffering entailed in displacement and use its resources of memory to help refugees cope with their loss. Fulkerson's insight that place endures through practices similarly challenges the church to sustain some memory of what can no longer be materially experienced: the lost land. As the Carteret Islander puts it, "Most of our culture will have to live in memory." *Liturgy* is one powerful way to preserve and care for these memories, and it has roots as far back as Israel maintaining its cultural identity while in exile.

Jennings's linkage of place and race warns us how powerful ideologies can supplant the identity-forming work previously handled by one's homeland. The profound precariousness of migrants' situation leaves them vulnerable to violent acts of Othering. The church, therefore, must work collaboratively to reshape the moral vision of communities as they take in ecological refugees. Jennings also shows how moral sensibilities are space-textured. As ecological refugees settle into new places, we cannot simply expect them to assimilate to their new culture; rather, both host and migrant must articulate their moral vision together. Phan's migrant theology teaches us how we are all migrants, prompting us to move beyond the host/guest binary and enter into what Jennings would call an "intimate joining."

Crucially, this reshaped moral vision demands a like-minded praxis. As Phan argues, "To be a migrant is to be on the move, and one of the most fundamental virtues required of people on the move is hope." Such hope is not a vague wish or a passive waiting for a future occurrence, but "a vigilant standing-on-tiptoe, a longing expectation, a leaning forward into the future. Above all, hope is embodied in actions to bring about, or at least prepare for and anticipate, the coming of the reality that is hoped for" (Phan, 864). By word and sacrament, this hope celebrates God's saving actions in history even as it looks forward to the eschatological future that God promises. Hope demands of a migrant church faced with ecological devastation that we remember the homelands lost and that we anticipate our future shared home. The two questions we must ask are: "What was the place you lost?" and "To what place are we all journeying together?"

The Role of the Church

In this last section, I would like to move to Phan's step of "practical mediation" by offering three concrete proposals for how the church can address ecological migration. In *Laudato Si'*, Pope Francis urges us to address the ecological crisis at the local community level, where "relationships develop or are recovered and a new social fabric emerges," where we can "cultivate a shared identity, with a story which can be remembered and handed on" (*LS* 232). The signs of the times call us to cultivate that shared identity as a migrant church, to embrace ecological refugees as we lean into the eschatological future together.

My first proposal, therefore, is liturgical: *the church should create space for sharing narratives that mourn lost places and that keep alive the memory of geographically constituted identities.* These narratives can serve to remember, lament, and protest the loss of place. The liturgy could accommodate this in a variety of ways: during the confession of sins, to admit our collective fault in permitting ecocide; during the prayers of the faithful, as we beseech God to have mercy on the ecologically vulnerable; and during the homily, when the pastor could invite individuals to share personal narratives. Such accommodations should prompt the existing community to take stock of its own relationship to place. This can lead to a newfound appreciation of how we are all tied to the land. By making newcomers feel welcome in the liturgy, we might begin to reformulate our new, shared moral vision together.

We have a literary trove to express such loss in the biblical tradition of lament. Bradford Hinze points out that lament can be a rich theological resource for expressing ecclesial pain and for calling responsible parties to accountability.[9] The prophet Jeremiah, for example, speaks about the land itself mourning its desolation, a desolation caused by human wickedness (Jer 12:4–11). Of course, the scriptural resources are not one-sidedly negative. Biblical scholar Richard Bauckham stresses that praise and lament go together.[10] As much as we draw on the tradition to mourn what has been lost, we must also appreciate what we still have.

My second proposal is catechetical: *the church should embrace the "ecological education" promoted by Pope Francis by listening to the voices of ecological refugees.* Phan calls the migrant the *imago Dei migratoris*; as we treat the migrant, so we treat God. The migrant and the ecological refugee enjoy privileged positions in the church's ongoing ecological pedagogy. This proposal is closely linked to the previous liturgical one because our manner of teaching is (or should be) bound up with our symbolic expressions and manifestations of beauty. Beyond simply informing us about the environmental crisis, ecological education should seek to establish harmony between ourselves and creation, cultivate ecological virtues, and reach for the transcendent. Francis says that ecological education must develop a vibrant aesthetic aspect, in which contemplation of creation is key: "If someone has not learned to stop and admire something beautiful, we should not be surprised if he or she treats everything as an object to be used and abused without scruple" (*LS* 215). This catechetical focus on ecological education would foster appreciation for holistic knowledge, for the relationships between creatures and their environments, for a spirituality that respects the importance of place and of the whole earth community. Refugees are the ones most keenly aware of the abuse of creation that we lament liturgically. While rejecting any type of soteriology that values the suffering of refugees for its own sake, we must learn from the tragedies they have endured and catechize toward a more sustainable future.

My third and final proposal is sacramental: *the church should deploy its sacramental logic to connect its universal body to each local instantiation in a particular place*. In our thinking about what the church is and must be, we need to contract and expand: *contract* to focus more intently on places and their meaning to us; *expand* to bring the whole Christian community and its vast, global resources to bear on the problem. The church must manifest this expansion not only in actionable discourse but in truly feeling sympathy, as a body, for the pain felt by each member.

In one sense, this proposal is simply acknowledging the global reality of the church in the twenty-first century. As Phan puts it, "The contemporary face of the church is that of a global migrant institution" (*"Deus Migrator,"* 853). It is a truly catholic (universal) or "glocal" church, increasingly diverse and polycentric. More than simply acknowledging de facto reality, however, I call my third proposal sacramental because it challenges us to think about the very essence of the church in a way that we can express only symbolically, through the sacraments. For example, the Eucharist is present to us materially, in a specific time and place, yet it is distributed everywhere throughout the ecclesial body simultaneously. We partake of one shared reality—the body and blood of Christ—yet each church partakes of a distinct instantiation of that reality, in the particular earthly materials provided by the priest and parish. By a similar logic, the church must learn to think locally and globally with a dialectical logic that values both particular places (which suffer from our sinful actions) and the universal body of Christ (which is far beyond our power to harm). Only then will the suffering of ecological refugees be fully recognized by the global church.

The message of my essay is simply this: places matter. As we consider "all the ends of the earth," let us remember the particular places of the church in all their specificity. We are already a migrant church, a church on the move. To what extent we become a *green* church on the move depends entirely on our ability to mourn with ecological refugees, to remember dearly the places they have lost, and to anticipate—in embodied eschatological hope—a future free of ecological harm.

Notes

[1]Coral Davenport and Campbell Robertson, "Resettling the First American 'Climate Refugees,'" *New York Times*, May 2, 2016, https://nytimes.com.

[2]Pope Francis, *Laudato Si': On Care for Our Common Home* (Vatican City: Libreria Editrice Vaticana, 2016). Hereafter cited parenthetically as *LS*.

[3]According to estimates by the United Nations University Institute for Environment and Human Security and the International Organization for Migration, as cited in Davenport and Robertson, "Climate Refugees."

[4]Jonathan Blitzer, "How Climate Change Is Fuelling the U.S. Border Crisis," *New Yorker*, April 3, 2019, https://www.newyorker.com.

[5]*Sun Come Up*, directed by Jennifer Redfearn (New Day Films, 2011).

[6]Mary McClintock Fulkerson, *Places of Redemption: Theology for a Worldly Church* (New York: Oxford University Press, 2007), 25. Further page references to this work are given parenthetically in the text.

[7]Willie James Jennings, *The Christian Imagination: Theology and the Origins of Race* (New Haven, CT: Yale University Press, 2010), 39. Further page references to this work are given parenthetically in the text.

[8]Peter C. Phan, "*Deus Migrator*—God the Migrant: Migration of Theology and Theology of Migration," *Theological Studies* 77, no. 4 (2016): 846. Further page references to this article are given parenthetically in the text.

[9]Bradford E. Hinze, "Ecclesial Impasse: What Can We Learn from Our Laments?" *Theological Studies* 72, no. 3 (2011): 470–95.

[10]Richard Bauckham, *The Bible and Ecology: Rediscovering the Community of Creation* (Waco, TX: Baylor University Press, 2010). For biblical praise of creation, see, e.g., Gen 1, Job 38–42, or Ps 148.

Pope Francis in Dialogue
with Vandana Shiva

John Sniegocki

Vandana Shiva is an ecofeminist activist/scholar from India who has been deeply influenced by Gandhi and by Hindu philosophy. She is one of the world's leading critics of current neoliberal capitalist forms of economic globalization. Her books include *Staying Alive: Women, Ecology, and Development*; *Monocultures of the Mind*; and *Earth Democracy*.[1] Of particular concern to Shiva are the negative impacts of dominant economic policies on women, the poor, and the environment.

In this essay I bring the work and writings of Shiva into dialogue with the thought of Pope Francis, especially as expressed in his encyclical *Laudato Si': On Care for Our Common Home*. I highlight numerous areas of convergence between Shiva and Francis, while also suggesting several ways that the incorporation of Shiva's distinctive insights could further enhance the analysis provided by Francis. Engaging in such dialogue with persons embodying the deepest insights of other cultures and traditions, I suggest, is a crucial task of the global church.

Vandana Shiva's Analysis
of the Roots of Our Problems

Vandana Shiva's writings and talks contain in-depth discussions of topics such as climate change; deforestation; desertification; the pollution of water, air, and soil; poverty; hunger; and violence. Shiva also stresses, however, the need to look beyond the details of each of these separate issues and to discern the deeper causes of these problems. She identifies two underlying and interdependent causes. These are, she suggests, the reductionist worldview that characterizes much of modern, Western science, and the oppressive realities of global capitalism that this science so often serves.

Shiva, whose professional training was as a physicist, strongly critiques the inadequacies of the dualistic, Cartesian worldview that she contends remains predominant in modern scientific practice despite more recent developments in theoretical physics that challenge this way of looking at the world. The most fundamental problem of modern science, Shiva argues, is contained in its conception of nature. Nature is generally viewed as inert, passive matter, whose use is subject to few if any ethical constraints. She contrasts this view of nature with traditional views held by many indigenous communities and rural dwellers throughout the world who understand nature as a living, vital reality whose fundamental integrity is to be respected.[2]

In her critique of modern science, Shiva builds on the pioneering analysis of historian of science Carolyn Merchant, especially as contained in her classic work *The Death of Nature: Women, Ecology, and the Scientific Revolution*.[3] Merchant traces a profound shift from organic to mechanistic views of nature as part of the scientific revolution and names this shift "the death of nature." This transformation of worldview, Merchant argues, paved the way for widespread ecological devastation:

> The image of the earth as a living organism and nurturing mother had served as a cultural constraint restricting the actions of human beings. One does not readily slay a mother, dig into her entrails for gold or mutilate her body. . . . The removal of animistic, organic assumptions about the cosmos constituted the death of nature—the most far-reaching effect of the Scientific Revolution.[4]

Echoing Merchant's views, Shiva states:

> The scientific revolution in Europe transformed nature from *terra mater* [mother earth] into a machine and a source of raw material; with this transformation it removed all

ethical and cognitive restraints against its violation and exploitation. . . . Industrialism created a limitless appetite for resource exploitation, and modern science provided the ethical and cognitive license to make such exploitation possible, acceptable—and desirable.[5]

In addition to describing modern science as "mechanistic," Shiva also describes it as "atomistic" and "reductionist."[6] The interconnectedness and interdependencies of nature, she contends, are too often ignored, with catastrophic results. This can be seen, for example, in the socially and ecologically devastating impacts of industrial agriculture. While certain variables are isolated and emphasized in industrial farming practices, such as maximizing production of monoculture crops through the use of various chemicals, the broader ecological and social contexts are often overlooked. This has resulted in massive soil erosion, depleted soil fertility, contaminated and depleted groundwater resources, poisoned farm workers, the massive displacement of small farmers, and many other negative consequences.[7]

In addition to being reductionist in its neglect of interconnections and interdependencies, modern science is reductionist, Shiva states, because of its exclusion of other ways of knowing, particularly those embodied in indigenous cultures. These alternative worldviews and associated practices in areas such as traditional agriculture and medicine are often disparagingly labeled "prescientific," "superstitious," or "backward," despite the insights based on long experience that these traditions contain.[8] Through this epistemological reductionism, says Shiva, sources of wisdom that could play an important role in addressing contemporary problems are overlooked or are contemptuously discarded. Shiva refers to this dismissal of indigenous and other sources of wisdom as the creation of "monocultures of the mind."[9]

These traits of atomism, reductionism, and mechanistic understandings of nature Shiva also connects to the gendered nature of modern Western science. She highlights, for example, the explicitly sexist conceptualizations of science contained in the thought of many modern scientific pioneers. A primary example is Francis Bacon, often referred to as the father of the modern scientific method. Bacon, like many early modern scientists, conceptualized nature as female and explicitly and positively equated the scientific method with images of rape, torture, and exploitation. Nature, Bacon states in his essay "The Masculine Birth of Time" (the title itself already clearly revealing a gendered framing), must be "bound into service" and made a "slave."[10] The discipline of scientific knowledge and the inventions it leads to, says Bacon, do not "merely exert a gentle guidance over nature's course; they have the power to conquer and subdue her, to shake her to her foundations."[11] Reflecting on Bacon's views, Shiva states:

> In Bacon's experimental method, which was central to this masculine project, there was a dichotomising between male and female, mind and matter, objective and subjective, rational and emotional, and a conjunction of masculine and scientific dominating over nature, women, and the non-west. His was not a "neutral," "objective," "scientific" method—it was a masculine mode of aggression against nature and domination over women. . . . Both nature and inquiry appear conceptualized in ways modelled on rape and torture . . . and this modelling is advanced as a reason to value science.[12]

It should be stressed that Shiva is not calling for a total rejection of modern science and technology. She is, however, calling for a much more critical approach, including the need for much greater humility on the part of humans in relation to nature and recognition of the need for much greater attentiveness to holistic perspectives (including the wisdom of traditional cultures) and to the negative side effects of conventional approaches.

Shiva argues that the reductionist version of science triumphed not because it was the most adequate (the ecological and social problems that it has given rise to disprove this) but rather, she says, because it best served the needs of the powerful, particularly owners of capital:

> Reductionist forestry has destroyed tropical forests, and reductionist farming is destroying tropical farming. As a system of knowledge about nature or life reductionist science is weak and inadequate; as a system of knowledge for the

market, it is powerful and profitable. Modern science, as
we have noted earlier, has a worldview that both supports
and is supported by the socio-political-economic system of
western capitalist patriarchy which dominates and exploits
nature, women, and the poor.[13]

The alliance of capitalism and patriarchal science, Shiva contends, has given rise to models of "development" and forms of globalization that have dispossessed huge numbers of people (small
farmers, indigenous communities, for example), undermined the
power of workers, and created widespread economic insecurity,
while concentrating ownership of land and other natural resources
in ever fewer hands. It has also created crises of meaning for many,
by undermining communal bonds and cultural values. And it has
created crises of democracy, as wealthy elites and corporations
have come to dominate political processes.[14] This combination of
economic insecurity, sociocultural displacement, and democratic
decay, Shiva suggests, is at the root of much contemporary ethnic conflict, racism, xenophobia, and violent fundamentalisms,
as scapegoats are sought to explain social problems rather than
challenging the true structural roots of these problems in unjust
economic systems. "When economic dictatorship is grafted onto
representative, electoral democracy," says Shiva, "a toxic growth
of religious fundamentalism and right-wing extremism is the
result. Thus, corporate globalization leads not just to the death
of democracy, but to the democracy of death, in which exclusion,
hate, and fear become the political means to mobilize votes and
power."[15]

As an alternative, says Shiva, what is needed are grassroots
efforts to build true democracy—economic, political, ecological,
what Shiva calls "earth democracy."[16] Drawing on Gandhi and
on what she terms the "feminine principle," which she understands as being an approach to life available to both men and
women, she articulates a vision based on nonviolence, mutual
interdependence, greater economic equity, and respect for all
species.[17] Through her activism—in the Chipko movement (a
women-led movement to protect forests), efforts in support of
organic, regenerative agriculture, campaigns against genetically
modified crops and in support of biodiversity, and movements

challenging current forms of globalization and in support of greater economic democracy—Vandana Shiva seeks to help to make this vision a reality.

Pope Francis and *Laudato Si'*

The similarities between the views of Vandana Shiva and Pope Francis are many and profound. Like Shiva, Francis highlights a long list of crises that our world is facing, among the most pressing of which are climate change and ecological devastation, wealth inequality, migration, and war. Francis also shares an understanding that these crises are rooted in a deeply flawed underlying worldview, which, like Shiva, he describes as reductionistic, focused on domination and control, and lacking adequate awareness of our profound interconnectedness with other humans, nonhuman creatures, and the natural world. Throughout *Laudato Si'* Francis repeatedly emphasizes the need to recognize that "everything is connected."[18] "Because all creatures are connected," Francis states, "each must be cherished with love and respect, for all of us as living creatures are dependent on one another."[19] Challenging anthropocentrism, Francis emphasizes the inherent value of all species as part of God's good creation. "It is not enough," he says, "to think of species merely as potential 'resources' to be exploited, while overlooking the fact that they have value in themselves."[20]

Francis highlights the need for an "integral ecology." Such an approach includes recognizing our interdependence with other creatures. It also includes recognizing that issues of social justice and ecological sustainability are fundamentally interrelated. There is a pressing need, Francis asserts, to heed "both the cry of the earth and the cry of the poor."[21] Thus Francis, like Shiva, stresses the importance of becoming aware of our interconnectedness with all of creation and acting in ways that foster both ecological sustainability and the true well-being of the poor.

Critique of the Technocratic Paradigm and of Capitalism

Francis also expresses views similar to those of Vandana Shiva in his claim that many of our problems are rooted in a deeply flawed approach to science and technology. Francis names these problematic understandings of science and technology the "technocratic paradigm."[22] This worldview, he argues, has domination of nature and economic gain as its main priorities. He warns that technology, when "linked to business interests," is "incapable of seeing the mysterious network of relations between things" and so results in enormous harm, especially to the environment and to the poor.[23] Like Shiva, Francis refers to this dominant, capitalist-scientific worldview as "reductionist":

> The effects of imposing this model on reality as a whole, human and social, are seen in the deterioration of the environment, but this is just one sign of a reductionism which affects every aspect of human and social life. We have to accept that technological products are not neutral, for they create a framework which ends up conditioning lifestyles and shaping social possibilities along the lines dictated by the interests of certain powerful groups.[24]

An essential part of Francis's critique of the technocratic paradigm is his critique of capitalism. Francis in fact presents at least eight main criticisms of the prevailing global capitalist economic order. These include the creation of excessive economic inequality, the development of a permanent undercaste of the "excluded," exploitation of workers, contributions to social conflict and war, the fostering of consumerism and the "globalization of indifference," ecological devastation, the undermining of democracy, and the promotion of a culture of fear and scapegoating.[25]

Like Shiva, Francis emphasizes how the insecurities created by neoliberal capitalist forms of globalization have contributed to an increase in the rise of right-wing movements of racism and hate around the world, as people fail to understand the true roots of the crises that they face (due in large part to the control of the media and government by powerful economic interests) and so are often susceptible to various forms of scapegoating. Francis notes:

> The wounds are there, they are a reality. The unemployment is real, the violence is real, the corruption is real, the identity crisis is real, the gutting of democracies is real. The system's gangrene cannot be whitewashed forever because sooner

or later the stench becomes too strong; and when it can no longer be denied, the same power that spawned this state of affairs sets about manipulating fear, insecurity, quarrels, and even people's justified indignation, in order to shift the responsibility for all these ills onto a "non-neighbor."[26]

The scapegoating of immigrants and of racial, religious, or ethnic minorities, which we see taking place throughout much of the world, including the United States, is understood by Francis to be one part of a fundamentally flawed system in need of profound structural change. "I wonder whether we can see that these destructive realities are part of a system which has become global," Francis states. "If such is the case, I would insist, let us not be afraid to say it: we want change, real change, structural change. This system is by now intolerable."[27]

Along with Shiva, Francis recognizes that the needed alternatives (true economic and political democracy, ecological sustainability) will only come about as a result of massive grassroots efforts:

> You, the lowly, the exploited, the poor and underprivileged, can do, and are doing, a lot. I would even say that the future of humanity is in great measure in your own hands . . . ; the future of humanity does not lie solely in the hands of great leaders, the great powers and the elites. It is fundamentally in the hands of peoples and in their ability to organize.[28]

Similarly, Francis states:

> You, the popular movements, are sowers of change, promoters of a process involving millions of actions, great and small, creatively intertwined like words in a poem; that is why I wanted to call you "social poets." . . . I congratulate you, I accompany you and I ask you to continue to blaze trails and to keep fighting.[29]

The type of "fighting" that Francis calls for is firm commitment to active, nonviolent struggle. "Let us . . . make active nonviolence our way of life," Francis urges. "Jesus marked out the path of nonviolence. . . . To be true followers of Jesus today includes embracing his teaching about nonviolence."[30]

How Vandana Shiva Could Contribute
to Deepening the Analyses of Pope Francis

As we have seen, there are many similarities between the thought of Pope Francis and Vandana Shiva. Shiva in fact suggests in an essay on *Laudato Si'* that Francis deeply articulates what she herself means when she calls for "earth democracy."[31] At the same time, some differences exist, and I suggest that there are a variety of ways that Francis's thought (and Catholic social teaching, or CST, more broadly) could be further enhanced through engagement with some of these distinctive elements of Shiva's thought and work.

More Detailed Analysis of Critical Issues

In the course of her many books, Shiva engages in more in-depth analysis of many issues than Pope Francis can do in his briefer encyclicals and speeches. In addition to her deep and insightful analyses of the problems with industrial farming and the promise of agroecological alternatives, discussed above, Shiva also explores the impacts of reductionist science in the service of capitalist elites in other realms such as industrial forestry, livestock-raising, fishing, and water management. With regard to industrial forestry, for example, Shiva contends that in its single-minded emphasis on maximizing yields of wood, the many other roles that forests have traditionally played—such as providing food, fodder, and medicine and contributing to processes of water and soil conservation—are ignored. Through such reductionism, the livelihoods of many have been undermined; millions who have depended upon the forest have been displaced; and ecological balance has been disrupted.[32] Shiva's work could provide Pope Francis with deepened insights into these and similar realities.[33]

Food Ethics and Dietary Choices

Other crucial insights contained in Shiva's work that Pope Francis could learn from concern food ethics and our dietary choices. The theological-ethical framework articulated in *Laudato Si'*, for example, would seem to have many implications for food ethics, but these implications remain largely unexplored. In particular, discussion of the negative impacts of the consumption of meat and other animal products is missing from Francis's reflections. This is despite the fact that the livestock industry is one of the major sources of climate change and, according to a UN report, "one of the top two or three most significant contributors to the most serious environmental problems, at every scale from the local to the global."[34] Among the other problems to which the livestock industry greatly contributes are deforestation, loss of biodiversity, land degradation, water scarcity, water pollution, and air pollution.[35]

Francis clearly articulates God's concern for animals and humanity's obligation to not cause unnecessary harm, citing for example the statement in the *Catechism of the Catholic Church* (no. 2418) that it is wrong "to cause animals to suffer or die needlessly."[36] Francis does not, however, examine the horrific maltreatment of animals in factory farms or, more fundamentally, explore the question of whether any killing of animals for food should not in fact be understood as causing unnecessary harm in contexts where alternatives are available.

Vandana Shiva, who is a vegetarian, does explore these food ethics issues. She highlights, for example, the suffering of animals in factory farms, the enormous inefficiency of feeding grains and beans to livestock (a process in which the vast majority of nutrients contained in the grains and beans are lost to human consumption), and the various profound ecological harms of the livestock industry.[37] The thought of Pope Francis and CST in general could greatly benefit from enhanced awareness of these issues.

Attention to the Lived Experiences of Women

Perhaps the most fundamental insight that CST could gain from engagement with the works of Vandana Shiva is deeper awareness of the experiences of women. Strikingly, while Pope Francis speaks very eloquently of solidarity with the poor and marginalized in *Laudato Si'*, he makes no specific references to the experiences of women, including the multifaceted realities of sexism. For Shiva, in contrast, these realities are at the center of her concern. In her book *Staying Alive,* she explores the many negative impacts of conventional capitalist development policies on women, especially rural women. She highlights, for example, how increased emphasis on the production of cash crops for export undermines women's food production and their ability to meet their own nutritional needs and those of their families.[38] She also emphasizes how the deforestation connected with these practices has increased the time women need to spend gathering firewood and how the drying up of wells has increased the time spent retrieving water.[39] Similarly, she highlights how the industrialization of the dairy industry has undermined the livelihoods of many rural women and harmed the nutritional status of their families.[40] Much can be learned through engagement with these analyses of the impacts of conventional capitalist development policies on rural women. Likewise, much can be learned from Shiva's emphasis on the central role that women have played and continue to play in movements for social justice and ecological sustainability around the world.

Engaging in Dialogue with Other Traditions

There is much that Pope Francis and the broader tradition of Catholic social teaching can learn from engagement with the life and thought of Vandana Shiva. This engagement could result especially in richer insights into ecology, food ethics, nonviolent social movements, and the negative impacts of current forms of capitalist globalization on women, especially rural women. Engaging in dialogue with persons such as Vandana Shiva is, I suggest, a crucial task of the global church.

Notes

[1]Vandana Shiva, *Staying Alive: Women, Ecology, and Development* (London: Zed Books, 1989); *Monocultures of the Mind* (London: Zed Books, 1993); *Earth Democracy* (Cambridge, MA: South End Press, 2005).

[2]See Shiva's discussion of these critiques of modern science in *Staying Alive,* 14–37.

[3]Carolyn Merchant, *The Death of Nature: Women, Ecology, and the Scientific Revolution* (New York: Harper and Row, 1980).

[4]Ibid., 3, 193.

[5]Shiva, *Staying Alive,* xvii.

[6]Ibid., 22.

[7]For extensive discussion of the negative impacts of industrial agriculture, see Vandana Shiva, *Who Really Feeds the World? The Failures of Agribusiness and the Promise of Agroecology* (Berkeley, CA: North Atlantic Books, 2016); *Soil Not Oil* (London: Zed Books, 2008).

[8]Shiva, *Staying Alive*, 20–22.

[9]See Shiva, *Monocultures of the Mind*.

[10]Francis Bacon, "The Masculine Birth of Time," in *The Philosophy of Francis Bacon*, ed. and trans. Benjamin Farrington (Liverpool: Liverpool University Press, 1964), 62. Quoted in Merchant, *Death of Nature*, 169.

[11]Francis Bacon, in *The Works of Francis Bacon*, ed. J. Spedding et al. (Stuttgart: Verlag, 1963), 5:506. Quoted in Shiva, *Staying Alive*, 16.

[12]Shiva, *Staying Alive*, 16. For a good discussion of the roles of gender and class in the construction of modern science, see Merchant, *Death of Nature*; Evelyn Fox Keller, *Reflections on Gender and Science* (New Haven, CT: Yale University Press, 1985); Sandra Harding, *Whose Science? Whose Knowledge? Thinking from Women's Lives* (Ithaca, NY: Cornell University Press, 1991) and *The Science Question in Feminism* (Ithaca, NY: Cornell University Press, 1986).

[13]Shiva, *Staying Alive*, 24–25.

[14]See Shiva, *Earth Democracy*, 1–9.

[15]Ibid., 6.

[16]Ibid.

[17]For Shiva's discussion of the "feminine principle," see *Staying Alive*, 52–54.

[18]Pope Francis, *Laudato Si': On Care for Our Common Home* (2015), nos. 91, 117, 138, 240.

[19]Ibid., no. 42.

[20]Ibid., no. 33.

[21]Ibid., no. 49. Also see Leonardo Boff, *Cry of the Earth, Cry of the Poor* (Maryknoll, NY: Orbis Books, 1997).

[22]For Francis's discussion of the technocratic paradigm, see *Laudato Si'*, nos. 106–14.

[23]Ibid., no. 20.

[24]Ibid., no. 107.

[25]For discussion of each of these critiques of capitalism by Pope Francis, see John Sniegocki, "Pope Francis and Alternative Economic Visions," *Journal of Catholic Social Thought* 16, no. 2 (Summer 2019): 209–23.

[26]Pope Francis, "Message to Meeting of Popular Movements in California" (2017), http://www.usccb.org.

[27]Pope Francis, "Address to Second World Meeting of Popular Movements" (2015), http://w2.vatican.va.

[28]Ibid.

[29]Pope Francis, "Address to Third World Meeting of Popular Movements" (2016), http://w2.vatican.va.

[30]Pope Francis, "Nonviolence: A Style of Politics for Peace" (2017), https://w2.vatican.va.

[31]Vandana Shiva, "A 21st-Century Manifesto for Earth Democracy," https://catholicclimatemovement.global.

[32]For Shiva's discussion of industrial forestry, see *Staying Alive*, 55–95.

[33]For discussion of various issues related to water, see Vandana Shiva, *Water Wars: Privatization, Pollution, and Profit*, 2nd ed. (Berkeley, CA: North Atlantic Books, 2016).

[34]UN Food and Agriculture Organization, *Livestock's Long Shadow* (2006), xx.

[35]For a good discussion of the negative ecological impacts of the livestock industry, in addition to the UN report cited above, see Richard Oppenlander, *Food Choice and Sustainability* (Minneapolis: Langdon Street Press, 2013).

[36]Pope Francis, *Laudato Si'*, no. 130.

[37]See Vandana Shiva, *Stolen Harvest: The Hijacking of the Global Food Supply* (Cambridge, MA: South End Press, 2000), 62–71.

[38]See Shiva's discussion of "Women in the Food Chain," in *Staying Alive*, 96–178.

[39]See Shiva's discussion of "Women in the Forest," ibid., 55–95.

[40]Ibid., 165–73.

Toward a Cosmopolitan Localism

Walter Mignolo and Pope Francis in Dialogue

Daniel A. Rober

In 2004, Joseph Cardinal Ratzinger and Jürgen Habermas took part in a debate concerning faith and reason. This debate, later published as *The Dialectics of Secularization*, in many ways set the tone for Benedict XVI's pontificate, particularly its key intellectual interventions such as the Regensburg Address and the Westminster Hall speech. Habermas represented an ideal dialogue partner in many ways to Ratzinger—a German intellectual of similar age and training whose fundamental concerns related in important ways to his own.[1] Pope Francis, who, as this essay describes, tends to distrust abstract intellectualism, has tended before and during his pontificate to focus more on personal engagements, for example with Rabbi Abraham Skorka and the Jewish community of Buenos Aires. If there were a contemporary thinker with whom he might have a fruitful such dialogue, however, his fellow Argentine Walter Mignolo, a professor of literature at Duke who has written extensively on issues concerning colonialism and its continuing effects, would be a strong candidate.

The pontificate of Pope Francis has brought an Argentinian perspective to the heart of the church hierarchy in ways that have been transformative for the life of the church. Amid much analysis of Francis and his thought, there has been little commentary about the intellectual connections between Francis and Mignolo.[2] Mignolo's thought parallels several important ideas of Francis—most notably the notion that the world is not a sphere but a polyhedron,[3] which Mignolo thinks of as "cosmopolitan localism"—while offering a significantly sharper critique of globalization and other phenomena that have come out of the "modern" West.[4]

Mignolo's widely read work, *The Darker Side of Western Modernity*, posits that the modern West has a twofold "darker" side—first, its legacy has been built on a series of "dark" deeds, particularly the slave trade and genocides of native peoples, and second, many of the people who have been victimized by modernity have been precisely those of darker complexion.[5] Here and elsewhere in Mignolo's work, he destabilizes notions such as center and periphery that have been essential to Western thinking, and indeed to much contemporary Christian thinking as seen in Pope Francis's repeated admonitions to go out to the peripheries. For Mignolo, these concepts are essentially imperial and Western, and decolonial thinking (which in Mignolo's thinking has much the same meaning as "postcolonial" in other cultural contexts) exposes the way in which these modes of discourse have assisted in the oppression of peoples not just politically but in their very epistemology.

Mignolo's Challenge to Coloniality

This essay argues that taking Mignolo's work seriously for theology would further radicalize the shift away from the traditional Western narratives that Francis has in many ways already begun to encourage. It means accepting and living with the destabilization of comfortable concepts and institutions. The challenge for those who have benefited from modernity and Western forms of postmodernity is to accept that even their apparently liberating aspects—particularly the ways they have eased the lives of many people in the developed world—have been accomplished at the expense of or with disregard for those of other peoples. This acceptance furthermore requires action, and Mignolo's thought acts as a spur toward a mystical politics of cosmopolitan localism that the church ought to model and advocate for.

Mignolo situates cosmopolitanism in regard to globalism: "While *globalism* is the term to designate the neo-liberal project, *cosmopolitanism*" is the term that names honest liberal projects (Mignolo, *The Darker Side of Western Modernity*, 255). Globalism, Mignolo argues, has its roots in early modern Christianity and its colonial project, having been succeeded by secular versions (256). Cosmopolitanism, likewise, has been part and parcel of Western expansionism and serves to hide coloniality (257–59). It must be replaced by a decolonial cosmopolitanism that "emerges from the borders, in exteriority, in the realm of colonial difference," rather than the version that "was concocted and enacted in and from the metropolitan centers" (285). This project is in pursuit of breaking the "colonial matrix" undergirding the contemporary world, which controls not only capital but also "the sphere of knowledge and subjectivity" (xix).

What, then, of cosmopolitanism? For Mignolo, decolonizing cosmopolitanism means pursuing a "decolonial cosmopolitan order" built on "various models of conviviality that Western cosmopolitanism suppressed" (270). Mignolo describes such an order in terms of a "world in which many worlds would coexist" (273). Rather than a globalized sameness, Mignolo is arguing for true difference interconnected by the potentially (but not always actually) positive elements of globalization such as communication systems. These worlds coexist while seeking each other's flourishing rather than destruction.

Mignolo's constructive proposal is for what he calls a "cosmopolitan localism," where an interconnected world is experienced on a local, indigenous level. He describes "localisms breaking away, delinking, building, and being in the world otherwise than the liberal or Marxist cosmopolitan" (276). Those latter cosmopolitanisms were and are hegemonic, built on ideas imposed or coerced from without. Mignolo envisions a world in which ideas from various localities come into constructive dialogue.

Mignolo uses the image in his description of cosmopolitan localism of "communal nodes . . . cooperating rather than competing with each other," with no node that "envisions itself extending all over the planet in a grand cosmopolitan salvation mission" (283). Mignolo here seems to be speaking of American cultural imperialism, where today corporations and technological platforms extend themselves around the world in search of customers and dominance. Those platforms often claim to value diversity, but even such diversity fully realized in what Mignolo calls a "polycentric capitalist world" would not be truly decolonial (285).

The thrust of Mignolo's thought is ultimately epistemological: he wants to pursue a way to think about the world otherwise than modern Western rationality would have it. Mignolo's thought continues and contributes to a trajectory of Latin American thought pioneered by Rodolfo Kusch, another Argentinian theorist. Kusch argues, in short, that Latin Americans need to retrieve and put forward the philosophy that he calls "an implicit way of thinking lived every day in the street or in the countryside."[6] Mignolo is admittedly indebted to Kusch, and speaks perhaps introspectively of an "immigrant consciousness" of those who, like his and Pope Francis's families (they are both Argentines of Italian background), are transplanted into societies with established societal hierarchies.

For Mignolo, then, decolonial thought requires a substantive uprooting of Western thought patterns in order to decenter them. It is ultimately about what he calls a de-coloniality of being, which implies "de-linking from the Western subject and from any pretense to uni-versality."[7] The situatedness of decolonial thought in Latin America gives it a sense of place, but does not elevate it over, or fundamentally put it in competition with, other forms of postcolonial thought that speak from their own contexts.

Pope Francis: The Sphere and the Polyhedron

In his apostolic exhortation *Evangelii Gaudium* ("The Joy of the Gospel"), which serves in many ways as a kind of constitution for his pontificate, Pope Francis lays out a set of four principles that inform his view of the world:

1. Time is greater than space.
2. Unity prevails over conflict.
3. Realities are more important than ideas.
4. The whole is greater than the parts. (*EG* 222–37)

These principles, while coming to the fore in this document, have been a major thread in the intellectual development of Jorge Mario Bergoglio. His intellectual biographer Massimo Borghesi traces these ideas to his study of Romano Guardini.[8]

Taken together, these maxims express a series of dualities or tensions that are then weighted according to importance. The idea that time is greater than space is important because, as Francis describes it, in many contexts "spaces and power are preferred to time and processes" (*EG* 222). When this happens, programs and agendas become more important than people and other higher values. But time is geared toward a future, what Borghesi calls the "patient construction of projects that are not limited to the present but keep in mind the future development of peoples."[9]

Unity prevailing over conflict is the formula Francis uses to, in his words, "build communion amid disagreement" (*EG* 228). This is not simply "agreeing to disagree" or putting aside disagreements for the sake of getting along, but rather a sign of the true greatness that comes with humility and the courage to face rather than sublimate conflict. Engaging in conflict rather than simply avoiding it allows us to pursue the true unity that comes from solidarity. Francis thus sees conflict as valuable, but not for its own sake or even for some political end in the Marxist sense of dialectic or heightening contradictions; rather, conflict must proceed from and move toward a desire for the common good of all.

In resolving the tension between reality and ideas, Francis puts it simply: "Realities simply are, whereas ideas are worked out" (*EG* 231). Realities thus have a kind of givenness to them that ideas do not—ideas need to be formulated, whereas reality places itself in front of us whether we care to notice it or not. As Francis says elsewhere, "*Reality* is. *Idea* is elaborated, induced."[10]

The duality of the whole and the part is described by Borghesi in terms of "*globalization-localization,*" which he views as Bergoglio's way of wrestling with post-1989 globalization and its relationship to various cultures.[11] This dichotomy, in some respects, adds up to Francis's other dictum, which is that the world is not a sphere but a polyhedron. As laid out in the following section of *The Joy of the Gospel*, this idea prioritizes the "polyhedron, which reflects the convergence of all its parts, each of which preserves its distinctiveness" (*EG* 236). With this concept, Francis resists the "flattening" effects of globalization in favor of a vision of the world and church enriched by the various points of the polyhedron.

Francis has also commented that the way the church can contribute to globalization today is dialogue, envisaged as a bridge between cultures.[12] On this point, he notes that in globalization, envisaged as the polyhedron, God is everywhere (Pope Francis, *Future of Faith*, 49). As a contrast to this, he borrows from Guardini a cyclical concept of "unculture" in which people take precultural forms and build them into a culture, only to then subsequently undo them through what Francis calls "monoculture," that is, a reduction of culture to select components (67). This is most notable in the liberal market economy, which Francis calls "madness" in the way it reduces people to their earning potential (68).

Much of Francis's thought boils down to an emphasis on lived experiences over abstract ideas that reduce those experiences to simplistic categories. In some sense, the idea that "reality is more important than ideas" serves as a keystone for much of his thought and pontificate. This explains to a large degree his resistance to liberation theology, which he views as an ideological intellectual movement with many strands over-indebted to Marxism.[13] Francis indeed has pointed out that the "danger in theology lies in making things over-ideological" (188). He has usually been seen—and indeed identified himself—as more sympathetic to the "theology of the people," an Argentine movement within liberation theology broadly construed. This movement, in the words of Rafael Luciani, argues that "theology has to be contextualized in peoples and their cultures, never outside them, or it will be insignificant and irrelevant, unable to speak to concrete human subjects who live out their personal history in the midst of their everyday life."[14] His sympathy for the theology of the people, then, is representative of Francis's priority for realities—particularly people—over what he would view as the danger of reduction to abstract ideas.

Ships Passing in the Night?

Given that Francis and Mignolo both hail from Argentina and demonstrate clear convergences in some key aspects of their thought, it is notable how in some senses there has been little direct convergence between them. For example, in an interview, Mignolo has argued that "Pope Francis feels the world from the Third World, and that makes a difference."[15] Mignolo has thus expressed a level of interest in Francis as a fellow Argentine and as someone bringing this perspective to bear on the governance of a major global institution. However, it is notable that Mignolo says that Francis "feels" rather than "thinks" from the Third World. This might reflect a judgment either that the intellectual approaches favored by Francis owe too much to European models such as Guardini's, or that the Latin American approaches he favors such as the theology of the people do not meet the standard for what Mignolo would consider an indigenous epistemology. I suggest later in this essay that Enrique Dussel's liberation theology, more so than the theology of the people, represents a closer approximation of Mignolo's vision for movement toward an indigenous epistemology.

Mignolo's thought has notably reflected on some of the explicit concepts found in Francis, particularly the duality of time and space. He argues that near the end of the nineteenth century "spatial boundaries" separating various civilizations "were transformed into chronological ones."[16] Thus, in a broadly Hegelian sense, civilization was viewed in terms of progress. As Mignolo puts it, "Time . . . reordered universal history and became the essence of modernity" such that "to be civilized is to be modern, and to be modern means to be in the present."[17] Mignolo's sense of time here is somewhat distinct from that of Francis, in cautioning about an important challenge, namely, how to think in terms of time while avoiding narratives assuming the inevitability of progress.

Perhaps the most potent connection between Francis and Mignolo is that between the polyhedron described by Francis and Mignolo's communal nodes. Both Mignolo and Pope Francis choose similar images connoting the way that different parts of the world ought to relate. Both seek to move beyond an image of the world centered only on certain cultures or discourses claiming universality on the basis of traditional power and prestige. There is thus a certain complementarity between Mignolo and Francis, in terms both of ideas that connect but also of possible correctives to one another. Mignolo offers a more intellectually rich and nuanced description of the situations he is describing. However, Francis, by virtue of his life of ministry, brings practical wisdom and experience to his analysis.

Two other Argentine thinkers help highlight the convergences and divergences between Pope Francis and decolonial theory.

Enrique Dussel and Marcella Althaus-Reid have been in conversation with Mignolo's intellectual currents while maintaining stronger ties to Catholic theology, particularly the movement of liberation theology, than Mignolo. Dussel in particular can be helpful for building connections between Francis and Mignolo, and Althaus-Reid challenges both of them in important ways.

Dussel's thought in many ways helps bridge the thought of Francis and Mignolo by engaging in a version of liberation theology that incorporates the kind of cultural analysis pioneered by Mignolo. Dussel thus performs in a Latin American context an approach that I think would be helpful on a broader scale. In particular, he makes these connections through his richly drawn ideas about history and language. As Dussel puts it, "We fail to take cognizance of the fact that language is not only a tool for communication, but also a trap" in that "the very words of a language conceal the experience of a people; they cover over that experience."[18] For Dussel, as for Mignolo, languages and concepts from outside have often served to oppress and elide experience. Dussel adds, however, an eschatological consciousness that bridges the gap and also deepens the conversation. As he puts it, even in the Western sphere, the "process of conceptualization began to give special emphasis to certain Christian experiences to which it could give expression. Other Christian experiences, for which Greek philosophic thought could not find any expression, were not conceptualized in an adequate way" (17). For Dussel, "Faith can never get to its last and ultimate horizon because that horizon is historical," and history is always moving (18). This construction of time helps bridge the gap between Mignolo and Francis on this point, since Dussel speaks both their languages.

Marcella Althaus-Reid subjects traditional Catholic theology and practice as well as male-produced liberation theology to a scathing critique; she has notably been a sympathetic critic of Dussel, drawing on his work while also critiquing it for being dismissive or critical around issues concerning sexuality.[19] Her work makes important contributions to a number of theological discourses, including particularly queer theology, but my essay focuses on the connections she draws between liberation theology and decolonial discourse.

Althaus-Reid argues that liberation theologies have done part of the work of separating Christian thought out from Western colonial discourses, but have not fully accomplished this task.[20] The danger, she argues, is a kind of fetishization in which liberation theology becomes a kind of "theme park theology," which "may be the theology of the poor, but it still obeys the tradition of the thinking and logic of the centre."[21] In this sense, Althaus-Reid echoes aspects of Mignolo's thinking, with an incisively drawn critique of both Western theologies and Latin American male theologies. She goes so far in another work as to point out that liberation theology was "a movement from the margins into the central discourse of theology," that was constituted as "a kind of cultural mirror act which considered any discourse from the south, barbaric."[22] Susan Abraham echoes this point with specific reference to Mignolo by critiquing his distinction between decolonial thought and South Asian postcolonial thought, particularly in the way that it tends to avoid categories of gender.[23]

Althaus-Reid's feminist thought also challenges narratives taken for granted particularly by Francis but also by Mignolo. For example, she describes Mary as a "symbol in prison" with respect to the way that imagery surrounding her is used to keep women in oppression in Latin America.[24] She describes how in Peru indigenous "institutions have been attacked by a patriarchal project of colonization, whose interpretation of Christianity has proved to be opposed to the ethos of the Andean regions."[25] Thus she deepens Mignolo's critique by bringing issues of gender to bear while raising questions that Francis scarcely treats. Althaus-Reid's ideas challenge Francis's pastoral praxis—and Mignolo's cosmopolitan localism—to be more true to their own best ideals with respect to the experiences and contributions of women.

Synodality and Cosmopolitan Localism

I would like to argue, then, that Francis and Mignolo might serve as effective conversation partners, insofar as Mignolo's ideas help theorize important aspects of Francis's agenda for the church. Cosmopolitan localism as an ideal connects strongly with the idea of synodality, which has been a hallmark of Francis's pontificate. Synodality allows all points of the polyhedron of the global church to bring their insights to bear on important matters.[26] While this might look different in a Catholic context than in certain other churches such as the Orthodox Church or Anglican Communion where it is arguably more integral to the structure of the church, it is still remarkable the degree to which Francis has emphasized and brought forward this element that was neglected during the previous two pontificates.

The Synod on the Amazon presents an important case in point with respect to Francis and Mignolo, and not only because it is located in Latin America. As the preparatory document argues, although the Amazon is one place on the planet, "It is a mirror of all humanity which, in defense of life, requires structural and personal changes by all human beings, by nations, and by the Church."[27] This point signifies the broader importance of the synod for cosmopolitan localism—it deals with issues in a particular locale that have significance for everyone, in a site (the Vatican) that has symbolic and juridical significance for the universal church. It thus represents an ideal place to begin performing this version of cosmopolitan localism by thinking through issues specific to the Amazon, even as their possible implications for others draw attention and critique.

Beyond the appeal of synodality, however, I would argue that the ideal of cosmopolitan localism effectively applied would have broader implications for the church, in which Mignolo's insights along with those of Dussel and Althaus-Reid would be particularly helpful. Cosmopolitan localism would mean embracing an epistemic humility that breaks down the relationship between center and periphery by refusing to assume that ideas mean the same thing, or apply in the same way, in different contexts.

The Truly Global Church

An essential challenge for contemporary Christians has been understanding what it means to live in a truly global church. This is particularly true for Catholics in Europe and North America, because many were implicitly raised on the assumption that, in Hilaire Belloc's words, "The Church is Europe, and Europe is the Church."[28] Mignolo's thought, while broadly unsympathetic to religion, opens a way forward in this discussion that avoids the nostalgia of many restorationist attempts to combat secularity, while avoiding overly optimistic attempts to apply modern or postmodern categories too sweepingly. Most notably, it upends the notion, shared by Pope Benedict among others, that Western thought, going back to Greco-Roman philosophers, has an exclusive purchase as the philosophical system par excellence undergirding Christian theology.[29]

The cosmopolitan localism sketched out above in dialogue with Mignolo and Pope Francis represents an ideal and one very much worth pursuing in an age in which globalization clearly has not brought about the kind of happiness that it promises, and various forms of nationalism have been offered as alternatives. Cosmopolitan localism presents a vision that emerges from a context and stays rooted in it while reaching out toward the universal, yet never claiming to possess it. Were Pope Francis and Walter Mignolo to engage in the dialogue discussed at the beginning of this essay, I believe they would agree that a shared framework on the basis of their thought in this area is possible and indeed perhaps necessary.

Notes

[1] Jürgen Habermas and Joseph Ratzinger, *The Dialectics of Secularization* (San Francisco: Ignatius Press, 2006).

[2] The most notable such comparison is Bradford E. Hinze, "Decolonizing Everyday Practices: Sites of Struggle in Church and Society," *CTSA Proceedings* 71 (2016).

[3] Pope Francis, *Evangelii Gaudium* ("The Joy of the Gospel"), 236. http://w2.vatican.va. Hereinafter referred to as *EG*; references to this work are given parenthetically in the text.

[4] For discussion of issues surrounding "cosmopolitanism," see Kwame Anthony Appiah, *Cosmopolitanism: Ethics in a World of Strangers* (New York: W. W. Norton, 2006), and Martha Nussbaum, *Cosmopolitanism: A Fragile but Flawed Ideal* (Cambridge, MA: Harvard University Press, 2019).

[5] Walter Mignolo, *The Darker Side of Western Modernity* (Durham, NC: Duke University Press, 2011), 2. Hereafter page references to this book are given parenthetically in the text.

[6] Rodolfo Kusch, *Indigenous and Popular Thinking in Latin America*, trans. María Lugones and Joshua M. Price (Durham, NC: Duke University Press, 2010), 1.

[7] Mignolo, Introduction to Kusch, *Indigenous and Popular Thinking*, xvii.

[8] Massimo Borghesi, *The Mind of Pope Francis*, trans. Barry Hudock (Collegeville, MN: Liturgical Press, 2018), 107.

[9] Ibid., 115.

[10]Jorge Mario Bergoglio, *Noi come cittadini, noi come popolo* (Vatican: Libreria Editrice Vaticana, 2010), 65. Cited in Borghesi, *Mind of Pope Francis*, 116.

[11]Borghesi, *Mind of Pope Francis*, 117.

[12]Pope Francis, with Dominique Wolton, *A Future of Faith*, trans. Shaun Whiteside (New York: St. Martin's Press, 2018), 47–48. Further page references are usually given parenthetically in the text.

[13]Ibid., 188: "And, within liberation theology, some components have gone missing, let's put it that way, along partisan paths, with far-left parties or with Marxist analysis."

[14]Rafael Luciani, *Pope Francis and the Theology of the People*, trans. Philip Berryman (Maryknoll, NY: Orbis Books, 2017), 9.

[15]Ignacio López-Calvo, "Coloniality Is Not Over, It Is All Over": Interview with Dr. Walter Mignolo, November 2014, part 1, *Transmodernity* 6, no. 1 (Spring 2016): 178.

[16]Mignolo, *Local Histories/Global Designs* (Princeton, NJ: Princeton University Press, 2012), 283.

[17]Ibid., 285.

[18]Enrique Dussel, *History and the Theology of Liberation*, trans. John Drury (Maryknoll, NY: Orbis Books, 1976), 13. Further page references are given parenthetically in the text.

[19]Marcella Althaus-Reid, *Indecent Theology* (London: Routledge, 2000), 194.

[20]Marcella Althaus-Reid, "Gustavo Gutiérrez Goes to Disneyland," in *From Feminist Theology to Indecent Theology* (London: SCM, 2004), 128.

[21]Ibid., 129.

[22]Althaus-Reid, *Indecent Theology*, 25.

[23]Susan Abraham, "Postcolonial Hermeneutics and a Catholic (Post) Modernity," in *Beyond Dogmatism and Innocence: Hermeneutics, Critique, and Catholic Theology*, ed. Anthony J. Godzieba and Bradford E. Hinze (Collegeville, MN: Liturgical Press, 2017), 223.

[24]Marcella Althaus-Reid, "Troubling Theology," in *From Feminist Theology to Indecent Theology*, 23.

[25]Ibid., 27.

[26]Francis describes his vision of synodality in his 2016 address to the Roman Curia, calling for greater conversation between different departments of the hierarchy and succinctly arguing, "A synodal Church is a listening Church." Pope Francis, "Presentation of Christmas Greetings to the Roman Curia," December 22, 2016, n. 30. https://w2.vatican.va.

[27]"Amazonia: New Paths for the Church and for an Integral Ecology," Preparatory Document, June 8, 2018. https://press.vatican.va.

[28]Hilaire Belloc, *Europe and the Faith*, http://www.gutenberg.org.

[29]Katie Grimes has argued effectively against this in "Does God Speak Greek?" *Theology Today* 75, no. 2 (2018): 193–213.

Postmodern Theological Curriculum Theory in a Globalized Context

Tracey Lamont

Students from around the world study theology in online and face-to-face classes. Cultural, racial, gender, and ethnic differences often focus our discussions—usually but not always in fruitful ways. I have witnessed graduate students in pastoral ministry courses misunderstand one another in online discussions over cultural, ideological, and ethnic differences; and in one face-to-face class, students had heated exchanges over issues of race, gender, and ethnicity. These experiences raise questions for me about how religious and theological educators can help students practice intercultural communication skills, more fully understand and value the voices of the other, undertake a constructive process of learning through the perspectives of diverse cultures and ways of knowing, and all this both in traditional face-to-face classes and virtually in online classes.

This essay explores the implicit and explicit influences of the modern Euro-American curriculum and pedagogy[1] on teaching religion and theology in Catholic higher education in a globalized context. William E. Doll Jr. describes how the modernist curriculum values and reinforces characteristics of progress, industry, empirical data, uniformity, and rational objectivity.[2] This modern curriculum emerges from white Western or Euro-American education and curriculum theory, which prizes empiricism, objectivity, and the scientific method, and downplays emotions, subjectivity, and the teachers' and students' experiences.[3]

From the perspective of the modern curriculum, these more subjective ways of teaching and learning can be characterized as less valuable, less academic, and therefore inappropriate in academic spaces. Dialogue on culture, race, ethnicity, and gender, however, involves emotions and experiences—including experiences of colonialism, racism, prejudice, and discrimination. Derald Wing Sue, in his research on the psychology of race talk, explores how educators cannot exclude experiential and emotional ways of knowing from their curricula if they are to address personal, institutional, or cultural racism and discrimination. He argues that such "attempt[s] to maintain objectivity . . . have resulted in separation of the person from the group (valuing of individualism and uniqueness), science from spirituality, man/woman from the universe, and thoughts from feelings."[4]

Theology as a discipline is subjective—it seeks truth and understanding through interpretation and the search for wisdom and meaning. Theology in a globalized context involves attentiveness to how theology and spirituality are lived and practiced through a myriad of diverse cultural forms and expressions. Therefore, theological educators are encouraged to embody cultural diversity and more subjective approaches in their teaching and learning. Curriculum theorist Patrick Slattery writes that "curriculum development in the postmodern era demands that we find a way around the hegemonic forces and institutional obstacles that limit our knowledge, reinforce our prejudices, and disconnect us from the global community."[5] Heeding Slattery's advice, this essay reenvisions the art and practice of teaching theology in higher education, and offers educators a way forward—beyond the dominant Western curriculum model prevalent in the Global North. It examines how a culturally responsive and constructive postmodern theological curriculum can enable educators to rethink their curriculum design and develop an intercultural pedagogy and other teaching strategies that integrate a reverence for cultural, racial, and ethnic diversity, as well as recognition of unity within a global context.

Overview

Teaching and learning theology in a globalized context necessitates that educators be attentive to curriculum development, which I, along with Doll and Slattery, define less as "a course to be run" and more as a "process of development, dialogue, inquiry, transformation" that envisions "education [as] a transformative enterprise."[6] This understanding encourages theological educators to explore how various pedagogies enhance or limit our curriculum in a global context. The first section of this essay provides a brief overview of the limits of some liberation pedagogies for teaching and learning in a globalized context.[7] Next, it explores the implicit and explicit influences on the modern Euro-American curriculum as contrasted with a postmodern curriculum framework, and concludes by offering strategies and methods for developing a culturally responsive postmodern theological curriculum.

Pedagogies of Liberation

Liberation pedagogies, or pedagogies of resistance, such as critical and antiracist pedagogies, seek to elevate the voices of the oppressed and marginalized as a way of "understand[ing] curriculum as a political text."[8] Critical pedagogy emerges from liberation theology, most notably from the work of Paulo Freire,[9] while antiracist pedagogies, according to Christine Sleeter, "emerged largely in opposition to multicultural education" framed from the perspective of "white educators."[10] The theories surrounding these pedagogies do not always explore the power dynamics involved in developing a postmodern theological curriculum for teaching and learning in a global context.

Antiracist pedagogies, for example, often refer to racism as it is experienced in the United States. However, in my online courses, I have several students from countries in East Africa, where they face challenges navigating tribal and religious diversity among people of the same race but from different cultures, religious traditions, or factions. It is, therefore, more advantageous to frame discussions on white privilege and cultural diversity in terms of power when teaching a globally diverse student body. Eric H. F. Law, in his work with multicultural communities, argues that multicultural groups should engage in a power analysis by first acknowledging that inequality exists, and then by examining and unpacking perceptions of power.[11] This method helps participants, in our case, students, explore doing justice in an "ethnorelative," rather than ethnocentric, way (Law, 35). In using an ethnorelative approach, Law states,

> We begin by accepting the reality that people's power perceptions are different because of cultural difference. By analyzing these power perceptions and how they are relative to each other, we will see that there is a great disparity of power between the two groups. . . . [Then] we need to create an environment that allows people to interact with equal power and therefore redistributes power evenly. (35)

In this way, theological educators can begin exploring systems of oppression first through an analysis of power and then through the diverse social and cultural contexts of the students, as a way of building a transformative curriculum that enables students to develop intercultural competencies in a variety of settings, in addition to committing to the work of dismantling racism.

Feminist scholars also offer an important critique of liberation or critical pedagogy, noting how it is framed in a modernist worldview that focuses more on class than on race and culture.[12] Elizabeth Ellsworth, for example, argues that, among other shortcomings, "The desire by the mostly white, middle-class men who write the literature on critical pedagogy to elicit 'full expression' of student voices . . . becomes voyeuristic when the voice of the pedagogue himself goes unexamined."[13] Ellsworth encourages educators, when developing a culturally responsive postmodern curriculum in a global context, to conduct an analysis of power between the students, the teacher, and—as intercultural pedagogy suggests—the text.

Ellsworth's critique also notes that "the literature on critical pedagogy implies that students and teachers can and should engage each other in the classroom as fully rational subjects."[14] If the literature on pedagogies of liberation fails to explore the depth of emotional reactions that can emerge from conversations on racism, colonialism, power, privilege, and oppression, it thus limits theological educators in creating transformative curricula and culturally responsive classrooms. Furthermore, as Slattery contends, "Curriculum scholars who were writing specifically about race, gender, ethics, [and] politics . . . were relatively small in number. Their voices were usually excluded from mainstream discourses, professional journals, and curriculum textbooks."[15] This suggests that very few educators have been encouraged to view curriculum as a political text, or to adopt liberation pedagogies; if they have been open to such pedagogies, they nevertheless may not have understood the implicit epistemological influences on the modern curriculum.

Many educators who find themselves in a heated exchange over topics of race, power, privilege, and oppression struggle, often because of fear and/or ignorance, to handle emotional outbursts in classroom settings and, thus, cease talking about these challenging topics. This presents a barrier to creating a culturally responsive classroom for teachers who are unsure about how to handle negative emotions, or who have tried and felt that they failed. Educators who experience the dichotomy between the expectation of holding rational, objective discussions and the subject matter—of those very discussions—that elicits strong emotions are likely unaware of the implicit curriculum of the modern worldview. This curriculum and its accompanying pedagogy value cognition and objectivity over emotions or experiential ways of knowing, and thus create an internal separation within the teacher and between the teacher and students. In sum, the literature on critical and antiracist pedagogies draws out noteworthy connections among epistemology, curriculum development, and pedagogy.

Modernism, Postmodernism, and Curriculum

Our worldview or understanding of curriculum and pedagogy frames our efforts in teaching and learning in a globalized context. Modern curriculum theories draw insight from advances in science and technology and from European Enlightenment philosophers such as René Descartes and his emphasis on ordered reason and observable truths. From this worldview emerged Ralph Tyler's *Basic Principles of Curriculum and Instruction* in 1949, still used as a primary source in curriculum programs in higher education.[16] In what became known as the Tyler rationale, this method of curriculum and instruction begins by identifying goals and objectives, or standards, then creates learning experiences aimed at achievement of the predetermined objectives, followed by an evaluation process to assess if the objectives have been met. Slattery provides a concise summary of the paradigm shifts giving rise to the modern and postmodern periods. He states, "We have been conditioned" by modernism and the modern curriculum "to believe that our goals, objectives, lesson plans, and educational outcomes must all be *measurable* and *behaviorally observable* in order to be valid."[17] He goes on to state:

> I have met very few teachers who actually believe this philosophy of education. However, the majority who do not ascribe to this educational ideology—rooted in scientific management and the Tylerian Rationale—have allowed themselves to be conditioned to behave as though they do. Postmodernism challenges educators to explore a worldview that envisions schooling through a different lens of indeterminacy, aesthetics, autobiography, intuition, eclecticism, and mystery.[18]

The espoused methodology in the modern curriculum views knowledge as the search for truth based on what one can prove— or, according to Doll, "Whatever is true, factual, real is discovered, not created."[19] The legacy and influence of the Tylerian model of education is evidenced in the national push for standardized testing in the United States and other countries such as South Korea and Nigeria. Characteristics of the modern Tyler rationale can also be found in the efforts by some school districts or state colleges and universities to remove the humanities and the arts from school curricula.[20] Many students in the United States are, as a result, accustomed to "showing what they know" through standardized tests, which often contain only multiple choice questions. There is nothing more prescribed or predetermined than choosing an "answer" from four or five predetermined choices.

Postmodernism, in contrast, is "a process of development, dialogue, inquiry, transformation," which, as Doll states, "moves beyond a spectator epistemology, beyond a process-product, subjective-objective split" that characterizes the modern curriculum framework.[21] Willie James Jennings, in his discussion on "renouncing the way Whiteness thinks," refers to a modernist strand in Christian education that he calls "pedagogical imperialism," which perceives Christianity to be a closed system in which "Christians entered the new world as imagining themselves as the teachers of the world, as the bringers of a civilization and sophistication, and the world as perpetual learners, as infants always in need of arriving at the truth"—a truth, I would argue, that is predetermined by the modern Euro-American curriculum. Jennings argues that "to be a learner is to enter the world of another's ecology of knowing, to be willing and eager to listen and to perceive the world through the senses and sensibilities of another people. The colonialist legacy we inherited, however, has fundamentally denied other ways of knowing and turned knowledge itself into a commodity."[22] Therefore, it is necessary to model teaching and learning across difference by employing a culturally responsive pedagogy that, according to Geneva Gay, "teaches *to and through* the strengths of [our] students."[23]

The objective, rational thinking that dominates the modern Euro-American curriculum also implicates theological educators to the extent that they are not prepared or willing to engage students in conversations of race, power, privilege, and oppression that have the potential to become emotionally charged. Derald Wing Sue argues that from the overemphasis in the United States on "Western science . . . we are often told to be objective, that rationality is the ability to separate ourselves from the issues, and not to let our emotions get in the way."[24] As a result, Sue states:

> Most people prefer to avoid discussing race for many reasons. White Americans are fearful that whatever they say or do in a racial dialogue might make them appear biased and racist. Thus, as observed by Kiselica (1999), they may enter a conversation on race with great trepidation, be very careful about what and how they say things, remain silent and guarded, minimize or dilute the importance of the racial issues, profess color blindness, and voice their thoughts and opinions in politically correct language.[25]

This emotional avoidance, for some theological educators, is not limited to conversations on race, but extends to class discussions on cultural and ethnic differences as well. Some educators fear that they will say the wrong thing and escalate the hostility in the classroom, making students of color feel marginalized, devalued, or hurt by hostility from white students. It is also the case that some teachers are not clear on the complexities of racism or colonialism, or themselves believe the false narratives perpetuated in US culture that espouse the myths of meritocracy or that everyone is equal and that therefore people can and should pull themselves up by their "bootstraps" to get ahead in life. Such educators are unable to engage productively in conversations related to racism, power, and privilege.

George Yancy acknowledges the struggles involved in dismantling racism. He calls the needed dismantling process "un-suturing," whereby white teachers can teach about race, power, privilege, and oppression by first "modeling white vulnerability, frank speech, and processes of mourning or lamenting the horrors that white racism has created and continues to generate."[26] Scholars who write on culturally responsive practices also model this sort of "un-suturing" in their writing. Law, for example, models vulnerability and honesty as he recounts how his efforts to develop culturally inclusive liturgies and trainings have not always gone the way he envisioned they should.[27] Similarly, Stephen Brookfield reflects on his efforts to teach about race in the classroom, and states, "The fundamental reality and experience of teaching race is feeling as if you're not getting it right. Once you accept that things will never go the way you anticipate, you start to reframe what success and failure means."[28] As Lucia Pawlowski once said, as recounted by Brookfield, "There are two ways to teach about race—badly, or not at all."[29] For theological educators, silence is not an option.

A Postmodern Theological Curriculum and Pedagogy

The polarizing tendencies in public politics and policy, along with, as Slattery notes, "intractable racism, sexism, heterosexism, xenophobia, and other prejudices, make the current climate for discussing issues of justice and compassion volatile . . . [rendering] the story of theology and curriculum in schools and society . . . a complex and complicated conversation."[30] Drawing on Slattery's understanding of curriculum as a postmodern theological text, Geneva Gay's culturally responsive teaching, and Boyung Lee's intercultural pedagogy, I argue that theological educators can create classroom spaces that encourage and value ontological or experiential and emotional ways of knowing and that include "storytelling or bearing witness to one's lived reality or experiences."[31]

Slattery proposes a "postmodern curriculum as theological text," which through its emphasis on "diversity, eclecticism, and ecumenism [can] bring us closer to wisdom and justice."[32] It includes "metaphysical dialogue . . . [where] self-reflection, intuition, nonrational discourse, nonlinear teaching methodologies, meditation, and wisdom are all encouraged and nurtured in the curriculum."[33] The postmodern curriculum recognizes, embraces, and encourages the dynamics of living in a globalized society where knowledge is socially constructed, deconstructed, and created among all elements of the curriculum, students, teacher, setting, and larger world. It is my contention, therefore, that theological educators, in becoming attentive to the implicit and explicit influences on their curricula, may come to embody more fully the curricula they espouse.[34]

Practicing intercultural communication skills in the classroom provides one way for students and teachers to learn from diverse perspectives and ways of knowing, in both face-to-face and online classrooms—a way of doing justice that "becomes embodied teaching."[35] Gay defines culturally responsive teaching as "using the cultural characteristics, prior experiences, frames of reference, and performance styles of ethnically diverse students to make learning encounters more relevant and effective for them. It teaches *to and through* the strengths of these students."[36] This teaching style corresponds to Law's experience with multicultural communities. He states that "to be interculturally sensitive, we need to examine the internal instinctual part of our own culture. This means revealing unconscious values and thought patterns so that we will not simply react from our cultural instinct."[37] In this way, the practice of "un-suturing" assists white theological educators, by shifting the power structure in teaching, to "give power away," by being humble, vulnerable, and honest about our own social location and privilege, as part of our commitment to intercultural learning with and through our students.[38]

Developing an intercultural pedagogy encourages theological

educators to create a culturally responsive, postmodern theological curriculum in a globalized context. Lee describes intercultural pedagogy as a way to "promote interaction between participants of different backgrounds, and remain cognizant of the merits of interculturality."[39] Citing Nami Kim's work *Liberating Interdependence*, Lee states:

> It is critical for us not to focus simply on the author's voice in the classroom or on the purported orthodoxy of church leaders. Instead we should investigate the ways different groups of people in Christian communities across history create meaning out of the text, using their different cultural backgrounds. We need to examine how these different interpretations create a multiplicity of meanings that interact with and condition one another.[40]

Lee provides an example based on teaching biblical studies: "It is essential to analyze how the West reads and interprets the Bible, and to study the Bible's modern-day interpreters' socio-political-economic assumptions, and their implications."[41]

Other strategies to help students and teachers unpack ontological knowing and grow in intercultural sensitivities include reflective journaling and using autobiographies to help students uncover their perceptions of power. In the beginning of the semester, I discuss and model Law's strategy of mutual invitation, and as the semester unfolds, I use this method of communication in small and large group discussions with my students. This ensures that each person has the power to invite someone else to contribute to the discussion, and, simultaneously, each person has the power either to remain silent or to contribute.[42]

To be effective in helping students and teachers recognize forces of power and oppression in their own contexts (their ministries, work, and social lives), this style of teaching must include attentiveness to the emotional dimensions of learning. As Law notes, our efforts to build intercultural sensitivity can feel unnerving. In working to "uncover our own internal culture," we can feel

> like a fish being pulled out of the water and discovering for the first time that the water had been its total life context.

A fish out of the water is not comfortable. Its life is in danger. That is how it feels sometimes when we are being pulled outside our cultural water so that we can see what our culture looks like from the other's point of view. We can feel very threatened and insecure.[43]

Ignoring these inner states, this affective dimension of knowing and doing, can have a deleterious effect on teaching and learning. Without acknowledging how one is feeling, a person's instinct is to retreat, "jump back into our cultural water . . . run and hide."[44] Students who are not encouraged to mine their experiences, to be attuned to their inner self and emotions, will struggle to translate what they are learning into the world they live in. Thus, they will not have practice developing what David Evans and Tobin Miller Shearer, with Carol Dweck, call "grit in the classroom," or the "capacity to learn about racial"—and, I would add, cultural—"dynamics and gain the tools to challenge racism," to fruitfully navigate polarizing and conflictual topics, and thus may never fully come to understand the dynamics of multicultural living and learning.[45]

A culturally responsive, postmodern theological curriculum enables teachers and students to practice intercultural communication skills in the classroom, to navigate ontological or emotional ways of knowing, to explore perceptions of power, to learn from and through diverse perspectives, and to work for justice in a global world.

Notes

[1]Although "pedagogy" refers to the practice of teaching and learning with children, "andragogy" is a more appropriate term for the practice of teaching and learning with adults; however, the majority of literature on postmodern curriculum uses the term "pedagogy." For consistency, I will use the term "pedagogy" in this essay to mean the art and practice of teaching all ages.

[2]William E. Doll Jr., *A Post-Modern Perspective on Curriculum* (New York: Teachers College Press, 1993). I have written elsewhere about the characteristics of the modernist curriculum as it compares with the postmodern curriculum, specifically on the limitations of the modern curriculum when it comes to including transformative learning theory and strategies for creating antiracist pedagogies in graduate programs in ministry and religious education; see Tracey Lamont, "Safe Spaces or Brave Spaces? Re-

Envisioning Practical Theology and Transformative Learning Theory," in *Religious Education* 114, no. 5 (November 15, 2018), https://doi.org/10.10 80/00344087.2019.1682452.

[3]See Stanley Aronowitz and Henry Giroux, *Postmodern Education: Politics, Culture, and Social Criticism* (Minneapolis: University of Minnesota Press, 1991); Derald Wing Sue, *Race Talk and the Conspiracy of Silence: Understanding and Facilitating Difficult Dialogues on Race* (Hoboken, NJ: Wiley 2015), 65–66.

[4]Sue, *Race Talk*, 66.

[5]Patrick Slattery, *Curriculum Development in the Postmodern Era*, 3rd ed. (New York: Routledge, 2013), 36.

[6]Doll, *Post-Modern Perspective*, 13; Slattery, *Curriculum Development*, xxi.

[7]Authors who critique these pedagogies include Christine Sleeter, *Power, Teaching, and Teacher Education: Confronting Injustice with Critical Research and Action* (New York: Peter Lang, 2013); bell hooks, *Teaching to Transgress: Education as the Practice of Freedom* (New York: Routledge, 1994); Carmen Luke and Jennifer Gore, eds., *Feminism and Critical Pedagogy* (New York: Routledge, 1992); Boyung Lee, "Toward Liberating Interdependence: Exploring an Intercultural Pedagogy," *Religious Education* 105, no. 3 (2010): 283–98; and Aronowitz and Giroux, *Postmodern Education*.

[8]William F. Pinar, William M. Reynolds, Patrick Slattery, and Peter M. Taubman, *Understanding Curriculum: An Introduction to the Study of Historical and Contemporary Curriculum Discourses* (New York: Peter Lang, 2013), 265.

[9]Ira Shor and Paulo Freire, *A Pedagogy for Liberation: Dialogues on Transforming Education* (New York: Bergin & Garvey, 1987).

[10]Sleeter, *Power, Teaching, and Teacher Education*, 132.

[11]Eric H. F. Law, *The Wolf Shall Dwell with the Lamb: A Spirituality for Leadership in a Multicultural Community* (St. Louis, MO: Chalice Press, 1993), 15, 35. Further page references are given parenthetically in the text.

[12]For a comprehensive discussion on this critique, see Mary Breuing, "Problematizing Critical Pedagogy," *International Journal of Critical Pedagogy* 3, no. 3 (2011): 2–23.

[13]Elizabeth Ellsworth, "Why Doesn't This Feel Empowering? Working through the Repressive Myths of Critical Pedagogy," in *Feminisms and Critical Pedagogy*, ed. Carmen Luke and Jennifer Gore (New York: Routledge, 2013), 104.

[14]Ibid., 93.

[15]Slattery, *Curriculum Development*, 11.

[16]For evidence of this see ibid., 8.

[17]Ibid., 24.

[18]Ibid.

[19]Doll, *Post-Modern Perspective*, 31.

[20]Evidence of this is found in the creation of S.T.E.M. programs: science, technology, engineering, and math in both secondary and postsecondary schools. The pendulum swung back, however, when some schools reincorporated the arts into their curricula, forming the acronym S.T.E.A.M. For

more on these trends, see Slattery, *Curriculum Development*, xii.

[21]Doll, *Post-Modern Perspective*, 13.

[22]Willie James Jennings, "Teaching and Living toward a Revolutionary Intimacy," in *"You Say You Want a Revolution?" 1968–2018 in Theological Perspective*, ed. Susie Paulik Babka, Elena Procario-Foley, and Sandra Yocum, College Theology Society, vol. 64 (Maryknoll, NY: Orbis Books, 2018), 8.

[23]Geneva Gay, *Culturally Responsive Teaching: Theory, Research, and Practice*, 2nd ed. (New York: Teachers College Press, 2010), 31.

[24]Sue, *Race Talk*, 72.

[25]Ibid., 13. See also Robin Di'Angelo, *White Fragility: Why It's So Hard for White People to Talk about Racism* (Boston: Beacon Press, 2018).

[26]George Yancy, "Guidelines for Whites Teaching about Whiteness," in *Teaching Race: How to Help Students Unmask and Challenge Racism*, ed. Stephen D. Brookfield and Associates (San Francisco: Jossey-Bass, 2019), 33.

[27]Law, *Wolf Shall Dwell*, ix–xi.

[28]Stephen Brookfield, "The Dynamics of Teaching Race," in *Teaching Race: How to Help Students Unmask and Challenge Racism*, 15. See also Karyn D. McKinney, "Whiteness on a White Canvas: Teaching Race in a Predominantly White University," in *Race in the College Classroom: Pedagogy and Politics*, ed. Bonnie TuSmith and Maureen T. Reddy (New Brunswick, NJ: Rutgers University Press, 2002), 126–39.

[29]Brookfield, "Dynamics," 15.

[30]Slattery, *Curriculum Development*, 77–78.

[31]Sue, *Race Talk*, 66.

[32]Slattery, *Curriculum Development*, 107.

[33]Ibid., 108.

[34]For more on embodying curriculum see Maria Harris, *Fashion Me a People: Curriculum in the Church* (Louisville, KY: Westminster John Knox Press, 1989); and Yolanda Smith, "'Let Freedom Ring!' Black Women's Spirituality: Shaping Prophetic Christian Education," *Religious Education* 107, no. 3 (2012): 220–24.

[35]Smith, "Let Freedom Ring," 223.

[36]Gay, *Culturally Responsive*, 31.

[37]Law, *Wolf Shall Dwell*, 9.

[38]Ibid., 84. Law also refers to giving power away as "practicing the spirituality of the cross."

[39]Lee, "Toward Liberating Interdependence," 292.

[40]Ibid.

[41]Ibid., 293.

[42]Law, *Wolf Shall Dwell*, 79–88. For a comprehensive list of strategies to help students unpack racism, power, privilege, and oppression, see Brookfield, *Teaching Race*.

[43]Law, *Wolf Shall Dwell*, 10.

[44]Ibid.

[45]David Evans and Tobin Miller Shearer, "A Principled Pedagogy for Religious Education," *Religious Education* 112, no. 1 (2017): 11. See also Carol S. Dweck, *Mindset: The New Psychology of Success* (New York: Random House, 2006).

PART II

NEGOTIATING BORDERS

AND BARRIERS

Inter-Ritual, Ecumenical, and Interfaith Living of Catholicism

An Indian Feminist Perspective

Shalini Mulackal, PBVM

Namasthe! I am happy to share with you my experience of living Catholicism in the Asian continent and particularly the Indian subcontinent. Being born as a female automatically placed me in a less privileged/inferior/unequal position, both within the church and also in a society that is patriarchal in its worldview, structures, customs, and traditions. I was born into an Oriental church that traces its origin to St. Thomas the Apostle. Later, when I joined the Presentation Sisters, I became a member of the Latin church.

My Christian faith is often challenged by a growing feminist worldview, theological education, and the multicultural, pluri-religious, caste-ridden, unjust socioeconomic and political context of India. At the same time, it is enriched by the study of other religions—especially Hinduism, its sacred texts, philosophy, and spirituality.[1] I also have Hindu neighbors with whom I maintain warm relationships. I had companions and friends at school and college who were Hindus.

It is from this standpoint that I present this essay, which is divided into three sections. The first section focuses on the present-day Indian context, and the second section gives an overview of Indian Christianity. The third section highlights how Indian Catholicism is lived inter-ritually, ecumenically, and in harmony with other religions.

Indian Context at a Glance

Using the methodology of "combination of opposites,"[2] I describe the situation of India in six different realms.

Sociocultural Realm

In the sociocultural realm India is known for having unity in diversity, simplicity and complexity, openness and intolerance, national integration and parochial regionalism, intellectual brilliance and the scourge of illiteracy, brilliant brains and the brain drain, passionate nationalism and regionalist lobbying, a magnificent Constitution and its ineffective implementation.

Socioeconomic Realm

In the socioeconomic realm we find the coexistence of economic development and abject poverty, of globalization and growing marginalization, of open markets and widening disparity, the improvement of living standards and the lack of basic needs, a largely agrarian nation and neglected farmers, affluent cities and discarded villages, sprawling skyscrapers and miserable slum dwellings, a handful of billionaires and hapless millions, a resourcefully huge young generation and worrying unemployment.[3] Despite several policies and programs to combat poverty, more than 400 million persons in India continue to live in conditions of extreme poverty, earning income of less than US $1 a day.

A number of studies have established that people belonging to Scheduled Castes, Scheduled Tribes, and Other Backward Castes have the largest share of the poor. Women of these vulnerable classes are the worst affected segment of the society. Poverty has a gender dimension.[4] India has exceptionally high rates of malnutrition, especially among women and girls. Tradition requires that women eat last and the least throughout their lives, even when pregnant or lactating.

Sociopolitical Realm

The combination of opposites in the sociopolitical realm includes democracy and pseudonationalism, secularity and growing religious fanaticism, promising election manifestos and vote-bank politics, urgency of progress and political squabbling, democratic governments and fascist tendencies, boom in the communication sector and the politically manipulated media, development programs and unbridled corruption, political consciousness and political vendetta, a strong sense of national security and unresolved boundary disputes.[5]

Socioreligious Realm

In the socioreligious realm there are religious diversity and growing fundamentalism, religiosity and superstition, spirituality and materialism, rituals authentically rooted in tradition and inhuman practices, asceticism and agnosticism, religious consciousness and communal flare-ups, communal harmony and political poisoning. The increasing hate campaign organized against those belonging to minority religions is a serious threat and challenge to Christianity in India.

Sociohumanitarian Realm

The combination of opposites in the sociohumanitarian realm includes the value of nonviolence (*ahimsa*) and violence, social awareness and structural failure, promotion of human rights and systemic exploitation, ancient systems of medicine and an inadequate health care system, veneration of goddesses and gender discrimination, human sensitivity and inhuman atrocities, liberation movements and oppressive institutions, constitutional equality and blatant caste discrimination, consciousness of fundamental rights and human rights violations, peoples' movements and civic indifference.[6]

Socioecological Realm

In the socioecological realm we are faced with natural beauty and alarming pollution, wealth of resources and undue exploitation of nature, abundance of rain and extended droughts, the "Clean-India Drive" and unscientific waste management, mighty rivers and dying riverbeds, deforestation and climatic changes, an accelerated growth in infrastructure and disappearance of wetlands, flourishing industrialization and hazardous living conditions, ecological movements and convenient opportunism, animal rights and disappearing wild species, rising temperatures and diminishing glaciers.[7]

Christianity in India

Two phases of Christianity on Indian soil can be distinguished. The first phase is the ancient Church of St. Thomas the Apostle. The second phase, from the fifteenth century onward, begins with the arrival of Western missionaries. Besides the Catholics, there are Christians belonging to various other denominations. India is also witnessing the emergence of a new form of community known as *Christbhaktas*.[8]

The Catholic Church in India is composed of three ritual churches.[9] The Church of Thomas Christians claims to have its origin in the preaching of the Apostle Thomas. The Persian or Chaldean bishops were the heads of the Thomas Christians in India until the arrival of the Portuguese. The section among St. Thomas Christians that maintains communion with Rome is the Syro-Malabar Church, which has thirty-one dioceses in India and four outside.[10] The Latin Rite came to India in the sixteenth century with the missionary work of the Portuguese and other Western missionaries. It is the largest Catholic Church in India with 132 dioceses.

The interference of the Portuguese and other Western missionaries in the affairs of the Thomas Christians led to divisions among them. The Jacobite Church in India originated in the aftermath of the Synod of Diamper (1599) and the Coonan Cross revolt (1653). Then in 1930, a group of Jacobites under the leadership of Archbishop Mar Ivanios reunited with the Catholic Church and became known as the Syro-Malankara Church, comprising eleven dioceses.[11]

St. Thomas Christians in India

According to the ancient South Indian tradition, St. Thomas arrived in India and landed in Cranganore[12] on the Kerala coast in the year 52 CE. He converted many Hindus and established

Christian communities.[13] He went to the eastern coast too and converted many, and then crossed over to China. He returned to Kerala and organized the Christian communities and proceeded again to the Coromandel Coast, where he was martyred. He was buried in Mylapore in Chennai (Madras). Although these traditions might have been written later in local languages and/or in Syriac, no written historical documents about them exist today.[14] Some of these traditions are found in ancient songs of Malabar, in some of the travel narratives, and in some Portuguese documents.[15]

Identity and Way of Life of Thomas Christians

St. Thomas Christians have a special devotional attachment to the Apostle Thomas. They have a living tradition and an unbroken continuity with the one, holy, catholic, and apostolic church.[16] They have been known as *Mar Thoma Nazranis*[17] from ancient times onward, and they seem to have enjoyed a higher status in society.[18]

The identity of the Thomas Christians as being part of an apostolic church has been well evolved through the *Mar Thomas Margam*.[19] It stands for the faith and the whole ecclesial life of Thomas Christians. It symbolizes the social, cultural, religious, theological, spiritual, liturgical, juridical, and administrative setup of the faith community. According to Paremmakkal, "We the *Nazranis* of Malabar, from ancient times until today have faultlessly observed these holy teachings."[20] According to Placid J. Podipara, the identity of the Thomas Christians was expressed in this way: "Hindu in Culture, Christian in Religion, Oriental in Worship."[21]

An eyewitness account of the life of the Malabar Christians between 1778 and 1786 is found in a book called *Varthamanap-pusthakam*.[22] Besides this book, there is another important and very rare document called *Joseph the Indian*,[23] which furnishes us with a source of information about the life and traditions of pre-Portuguese Christianity in India.[24] It also contains information on the relation of these Christians to the Pope and the Patriarch of Babylon.[25]

There is a belief among Thomas Christians that St. Thomas

converted some Brahmins. This has become problematic. First of all, there is real doubt about its historicity, and, second, this belief has created caste consciousness among many Syro-Malabar Christians even to this day. As a result, there are seldom any marriages between Syro-Malabar Christians and Latin Rite Christians, since most Latin Rite Christians are supposed to be converts from the so-called lower castes, Dalits, and fisher people in Kerala. As a result, there is a false superiority complex among Thomas Christians. Although many priests and religious belonging to the Syro-Malabar Church work for the uplifting of Dalits and Adivasis elsewhere in the country, it is not a guarantee that they have shed their caste consciousness. This caste factor comes into play at various levels within the church.[26]

Liturgical Life of Thomas Christians

The liturgical life of Thomas Christians was in accordance with the East Syrian tradition, using the East Syrian language in the liturgy with certain adaptations to their context. For instance, the Thomas Christians used to take baths and put on clean clothes before they went to church. They used to prostrate themselves and kiss the floor as soon as they entered the church. The clergy and laity, together, used to chant the divine office every morning. They celebrated the Holy Eucharist rarely. They used leavened bread and wine made from raisins soaked in water for consecration.[27] It was these differences in the customs, practices, and ritual traditions of the Thomas Christians that were considered errors and heresies by the Western missionaries, and they imposed the teachings of the Council of Trent upon the Thomas Christians.

Formation of Priests among Thomas Christians

The tradition among the Thomas Christians was that the candidates for priesthood were trained in the local community under the care of local priests called *malpans*.[28] In the early centuries there was no organized seminary system among the *Nazranis* for the training of their priests. The boy who wished to become a priest would go to an erudite priest—his Malpan-teacher—and would stay with him for several years for training.[29]

Communion with Rome

There was communion between the Thomas Christians in India and Rome from the beginning. The Malabar Church founded by the Apostle Thomas grew outside the Greco-Roman world.[30] The distance was a big problem for these churches. It might not have been easy to have a juridical relationship between Rome and the St. Thomas Christians until the fifteenth century. But this lack of juridical relationship with Rome does not mean unorthodoxy in faith matters. "There is nothing in history to suggest that the Church of St. Thomas Christians was in conflict with the Church of Rome. It maintained faith communion."[31]

Ecclesiastical Governance

The administrative and organizational structures of the St. Thomas community were indigenous adaptations of East-Syrian and local systems. The community had a spiritual head in the person of the metropolitan. He enjoyed quasi-patriarchal authority. But he was only a spiritual head, exercising mainly the powers of Holy Orders, such as ordinations, blessings, the consecration of churches, and so forth.[32] Administration was completely in the hands of the archdeacon, who was always a native. He was responsible for the whole community before the government and nation.

Thomas Christians exercised their rights through *yogams* or assemblies. This indigenous institution was the synod of the whole church, which had the ultimate authority in dealing with all the matters of the church. It consisted of the representatives of all the parishes and priests, and the archdeacon had the decisive role in it.[33] Similarly, all the parishes had parish assemblies called *Palliyogams*, consisting of all the heads of the families, local priests, and others in sacred orders. These assemblies were the decision-making bodies.

Latin Church in India

There were no Latin Rite Christians in India until the end of the fifteenth century.[34] Their presence started with the missionary work of the Portuguese. Though the Franciscans were the first ones to come, it is St. Francis Xavier who is known as the Apostle of Latin Christianity in India.[35] The kings of Portugal, and the rights given to them by the Holy See (*Padroado*), played a vital role in the success of their mission. The colonial method of planting the church in India in the Western style had a long-standing negative impact on Indian Christianity.

Then in the seventeenth century, when the rival colonial powers of Holland and England began to wipe out the Portuguese presence, the missionaries were forced to return. Rome began to undertake the Indian mission directly, under the supervision of its new Congregation for the Propagation of Faith (*Propaganda*), which was established in 1622. Several Apostolic Vicariates were erected in India under the *Propaganda Fide*, which led to long-standing conflicts and rivalries between the clergy of *Padroado* and *Propaganda* jurisdictions.

Protestant Christianity in India

The first Protestant missionaries, two German Lutherans, came to India in 1706. In 1793, William Carey, an English missionary of the Baptist Church, came to Kolkata along with two others. The London Missionary Society (LMS) arrived in 1806, followed by the Church Missionary Society (CMS) of the Anglicans in 1813.

The twentieth century witnessed the great ecumenical movements among the Protestant churches. Four different denominations in South India—the Anglicans, the Presbyterians, the Congregational churches, and the Methodists—united to form the Church of South India (CSI) in 1947. Today they number about 38 million. In a similar way, seven different denominations[36] united to form the Church of North India (CNI) in 1970. They number about 12.5 million. The powerful American Baptist Churches in both the North East and Andhra, the American Methodist Churches in both the North and the South, and the Lutheran Churches in India did not join in the union.

Catholicism in India Today:
Threats, Opportunities, and Challenges

I now take a critical look at Christianity as it is lived in twenty-first-century India, using a feminist lens. The joy and gratitude one feels because of the long history of Christian presence is eclipsed when we realize that we are not as fully at the service of the Reign of God as we should be.

Reasons to Celebrate Christian Presence in India

We need to celebrate the strong faith of the people, beginning with St. Thomas Christians in the first century and Dalit and Tribal Christians of Kandhamal, Orissa, in the twenty-first century.[37] Women, in their multiple roles, have contributed immensely in passing on the faith to successive generations.

Though Christians are a tiny minority,[38] their contribution to the nation in terms of providing education, health care, and social and humanitarian work is immense. Almost 20 percent of educational institutions are run by Christians, providing education especially for the marginalized sections in rural areas. Of course, there are also some elite Catholic institutions in the urban centers catering to the rich and middle class. Catholics are known for the services they render in taking care of the poor, the destitute, the mentally and physically challenged, the differently abled, the orphans, the abandoned, and the elderly. Scholars say that the greatest impact of Christian evangelization in India has been on the marginalized sections of society.[39] St. Mother Teresa of Kolkata stands as a shining example.

Catholic Christianity in India has produced thousands of missionaries who serve in the remote areas of the country and abroad. It has nurtured many vocations and also has given birth to saints and martyrs.[40]

Inter-Ritual Living

The Catholic Church in India is a communion of three different individual churches. The Catholic Bishops' Conference of India (CBCI), which was founded in 1944, is the assembly of all the Catholic Bishops of India. In 1988 three separate episcopal bodies were created, representing the three ritual churches. However, the CBCI still functions as an overarching body of the three churches for national and supraritual matters. The Syro-Malabar and Syro-Malankara Churches were raised to Major-Archiepiscopal Churches in 1992 and 2005 respectively, and their synods have full and independent powers in all matters, including the election of the major archbishops. All three ritual churches work in unity, to a great extent, for the common good of the church.

The Indian Theological Association (ITA), founded in 1976, is composed of members belonging to all three ritual churches. During its annual conference, Eucharist is celebrated in different rites on different days, so that members have an experience of celebrating liturgy in a rite other than their own. There are women and men who belong to one rite, yet join a diocese or a congregation that belongs to another rite. They do not experience any conflict in living inter-ritually; on the contrary, they feel enriched by such experiences. Not only clerics and religious, but also lay faithful have occasions to live inter-ritually. Often, those who migrate to another place, within the country or beyond, join a parish that need not be of their native rite.

In most seminaries, theological faculties, and formation houses, there are students who belong to different ritual churches. As long as there is no competition or feelings of superiority, inter-ritual living can be quite enriching.

Interfaith Living

India is blessed with many ancient religions, and each of these religions has something unique to offer. All Indic religions emphasize silence, solitude, and interiority. These help individuals to find the divine within, through the practice of various *sadhanas* or methods. Indian Christians are called to respect the diversity of religions and recognize their unity in spirituality. We are co-pilgrims with people of other faiths in search of the height and depth, length and breadth of the mystery of the divine presence within and around us.[41]

Other religions are no longer considered false, "magic," or the devil's work. Plurality of religions is accepted today, not only as an irreversible historical fact, but also as a legitimate theological principle. Different religions have their origins not only in different historical and cultural contexts and in a variety of human responses, but in the very inexhaustible mystery of God, who cannot be contained in any one religion.[42]

Soon after Vatican II, Indian Christians took the initiative to begin an *ashram* movement. Like the Hindu *Sanyasis* (renouncers), some Catholic priests and a few religious women started to live in ashrams, following the Hindu way of living, and to give expression to Christian faith through rituals and symbols taken from Hindu tradition and Hindu spirituality. Today there are a few ashrams run by Catholics where anyone can go for an experience. One of the most famous is Kurisumala Ashram, situated in Kerala. In the holy city of Rishikesh, Ma Turia, who is a religious sister, spends her life in an ashram.

Efforts were also made to inculturate Christian faith in various ways soon after Vatican II. Many religious sisters replaced their religious habit with the Indian *saree* with a beige color symbolizing their life, like that of Indian *Sanyasis*. Certain aspects of Indian culture began to enter into Christian liturgical worship. The Indian Church also opened various centers for interreligious dialogue and encouraged the faithful to enter actively into such dialogue.

Efforts in Ecumenical Living

Though the Catholic Church in India is not yet a member of the National Council of Churches in India (NCCI),[43] there is some collaboration between the NCCI and CBCI, especially for dealing with national and social issues, especially with regard to reservation (affirmative action) for Dalit Christians. Attempts are made at various levels to work together—for example, the Christian Institute for the Study of Religion and Society (CISRS), which is an ecumenical body, organizes programs on a regular basis in which the participants and the resource persons are from various churches. Since 2014, women with a feminist consciousness have been trying to work together as an ecumenical group to raise their voices against violence and the abuse of women, both in society and in the church.[44] The Centre for Dalit/Subaltern Studies, located in Delhi, is ecumenical in its functioning. This center has published Bible commentaries for the entire Bible (twenty volumes) from a Dalit perspective; scholars belonging to various churches contributed to this study.

Threats Facing Indian Christians

The fast-growing Hindu Fundamentalism and Hindutva ideology pose a serious threat to Indian Christianity. Even before Independence, there were a few who wanted to make India a Hindu nation. They had been working and spreading their ideology for several decades. It is this group that has now captured political power, and they have passed anti-conversion bills in many states. The democratic and secular fabric of India has been systematically brushed aside. If this trend continues, it will be difficult for Christians and other religious minorities to live as free citizens.

Moreover, the Christian church in India is going through a crisis. Sexual abuse in the church has taken a very ugly turn, and the church leadership has been accused of covering up sexual offenders, land scams, and other wrongdoings. There is a lack of unity and collaboration among the various ritual churches, especially where their jurisdictions overlap in the same geographical area.

Opportunities and Challenges

The present context beckons Indian Catholics to become the "little flock" and bear witness to the values of the Reign of God, of justice, fellowship, sister/brotherhood, peace, equality, harmony, and unity. It is a call to be the salt, light, and leaven. In the present political context, it is going to be all the more challenging to bear witness and to be prophetic, denouncing evil and announcing the good news.

The call of Vatican II to become the "people of God" (*Lumen Gentium*, 2) remains a great challenge for the Indian Church, which is very patriarchal and hierarchical. Each individual member of the church is called to take responsibility for living one's Christian call to the fullest. We need to struggle against the tendencies to perceive the hierarchical church as "the church" and to see the rest of the faithful as passive subjects to be taken care of, taught, governed, and sanctified. The challenge is for all the members to be active agents.

The Indian Catholic Church has been given an opportunity to put into practice the communion ecclesiology of Vatican II, since it is blessed with three different ritual churches. There is much room for accepting each church with its individuality and uniqueness and to cooperate and learn from one another.

Another major challenge for Indian Catholic Christianity is to inculturate its faith in diverse cultural contexts. There cannot be only one way of inculturation. We need to focus on how to have a Dalit church, a Tribal church, an Adivasi church, a North Indian church, and so forth. We need to explore diverse ways of inculturating our faith, and, in the process, of transforming and purifying various cultures and learning from them, knowing that inculturation and evangelization of cultures is at the heart of the mission of the church as it is expressed in Pope John Paul II's *Redemptoris Missio*.

Only when the mystery of Christ becomes incarnate in all the cultures of the world and when they are fecundated with the values of the gospel, will evangelization of cultures take place. This calls the church to have a positive appreciation of the different cultures of humanity, on the one hand, and, on the other, awareness of a new mission for evangelizing the cultures. Jesus and his gospel can be at home in all cultures, though the gospel's origins are closely connected with the Hebrew culture. All cultures, because of human sin, need to be healed, ennobled, and perfected. Such a purifying process has to take place in all cultures, in encounter with Jesus and his gospel.[45]

Dialogue with other religions is another very important aspect of mission. Religions are the expressions of the presence and work of God, and they contain spiritual riches, although there may be "gaps, insufficiencies and errors."[46] Proclamation and dialogue are not opposed, but closely related, although distinct.[47] "There are many ways and expressions of dialogue, dialogue of experts, dialogue for integral development and for safeguarding religious values, dialogue of sharing spiritual experience, dialogue of life."[48]

Christian presence in India is found in many churches, those in communion with Rome, Orthodox churches, the mainline Protestant churches, Pentecostal churches, and many other denominations. Diversity of the different local churches was an essential part of the original vision of Christianity. In fact, the historical divisions in the church came almost as a result of the insistence on uniformity and the tendency to condemn all diversity in doctrinal and theological formulations.[49] Working for Christian unity becomes a task for us, while we acknowledge that it is a gift from God.

The church is the sacrament of salvation for the whole world, and the unity of the church is the sign of the coming unity of humankind. The unity proclaimed by the church points to and anticipates the final unity of all humankind, which is the ultimate goal of the ecumenical movement. Therefore, the churches in India should by all means, and without fear or scruples, dedicate themselves to the task of the restoration of the visible unity—of course, always by making the character of the church visible and credible to the world through a common commitment to mission, witness, and service, and by keeping in mind the ultimate goal of the unity of all humankind.[50] This goal, which will be a real challenge for the churches in India, should begin with mutual recognition among the churches.

The church in India can never be complacent in the face of multiple oppressions suffered by the marginalized groups. Their situation challenges the church to be on their side, putting itself at risk, and to work for the transformation of sinful structures such as the caste system, patriarchy, and unjust economic, political, and social systems.

Women in the Indian Church

As mentioned earlier in our discussion, the situation of women in Indian society is rather pathetic.[51] A few urban, educated, and employed women may be an exception to the general situation of subjugation, oppression, and violence inflicted on women and girls in our society. According to an economic survey conducted in 2016–17 by the Indian government, there were more than 63 million women "missing" from its population and 21 million unwanted girls. Two million go "missing" across all age groups every year because of selective female feticide, disease, neglect, and inadequate nutrition.[52]

The church in India is responding to this situation in a number of ways. It is providing education for girls, especially in remote villages. The church is also involved in empowering women, especially in making them economically independent, through organizing self-help groups, providing skills training, and helping them get loans from the government. However, the church also practices discrimination against women in various ways.

Women's active participation in basic Christian communities (BCCs) in recent times has given them a bit more visibility in parish and diocesan councils, as compared with a few decades ago. They take part actively in the Eucharistic celebration and other parish activities. However, these positive changes seem to be taking place only at a superficial level—they give the appearance of women's participation in the life and mission of the church, but if we go deeper, we are confronted with the secondary status of women in the church.

In some of the parishes that belong to the Syro-Malabar Church, women are not allowed to enter the church sanctuary. However, they are allowed to distribute communion. The priest comes down from the sanctuary to hand over the ciborium to the religious sister who is appointed as the communion minister. One wonders what is more sacred, the body of Christ or the sanctuary?

In 2016 Pope Francis invited the church to include women and other marginalized groups in the foot washing ritual on Holy Thursday; however, the two Oriental churches in India clarified the matter with Rome and obtained an exemption from allowing women in the ritual. Their argument was that, in matters of worship and liturgy, they enjoy autonomy.

All women experience exclusion in the present institutional church.[53] This exclusion is visible in its structures, theology, and liturgy. Due to the persistent use of exclusive language, women are made invisible even in worshipping congregations where they form the majority. This exclusion communicates to them that they are inferior and not equal in status to men. Theological and theoretical affirmation of their created equality, or their equality as members of the Body of Christ through baptism, cannot bridge this gap of inequality.

One of the main areas in which women experience exclusion in the church, and which has far-reaching consequences, is the exclusion from ordained ministries. It means exclusion from interpreting the word of God through their experiences, and also from the decision-making structures of the church. The ordained ministers are not only the presidents of the liturgical assemblies but also the leaders and ultimate decision makers in the church. As a result, women's experiences are not sufficiently reflected in most decisions made at various levels of the church, even when these decisions affect them directly.

Called to Be Salt and Light as Co-Pilgrims

In India Christianity is perceived as one of the foreign religions that came with colonialism, even though Christianity existed here from the first century onward. The Catholic Church in India comprises three ritual churches, of which two are of Eastern origin. The Oriental church in India lived in this land for fifteen centuries without any disturbance. It was adapted to the local culture and had indigenous ways of expressing its faith and other practices.

The coming of Portuguese missionaries disturbed the peaceful existence of St. Thomas Christians. Using *Padroado* rights, the Western missionaries tried to Latinize the Thomas Christians, which led to the fragmentation of the Thomas Christians. A few centuries of *Padroado* rule destroyed many of the customs and traditions of Thomas Christians, which were more participative and inculturated. Though the two Oriental churches enjoy autonomy in their governance, they are very much like the Latin church, where the participation of lay faithful in decision making is almost nonexistent.

Today the church in India is faced with many challenges, but also opportunities. The major challenge is to be the "little flock" under threat in the present sociopolitical situation of India. Yet it is also called to be the salt and light, to keep the memory of Jesus alive in this nation, and to live the values of the Reign of God. It must be a sign of God's Reign by joining hands with all Christians and walking with people of other faiths as co-pilgrims, respecting their faith and learning from them the mysterious ways God is leading them to the ultimate human destiny.

Notes

[1] I have studied Indian spirituality, lived in an ashram, and was initiated into yoga.

[2] See Cyriac Joseph Thayil, SDB, *The Church in the New Testament according to Raymond Brown* (Bengaluru: Kristu Jyoti Publications, 2018), 397.

[3] Ibid.

[4] According to the former UN Secretary General Kofi Annan, "Gender equality is more than a goal in itself. It is a precondition for meeting the challenge of reducing poverty, promoting sustainable development and building good governance." Statement delivered at the Conference on African Women and Economic Development, in Addis Ababa, Ethiopia, April 30, 1998.

[5] See Thayil, *Church in the New Testament*, 397.

[6] Ibid., 398.

[7] Ibid.

[8] *Christbhaktas* are devotees of Jesus who are not baptized and are not members of any church. They come together to pray and read the Bible, and

have a unique identity of their own. They are mostly found in North India, especially in and around Varanasi.

[9]These are the Latin Rite, Syro-Malabar, and Syro-Malankara rites. These different rites have distinct identities with regard to their origin, historical development, catechetical traditions, structural specificities, theologies, cultural orientations, spiritualities, canonical regulations, inter-ritual engagements, particular and universal relations, contextualizing methodologies, inner struggles, misunderstandings, and mutual grievances. See Thayil, *Church in the New Testament*, 410.

[10]There are four Eparchies outside India—in the United States, Canada, Australia, and England. These serve the migrated Thomas Christians in these areas.

[11]See Kuncheria Pathil, "Ecumenical Reality of the Indian Church," in *The Church in India in Search of New Identity*, ed. K. Kunnumpuram, Errol D'Lima, and Jacob Parappally, 19th Annual Meeting of the Indian Theological Association, May 4–8, 1996 (Bangalore: Dharmaram Publications, 1997), 296–98.

[12]This place was known in ancient times as *Malabar*. Hence these Christians are also referred to as Malabar Christians or Syro-Malabar Christians to indicate their connection with the Syrian Church.

[13]"The living tradition among the St. Thomas Christians attributes that St. Thomas converted some of the Brahmins into Christianity and established seven Christian settlements in Malabar. The seven Christian settlements attached to the apostolic work of St. Thomas are Cranganore (Muziris), Playur (Palur), Parur (Kottakavil), Kokkamangalam, Niranam, Nilakkal (Chayal), and Quilon." Pius Malekandathil, "St. Thomas Christians: A Historical Analysis of Their Origin and Development up to 9th Century AD," in *St. Thomas Christians and Nambudiris Jews and Sangam Literature: A Historical Appraisal*, ed. Bosco Puthur (Kochi: LRC Publications, 2003), 6–7. A Syriac manuscript of the year 1770 refers to these seven churches. This manuscript is available in W. J. Richards, *The Indian Christians of St. Thomas* (London, 1908), 72–77.

[14]See Kuncheria Pathil, "Christian Presence in India: A Historical Overview," in *Church on Pilgrimage: Trajectories of Intercultural Encounter*, ed. Kuncheria Pathil (Bengaluru: Dharmaram Publications, 2016), 315. It is important to note that during the Portuguese rule when Thomas Christians were brought under the jurisdiction of *Padroado* rule, the Portuguese missionaries destroyed many of the books of Thomas Christians that were written in Syriac.

[15]Ancient songs of the Malabar region where we find the traditions of the Thomas Christians are the *Rabban Pattu, Veeradiyan Pattu,* and the *Margam Kali Pattu*. Some of the travel narratives, like those of Cosmas Indicopleustes, an Egyptian who visited Arabia, East Africa, and India around 530 CE, John of Monte Corvino (1292), and Jordan Catalani (1319), recorded information about the mission of St. Thomas and the presence of Christianity in India. The Portuguese documents of the sixteenth and seventeenth centuries are the most important and richest sources about Malabar Christians. See A.

M. Mundadan, *The Sixteenth-Century Traditions of St. Thomas Christians* (Bangalore: Dharmaram College, 1970).

[16]See Jose Valiamangalam, MST, *Ecclesial Vision of St. Thomas Christians in the Light of Varthamanappusthakam: A Historico-Theological Study* (Kottayam, Kerala: Oriental Institute of Religious Studies, India, 2018), 188–89.

[17]The name *Nazrani* came from Jesus of Nazareth.

[18]This is because the great king Cheraman Perumal conferred on the *Mar Thoma Nazranis* greater honors and dignities than all other communities. He gave them the title of "*Maha Pilla*," which eventually turned into *Mappila*, i.e., "Sons of the King." Thomman Paremmakkal, *Varthamanappusthakam*, trans. Placid J. Podipara, Orientalia Christiana Analecta 190 (Rome: Pontificium Institutum Orientalium Studiorum, 1971), 255. As quoted by Valiamangalam, *Ecclesial Vision of St. Thomas Christians*, 190.

[19]*Mar Thomas Margam* literally means "the way of Thomas" or "the law of Thomas."

[20]Paremmakkal, *Varthamanappusthakam*, 255. As quoted by Valiamangalam, *Ecclesial Vision of St. Thomas Christians*, 191.

[21]Placid J. Podipara, *The Malabar Christians* (Alleppey, Kerala: Prakasham Publications, 1977), 27.

[22]*Varthamanappusthakam* is a travelogue written by Cathanar Thomman Paremmakkal in 1785. Its original vernacular is Malayalam, but an accurate English translation is given by Rev. Fr. Placid J. Podipara, *Varthamanappusthakam*. In order to find a solution for the problems faced by Thomas Christians under the *Padroado* rule of the Portuguese, two representatives were chosen to make a trip to Lisbon and then to Rome. They were Mar Cariattil and Cathanar Thomman Paremmakkal. Their long and risky voyage is depicted in *Varthamanappusthakam*.

[23]Joseph the Indian was a native of Cranganore or Kodungallor in Kerala. He was a priest belonging to the Thomas Christians of Malabar, who went to Europe in 1501. He went by ship from Cochin to Lisbon. After staying six months in Portugal, he proceeded to Rome and visited Pope Alexander VI. See George Schurhammer, *The Malabar Church and Rome: During the Early Portuguese Period and Before* (Trichinopoly: St. Joseph's Industrial School Press, 1934), 26.

[24]The narratives of Joseph the Indian reveal the ecclesial system and sacramental and liturgical life of St. Thomas Christians of Malabar, with their faith and traditions, feasts and fasts, customs and manners.

[25]See Antony Vallavanthara, *India in 1500 AD: The Narratives of Joseph the Indian* (Kottayam: OIRSI, 1984), xx–xxi. See also Schurhammer, *Malabar Church and Rome*, 26.

[26]Dalits and Adivasis/Tribals form the majority of Catholics in India. But this reality is not sufficiently reflected when it comes to leadership or other areas of church life. Dalit Christians are discriminated against, even within the church, in different ways, by the so-called high-caste Christians, including clergy and religious.

[27]See Jacob Kollaparambil, *The St. Thomas Christians' Revolution in 1653* (Kottayam: Catholic Bishop's House, 1981), 7.

[28]*Malpan* is a Syriac word that means "guru" or "teacher." See Joseph Kallarangatt, "Ecclesiological Perspectives of St. Thomas Christians," in *Mar Thoma Margam: The Ecclesial Heritage of the St. Thomas Christians*, ed. Andrews Mekkattukunnel (Kottayam, Kerala: OIRSI, 2012), 147.

[29]See Thomas Kalayil, "Priesthood in the Tradition of the St. Thomas Christians of India," *Asian Horizons* 3, no. 2 (December 2009): 28. This *malpanate* system was similar to Gurukulam education. In this system the boy would come and stay with the guru and perform household tasks. The metropolitan and archdeacon were considered ex-officio teachers. Most of the clergy received their ecclesiastical education from *malpans*. Only after the arrival of Western missionaries was the first seminary opened in 1587, with the intention of introducing Latin training for the priests.

[30]See Xavier Koodapuzha, "The Ecclesial Communion of the St. Thomas Christians of India before the 16th Century," *Harp* 22 (September 2006): 107.

[31]John Kudiyiruppil, *Oriental Theology* (Bangalore: ATC, 2010), 100.

[32]See Pathil, "Christian Presence in India," 317.

[33]Paremmakkal, *Varthamanappusthakam*, 3–4. See Kuncheria Pathil, "Theology of the Role of the Laity in Vatican II," *Jeevadhara* 26, no. 154 (July 1996): 262.

[34]Even though John of Monte Corvino (1291) reports the presence of Western missionaries in the thirteenth and fourteenth centuries who had planted a few communities in some parts of the country such as Mylapore, Thana, and Quilon, there were no Latin Rite Christians when the Portuguese arrived.

[35]See Pathil, "Christian Presence in India," 318.

[36]They are the Anglicans, Presbyterians, Congregational Churches, Methodists, Baptists, Disciples of Christ, and Church of the Brethren.

[37]During the Kandhamal violence against Christians, in 2008–9, the Christians bore witness to their deep faith. See Anto Akkara, *Early Christians of 21st Century: Stories of Incredible Christian Witness from Kandhamal Jungles* (Delhi: Veritas India Books, 2013).

[38]Christians form only 2.3 percent of the total population of India.

[39]See Jose Kalapura, "Christianity and Marginalized Communities in India: A Subaltern Historical Overview," *Indian Church History Review* 43, no. 1 (June 2009): 7.

[40]Some of the Indian saints include St. Alphonsa, St. Kuriakose Elias Chavara, St. Euphrasia Eluvathingal, St. Joseph Vaz, and St. Mariam Thresia. Indian Christianity can celebrate lives of those like Blessed Rani Maria, Fr. A. T. Thomas, and Sr. Valsa John, who sacrificed their lives for taking up the cause of the poor and the exploited, and the martyrs of Kandhamal for witnessing to their faith.

[41]See Sebastian Painadath, "Christianity's Relationship with Other Religions—Emerging New Paradigms," in *Church on Pilgrimage: Trajectories of Intercultural Encounter*, ed. Kuncheria Pathil (Bengaluru: Dharmaram Publications, 2016), 491.

[42]See Pathil, "Christian Presence in India," 336.

[43]The Protestant and other churches in India have a common ecumenical forum or council of churches in the National Council of Churches in India

(NCCI), which was founded in 1914. The NCCI brings together most of the churches and Christian organizations in India, except the Catholic churches, for mutual consultation, assistance, and action in all matters related to the life and witness of the churches.

[44]It is called the Indian Christian Women's Movement (ICWM).

[45]See Pathil, "Christian Presence in India," 339.

[46]John Paul II, Encyclical Letter *Redemptoris Missio, 55*; cf. 56, and Paul VI, Apostolic Exhortation *Evangelii Nuntiandi*, 53, later quoted in Congregation for the Doctrine of the Faith, *Dominus Iesus* (2000), 1.8.

[47]See the Pontifical Council for Interreligious Dialogue's document, *Dialogue and Proclamation*, 1991.

[48]See Pathil, "Christian Presence in India," 342.

[49]See Kuncheria Pathil, *Ecumenism: Unity in Diversity* (Bangalore: Dharmaram Publications, 2006), 4–5.

[50]Ibid., 49.

[51]For a short overview of women's situation in India see Shalini Mulackal, "Role of Women in Ecclesiogenesis: A Historical, Hermeneutical, and Critical Study," in *Church on Pilgrimage: Trajectories of Intercultural Encounter*, ed. Kuncheria Pathil (Bengaluru: Dharmaram Publications, 2016), 467–69.

[52]See https://www.indiabudget.gov.in/budget2017-2018/survey.asp#content.

[53]For a short discussion of women's exclusion in the church, see Shalini Mulackal, "Political Economy of Participation: Women in the Life and Mission of the Church," in *Ecclesia of Women in Asia: Gathering the Voices of the Silenced*, ed. Evelyn Monterio, SC, and Antoinette Gutzler, MM (Delhi: ISPCK, 2005), 189–90.

From the Sphere to the Polyhedron

Shaping Communion in a Synodal Church

Michael L. Hahn

In the United States, synodality is a concept that requires further understanding and broader practice. Synodality is sometimes confused with ecclesial democracy, a reductive distortion of what "walking together" really demands from the church as the people of God.[1] Synodality is also too often seen as a naïve ideal, even though in many other parts of the global church, especially in Latin America, it has been the ecclesial way of proceeding since well before the Second Vatican Council.

When we consider the topic of global Catholicism, the church's expanding geographic boundaries might come to mind first, for the church today is certainly less Europe-centered than it was before and during Vatican II. The challenge of global Catholicism, however, becomes apparent when, in addition to the expansion of geographic boundaries, we also consider the deepening of ecclesial communion. The challenge of global Catholicism is twofold. On the one hand, regardless of the degree of geographic expansion, Catholicism requires that ecclesial communion is maintained. Yet, on the other hand, if safeguarding ecclesial communion becomes too restrictive, the global dimensions of Catholicism can be stifled or lost.

Following the initial reception of Vatican II, which signaled hopeful possibilities for global Catholicism, the understanding of ecclesial communion that emerged from the 1985 Extraordinary Synod of Bishops restrained this progress. However, the ecclesiological commitments of Pope Francis mark a new era for the possibilities of global Catholicism. In support of this argument, I briefly sketch the understanding of ecclesial communion that emerged from the 1985 Synod. I then identify key features of the ecclesiological vision of Pope Francis under the heading of synodality. Finally, I suggest several ways that ecclesial communion operates differently in a synodal church.

The 1985 Synod and Communion Ecclesiology

On January 25, 1985, Pope John Paul II announced his intention to call an Extraordinary General Assembly of the Synod of Bishops to be held in Rome to commemorate the twentieth anniversary of Vatican II. An indication of the synod's eventual direction is found in the document "The One Church of Christ" released in advance of the synod by the International Theological Commission (ITC), which reviewed the ecclesiological themes of *Lumen Gentium*. Not surprisingly, given the significance of *Lumen Gentium*'s second chapter, the expression "people of God" is given considerable attention. However, the ITC document explains that "[people of God] requires reflection, deepening, and clarification if falsifying interpretations are to be avoided."[2] In particular, the ITC document seems concerned with a sociological interpretation of "people of God." Section VI of the ITC document defines the people of God as a "hierarchically ordered society," affirming that "the people of God, the Church, cannot be disassociated from the ministries that give her structure, and especially the episcopate."[3] The concept of "communion" is then introduced to describe the organization and structure of the people of God. Here we find the focus of the ITC's understanding of communion: "The communion that gives definition to the new people of God is therefore a social communion of a hierarchically ordered sort."[4]

Chilean theologian Ronaldo Muñoz argues that the understanding of communion in the ITC document returns to the ecclesiocentrism that Vatican II's emphasis on a missionary church engaged in the world attempted to reform.[5] In response to sociological interpretations of ecclesiological expressions, Muñoz further observes that the document "speaks of 'people,' 'community' and 'institution' at a symbolic level which appears sociologically neutral."[6] The problem, according to Muñoz, is that "the text shows an inability to envisage real ecclesial communities and believing peoples which are *not mere projections of the hierarchico-sacramental institution.*"[7]

The stated purpose of the 1985 Synod was to assess the reception and implementation of Vatican II. Yet, as Jean-Marie Tillard observes, "It is noteworthy that the final report of the 1985 Synod, two decades after the end of Vatican II, already indicates a *shift from, a re-reading of, some of its conspicuous points.*"[8] As examples, Tillard cites the synod's pessimistic view of the world,[9] the eclipsing of the ecclesiology of "people of God,"[10] and a return to ecclesiocentrism.[11] If the synod, in fact, represents an attempt to rein in some of the more audacious conciliar reforms, while also setting parameters for the future reception of Vatican II, then communion ecclesiology is the instrument it used. Noting the shift that had taken place since Vatican II, Hermann Pottmeyer concludes, "Whereas the Council's communio-ecclesiology yielded a synodal movement and structural creativity, the Synod's statements are guarded in this area."[12]

After declaring communion ecclesiology to be "the central and fundamental idea of the Council's documents," the synod provides a theologically rich definition of communion that begins with Trinitarian communion into which, through sacramental participation, human beings are incorporated.[13] Given this understanding of the church as a network of both vertical and horizontal relationships, it is surprising when the synod subsequently displays a hesitation, and even antipathy, toward the consideration of concrete questions concerning the structure of the church.[14] Indeed, after studying the responses to the pre-synodal questionnaire, the initial and second reports, and the discussion by language groups at the synod, Joseph Komonchak concludes, "By the Final Report, almost all of the serious questions raised about the concrete structural implications of ecclesial communion have either disappeared or been translated into questions of vague collegial 'spirit.' "[15] Komonchak argues that the horizontal dimension of communion, particularly consideration of the cultural and structural implications of communion, is neglected in the Final Report as a result of its nearly exclusive focus on the vertical dimension of communion.[16]

Dennis Doyle defines the broad approach of communion ecclesiology as "an attempt to move beyond the merely juridical and institutional understandings by emphasizing the mystical, sacramental, and historical dimensions of the Church."[17] Even though the synod defines communion theologically and relationally, its operative understanding remains hierarchical and juridical. This particular form of communion ecclesiology, which emerges from the synod, is further developed during John Paul II's papacy through several disciplinary notifications and instructions by the Congregation for the Doctrine of the Faith (CDF). In fact, the "CDF version" is one of six contemporary Catholic versions of communion ecclesiology that Doyle identifies in his magisterial text.[18] After reviewing the 1984 ITC document, the Final Report of the 1985 Synod, and several CDF documents from this era,[19] I suggest five distinctive characteristics of the CDF version of communion ecclesiology: (1) hyperconcern about sociological understandings of ecclesial communion; (2) visible expression and hierarchical structure of ecclesial communion; (3) sole emphasis on episcopal teaching authority; (4) unity over diversity—diversity of particular churches or of various charisms; and (5) the ontological and chronological priority of the universal church.

Synodality and the Ecclesiological Vision of Pope Francis

Unlike John Paul II and Benedict XVI who participated in Vatican II, Francis is the first pope since the council was held who did not attend. Perhaps an even more significant biographical difference is that Francis is the first pope from Latin America. This difference explains his unique approach to implementing Vatican II because, as Massimo Faggioli argues, "For a Latin American bishop like Bergoglio, Vatican II is an essential and obvious part of the experience of the church."[20] In comparison to his European predecessors, Francis is deeply indebted to his experience of the reception of Vatican II in Latin America generally and, in particular, the theology of the people as it developed in Argentina.[21]

The apostolic exhortation *Evangelii Gaudium*, the document referred to as the "roadmap" of his pontificate,[22] suggests that Francis intends an ambitious project of ecclesial reform and renewal. Francis refers to this project as "synodality," which Ormond Rush explains is Francis's "catch-all phrase for how he believes the Second Vatican Council is envisioning the church *ad intra*—in its inner workings—without wanting to separate the church's inner life from the effectiveness of its outward (*ad extra*) mission in the world."[23]

The most obvious feature of *Evangelii Gaudium* is Francis's repeated reference to the whole people of God. Francis emphasizes that "the Church, as the agent of evangelization, is more than an organic and hierarchical institution; she is first and foremost a people advancing on its pilgrim way toward God" (*EG* 111).[24]

Francis's definition of the church offers a balanced perspective, neglecting neither the church's vertical nor horizontal dimensions. For instance, calling attention to its divine communion, Francis insists, "Being church means being God's people" (*EG* 114). Yet this fundamental alignment in no way diminishes the church's responsibility to be in communion with the world. Francis affirms, "The People of God is incarnate in the people of the earth, each of which has its own culture" (*EG* 115). Here we see the influence of the theology of the people, which is also known as the theology of culture, given its attention to the sociocultural location of people.[25]

At the heart of *Evangelii Gaudium* is the affirmation that the whole people of God participates in the *sensus fidei*.[26] Paragraph 119, citing *Lumen Gentium* 12, is a critical passage reflecting Francis's "mature pneumatology," which also appears throughout *Evangelii Gaudium*, and has been named by Richard Gaillardetz as "one of the more unappreciated features of his theological vision."[27] Francis explicitly affirms elsewhere that every member of the church is endowed by the Holy Spirit with different charisms (*EG* 130).

The responsibility given to the whole people of God in *Evangelii Gaudium* flows from recovering the priority of baptism. As with the pneumatological emphasis in *Evangelii Gaudium*, Francis affirms the priority of baptism throughout the apostolic exhortation. In one particularly consequential passage, Francis writes, "In virtue of their baptism, all members of the People of God have become missionary disciples" (*EG* 120). Here we discover the connection between the recovery of baptismal significance and the missionary nature of the church. In other words, baptism calls the people of God to go forth "in order to reach all the 'peripheries' in need of the light of the Gospel" (*EG* 20). In contrast to a self-referential and self-centered church, Francis writes, "I prefer a Church which is bruised, hurting and dirty because it has been out on the streets, rather than a Church which is unhealthy from being confined and from clinging to its own security" (*EG* 49). Here again we observe the influence of the theology of the people in Francis's depiction of a missionary church going forth toward the periphery.

Missionary outreach is not one activity alongside many in the church, as Francis makes clear, but is rather *"paradigmatic for all the Church's activity"* (*EG* 15). For this reason, Massimo Faggioli rightly calls the ecclesiology in *Evangelii Gaudium* "a missionary ecclesiology faithful to the message of Vatican II."[28] Drawing attention to the connection between the missionary nature of the church and ecclesial reform, Francis contends that the "missionary option" has the potential to transform all of the church's structures and practices (*EG* 27). *Evangelii Gaudium* does not provide an exhaustive blueprint for ecclesial reform, but one concrete example suggests that Francis intends a far-reaching and ongoing reform. "Excessive centralization," Francis insists, "rather than proving helpful, complicates the Church's life and her missionary outreach" (*EG* 32). In unprecedented fashion, but consistent with his own teaching, Francis cites documents by national episcopal conferences including Brazil, Congo, France, India, the Philippines, and the United States, as well as regional conferences in Africa, Asia, Latin America, and Oceania.

The objective of the ecclesial reform that Francis initiates in *Evangelii Gaudium* is a more participatory and dialogical church. Throughout the apostolic exhortation, Francis affirms the value of listening, so much so that Gaillardetz names "a listening church" as a primary feature of Francis's "emerging ecclesiological vision."[29] Indeed, when Francis calls for the doors of the church to be open to the world, the primary mission he names is listening (*EG* 46).

Yet we often understand the practice of ecclesial listening only in a pastoral key. Clemens Sedmak helpfully expands this view by reading *Evangelii Gaudium* as proposing a renewed epistemic practice. When Francis describes a "church of the poor" (*EG* 49), Sedmak, exploring the epistemological consequences, asks: "If we think of the image of a church that is stripped of its power, would that also imply 'epistemic power,' 'power of judgment'? What does it mean for the church's capacity to judge the world?"[30] At the very least, it calls for a greater practice of ecclesial humility, which recognizes that genuine ecclesial communion is not imposed top-down or enforced juridically but is instead the result of sustained ecclesial listening.

This type of ecclesial listening requires a relative comfort with disagreement and conflict in the church. In a volume on Francis's intellectual influences, published in 2017, Massimo Borghesi argues that "the whole system of Bergoglio's thought is dominated by the overarching idea of the polarity of life."[31] We can see Francis's "tensioned thought" in *Evangelii Gaudium*'s well-known four principles (*EG* 222–37). Francis illustrates the final principle with the polyhedron, which "reflects the convergence of all its parts, each of which preserves its distinctiveness" (*EG* 236). In contrast with the sphere, "which is no greater than its parts, where every part is equidistant from the center, and there are no differences between them," a polyhedron does not need to enforce rigid uniformity in order to achieve unity (*EG* 236). Indeed, the polyhedron is an apt image because it points toward, as Juan Carlos Scannone explains, "a higher synthesis that does not erase tensions, but understands them, makes them fruitful, and opens them up to the future."[32]

Communion in a Synodal Church

In this final section, I argue that synodality provides a mature understanding of ecclesial communion. On October 17, 2015, in his address marking the fiftieth anniversary of the establishment of the Synod of Bishops,[33] an address that has been called "one of the most important speeches of his pontificate,"[34] Francis spoke of an "entirely synodal church" and broadly about the "path of *synodality*."[35] Here Francis is not referring to the Synod of Bishops or even the ancient synodal structures of the church.[36] Synodality is an all-encompassing proposal that involves the whole people of God. Francis defines synodality as the whole people of God "journeying together," and uses the image of an inverted pyramid, with the whole people of God forming the top of the pyramid, to illustrate a synodal church.[37]

The relationship between synodality and communion is not one of competing ecclesiological frameworks such that we choose either synodality or communion. Synodality also aims for communion, but it realizes that the way that ecclesial communion is achieved is more complex than the CDF version of communion permits. I agree with Ormond Rush, who contends that *communio* ecclesiology at Vatican II is "inchoate" and requiring synthesis—a synthesis that I believe Francis's understanding of synodality can provide.[38] Using the five characteristics of the CDF version of communion ecclesiology that I suggested above, I will suggest briefly how synodality might reshape ecclesial communion.

Theological Reductionism → Ecclesiological Realism

Although concern for sociological reductionism is valid, the limitation of the CDF version of communion ecclesiology is that it ignores the parallel concern of theological reductionism, resulting in overly idealized accounts of church life. The first shift in a synodal church is from hyperconcern about sociological understandings of the church to ecclesiological realism. Rather than following a "blueprint approach"[39] that uncritically applies the theological concept of communion to the church, the practice of synodality begins from below with an honest account of ecclesial experience. More recent ecclesiological texts demonstrate the value of an inductive approach to understanding the reality of the people of God.[40]

Hierarchical Expression of Communion → Inverted Pyramid

Second, synodality does not equate the much broader understanding of ecclesial communion with merely hierarchical communion. By recovering the priority of the whole people of God, the traditional pyramid is inverted, and focus shifts from power and status toward charisms and ministries. Ecclesial communion in a synodal church is not imposed from the top down but arises from the practice of synodality at the local, national/regional, and universal levels of the church—including, as Francis states, the exercise of the Petrine ministry.[41]

Teaching Authority of Bishops → A Listening Church and the Sensus Fidelium

Third, teaching authority is not limited to the role of bishops but involves the whole people of God reaching consensus through the *sensus fidelium.* A synodal church is a church that listens—bishops, theologians, and people. Indeed, "orthodoxy is in its communal aspect primarily a spiritual task of listening," but as Sedmak rightly insists, listening not only by "the faithful as the flock" but also the "shepherds leading."[42]

Diversity Oriented toward Unity → Polycentric Unity

Fourth, whereas the CDF version of communion ecclesiology accepts diversity so long as it does not threaten unity, synodality views diversity as essential, for polycentric unity is sustained by difference. The ecclesial listening required by synodality involves listening to diverse, neglected, and opposing voices: those who disagree are not immediately accused of "breaking communion." Francis's image of the polyhedron illustrates "the importance of listening to *everyone* in the church (all of the facets constitute the polyhedron) and the importance of *diversity* for the health of the church (all sides are distinct yet are part of the whole)."[43]

Ontological and Chronological Priority of the Universal Church → A Church of the Poor

Fifth, the insistence on the ontological and chronological priority of the universal church, a final feature of the CDF version of communion ecclesiology, is a consequence of its ecclesiocentric vision. Synodality pays more attention to the local church. "The synodal process," as Walter Kasper explains, "gives expression to the idea that the church is a unity in the multiplicity of local churches, of communities in the church, and of charisms."[44] Even more significant, however, is that synodality allows for a critical awareness of the church's epistemic poverty on every level, shifting the church away from being self-referential and self-centered and toward the peripheries.

Reshaping Ecclesial Communion

The fundamental weakness of the version of communion endorsed by the Congregation for the Doctrine of the Faith is that it proceeds as if ecclesial communion is already achieved and only needs to be protected. What results is a fragile understanding of communion that cannot adequately respond to the challenges and contributions of global Catholicism.

Synodality has the potential to reshape the way that ecclesial communion is understood and practiced. An honest examination of areas of difference and sinfulness in the church is not a threat to the church's communion but a necessary step in achieving genuine unity. Reclaiming the priority of the whole people of God does not eliminate the need for the hierarchical magisterium but provides it with its proper context. Listening and responding to the *sensus fidelium* does not weaken the teaching authority of bishops but increases its credibility. Diversity in the church is no longer viewed as a threat to communion but a natural consequence of the outpouring of the Holy Spirit. Communion is not the result of a centralized church that never moves or changes but rather the uniting of peripheries, geographic as well as epistemic.

In a synodal church, ecclesial communion remains the goal but the extent to which it is achieved depends on the whole people of God journeying together.

Notes

[1] The origin of "synod" is the Greek word *synodos*, which connotes "walking together."

[2] International Theological Commission, "The One Church of Jesus Christ: Select Themes in Ecclesiology on the Occasion of the 20th Anniversary of the End of the Second Vatican Council" (1984), II.2, available online at www.vatican.va.

[3] Ibid., VI.1.

[4] Ibid.

[5] Ronaldo Muñoz, "The Ecclesiology of the International Theological Commission," in *Synod 1985—An Evaluation*, ed. Giuseppe Alberigo and James Provost (Edinburgh: T&T Clark, 1986), 38.

[6] Ibid., 39.

[7] Ibid., 40.

[8] Jean-Marie Tillard, "Final Report of the Last Synod," in *Synod 1985—An Evaluation*, 65.

[9] Ibid., 66.

[10] Ibid., 68. Joseph Komonchak refers to the synod having "entombed" the concept, writing, "from the Final Report one could suspect that 'People of God' had been the title of a whole chapter of *Lumen Gentium*, that it had served as one of the architectonic themes of the Council's ecclesiology, and that it had been introduced precisely as an articulation of the very mystery of the Church in the time between Ascension and Parousia" ("The Theologi-

cal Debate," in *Synod 1985—An Evaluation*, 55). To clarify the meaning of this quote, I believe that Komonchak intends "suspect" as in "doubt" rather than "believe," since this passage and its context argue that the ecclesiology of "people of God" received far less attention at the 1985 Synod than it did at Vatican II.

[11]Tillard, "Final Report," 70.

[12]Hermann Pottmeyer, "The Church as Mysterium and as Institution," in *Synod 1985—An Evaluation*, 106.

[13]The text of the Synod's Final Report can be found in *Extraordinary Synod—1985* (Boston: Daughters of St. Paul, 1985), 37–68; here, II.C.1.

[14]Ibid.

[15]Komonchak, "Theological Debate," 57–58.

[16]Ibid., 61.

[17]Dennis M. Doyle, *Communion Ecclesiology: Vision and Versions* (Maryknoll, NY: Orbis Books, 2000), 12.

[18]Ibid., 19.

[19]"Instruction on Certain Aspects of the 'Theology of Liberation' " (1984); "Notification on the Book 'Church: Charism and Power' by Father Leonardo Boff" (1985); "Letter to Father Charles Curran" (1986); Profession of Faith and Oath of Fidelity (1989); *Donum Veritatis* (1990); and "Letter to the Bishops of the Catholic Church on Some Aspects of the Church Understood as Communion" (1992). The official version of these documents can be found on the Vatican's website.

[20]Massimo Faggioli, *Pope Francis: Tradition in Transition* (New York: Paulist Press, 2013), 11.

[21]Elisabetta Piqu, *Pope Francis: Life and Revolution* (Chicago: Loyola Press, 2013), 225–26.

[22]Juan Carlos Scannone, SJ, "Pope Francis and the Theology of the People," *Theological Studies* 77 (2016): 126.

[23]Ormond Rush, "Inverting the Pyramid: The *Sensus Fidelium* in a Synodal Church," *Theological Studies* 78 (2017): 303.

[24]Pope Francis, *Evangelii Gaudium: Apostolic Exhortation on the Proclamation of the Gospel in Today's World* (November 24, 2013), w2.vatican.va. All references to *Evangelii Gaudium* in the body of this essay will be denoted as *EG* followed by the article number.

[25]Rafael Luciani, *Pope Francis and the Theology of the People* (Maryknoll, NY: Orbis Books, 2017), xiii.

[26]Walter Kasper argues that Francis recovers the *sensus fidei*, which was neglected after the council, and this significant teaching requires a magisterium that can listen. Walter Kasper, *Pope Francis' Revolution of Tenderness and Love: Theological and Pastoral Perspectives* (New York: Paulist Press, 2015), 41.

[27]Richard R. Gaillardetz, *An Unfinished Council: Vatican II, Pope Francis, and the Renewal of Catholicism* (Collegeville, MN: Liturgical Press, 2015), 122.

[28]Massimo Faggioli, "*Evangelii Gaudium* as an Act of Reception of Vatican II," in *Pope Francis and the Future of Catholicism*: Evangelii Gaudium *and*

the Papal Agenda, ed. Gerard Mannion (New York: Cambridge University Press, 2017), 42.

²⁹Gaillardetz, *Unfinished Council*, 122.

³⁰Clemens Sedmak, *A Church of the Poor: Pope Francis and the Transformation of Orthodoxy* (Maryknoll, NY: Orbis Books, 2016), xvi.

³¹Massimo Borghesi, *The Mind of Pope Francis: Jorge Mario Bergoglio's Intellectual Journey* (Collegeville, MN: Liturgical Press, 2017), 141.

³²Scannone, "Pope Francis and the Theology of the People," 130.

³³For more on the establishment of the Synod of Bishops in 1965, see Massimo Faggioli, *A Council for the Global Church: Receiving Vatican II in History* (Minneapolis: Fortress, 2015), 232–38.

³⁴Richard R. Gaillardetz, "Pope Francis and the Rise of a Pastoral Magisterium," *Offerings: Journal of Oblate School of Theology* 10 (2017): 66.

³⁵Pope Francis, "Address of His Holiness Pope Francis: Ceremony Commemorating the 50th Anniversary of the Institution of the Synod of Bishops" (October 17, 2015), w2.vatican.va.

³⁶For more on the synodal structure of the early church, see John R. Quinn, *Ever Ancient, Ever New: Structures of Communion in the Church* (New York: Paulist Press, 2013), 8–12. It is widely known that Bergoglio praised Quinn's earlier book *The Reform of the Papacy: The Costly Call to Christian Unity* (New York: Crossroad, 1999).

³⁷Pope Francis, "Address," October 17, 2015.

³⁸Rush, "Inverting the Pyramid," 312.

³⁹Nicholas M. Healy, "Ecclesiology and Communion," *Perspectives in Religious Studies* 3 (2004): 274.

⁴⁰Natalia Imperatori-Lee, *Cuéntame: Narrative in the Ecclesial Present* (Maryknoll, NY: Orbis Books, 2018), xv–xviii.

⁴¹Pope Francis, "Address," October 17, 2015.

⁴²Sedmak, *Church of the Poor*, 158.

⁴³Rush, "Inverting the Pyramid," 324.

⁴⁴Kasper, *Pope Francis' Revolution of Tenderness and Love*, 52.

Is Paul's Inculturation in Acts 17:16–34 Actually Cultural Appropriation?

Discerning Models of Evangelization for the Future

Stewart L. Heatwole

One of the many challenges facing global Catholicism today has been and will continue to be ensuring that the Christian scriptures are accessible to believers and nonbelievers alike. Historically, the church has used numerous methods to make its message known, but in the years after the Second Vatican Council, an ancient model has been revived. This model is known as inculturation, and scriptural scholars have often looked to the biblical text itself for examples of this method. One of the most famous of these examples is Paul's sermon in Acts 17:16–34, where he addresses the scholars of Athens at the Areopagus. It is a powerful illustration because it clearly displays the spirit of inculturation, which allows for mutual exchange between two cultures so that the gospel message can transform the cultures in which it is embodied.[1] In other words, the reason Paul's speech is so notable is because he meets his audience in their context, using artifacts from their own cultural and religious landscape, and from this place reveals the ways in which Jesus Christ is the source and completion of their every desire.[2] The church now looks back at this episode in Acts 17 as a model of what good inculturation looks like and therefore how evangelization is to be approached.[3]

As a prominent model of how the church should evangelize, however, Paul's actions in Athens demand continued scrutiny. Such scrutiny would ensure that Paul's actions either remain as an unqualified model or become a qualified model for the church's mission of evangelization. I will not attempt to establish a moralistic evaluation of Paul's actions by modern standards—instead, I will use a modern lens to examine Paul's actions, so that the church today does not fall into pitfalls that will ultimately compromise its mission.

Recent studies in the social sciences have addressed situations where inculturation has "gone too far" and violates the culture into which a message and its messenger have entered.[4] This phenomenon has been named "cultural appropriation" because, instead of simply entering into another culture, something is taken from the encountered culture in the interaction. Given this development in the social sciences and the importance of Paul's actions in Acts 17 for the way in which the global church fulfills its mission, it is important to establish whether Paul goes beyond inculturation and is in fact appropriating the Athenian culture in his address at the Areopagus. If this were the case, it would call into question many of the church's contemporary practices modeled after Paul's example.

I argue that Paul is not culturally appropriating Greek religious culture (1) because of the power dynamic between Paul and his audience and (2) because of Paul's failure to exhibit any of the characteristics of appropriation in his speech. Before my case is made in full, a few basic details need to be established. First, the context of Paul's preaching and an account of Paul's words at the Areopagus need to be addressed. Second, the concept of cultural appropriation and its nuances need to be examined in light of recent literature on the subject. Finally, with these details sorted, I can apply a modern social critique to the biblical text to argue that Paul was not culturally appropriating the Greeks when he gave his sermon at the Areopagus.

Paul's Words at the Areopagus

When he arrives in Athens, Paul begins debating in the synagogues with the Jews and in the public squares with the representatives of different philosophical schools (Acts 17:17). After debating with these philosophers in the city center, he is invited to the Areopagus to give a full account of his beliefs in what they understood to be the plural gods of "Jesus" and "Resurrection" (Acts 17:18). The Areopagus at this time served a role similar to that of the Sanhedrin in Jerusalem because it was the site of religious debate and clarification.[5] It is fitting, then, that Paul and his promotion of "foreign divinities" (Acts 17:18) were brought here to be clarified and questioned. At the Areopagus, Paul begins by referencing the piety of the Athenians as displayed in an altar to an "Unknown God" and continues by describing God as the "Lord of heaven and earth," the giver and sustainer of life, and the one who, now known beyond natural revelation, demands repentance from the worship of idols (Acts 17:22–31). At the end of Paul's remarks to the Athenians, the crowd is divided. Some deride the notion of the resurrection proclaimed by Paul, and yet others are curious to hear more. As this episode in Paul's missionary work unfolds, we find an outsider with knowledge of Greek culture proclaiming a message that he believes can be heard by the people of Athens, but that is radically different from the beliefs professed at the time by the Athenians.

Paul's social standing among the Greeks is certainly one of the more interesting elements of this story. He makes himself known as a social outsider, but he actually resides in the liminal space between insider and outsider because of his position by birth and education. Born in the tribe of Benjamin in the city of Tarsus, Paul is both a Jew and a Roman citizen.[6] It is clear in Acts that Jews hold no place of privilege within Greek society, but, owing to his citizenship, he is afforded some degree of privilege, if only among the Roman officials in charge.

One episode in Acts 16 illustrates nicely the complexity of Paul's position. While preaching in Philippi, Paul commands a spirit to leave a slave girl who had gained great profit for her owners owing to her oracular abilities. When the owners of the slave girl realize their loss of income now that the spirit has left the girl, they seize Paul and his companion Silas and take them to the local Roman magistrates (Acts 16:19). The magistrates have them imprisoned on account of their being Jews and disturbing the peace by promoting customs contrary to Roman practice (Acts 16:23). After being released, Paul makes it known that he and Silas are both Roman citizens and have not been given the trial they are owed as citizens and therefore will not leave quietly, to the shame of the magistrates (Acts 16:38). Not only does this passage show the lowly status of the Jews in Macedonia, but it also highlights the great privilege that came with being a Roman citizen. Finally, Paul was not ignorant of Greek culture, but had studied Greek as a young man in Tarsus and therefore was familiar with their poets and teachings. This helps explain his use of the poet Aratus of Soli in Acts 17:28 and will prove to be important in our subsequent discussion on appropriation. This argument is benefited by further analysis of Paul's speech.

The speech that Paul gives in Athens is typical, considering his Jewish identity and training.[7] His proclamation is complex in character because it highlights the religious sensitivity of the Athenians, offers criticism of their practices, and utilizes the theology and poetry of the Greeks.[8]

Paul begins his speech with the popular religious artifacts of Greece—namely, the dedicated altars at which devotees of the different gods worshiped. The altar that Paul references to ingratiate himself with the Athenians could have been a dedicated altar to an "Unknown God" or it could have simply been an undedicated altar. Regardless, the effect remains the same: Paul goes out of his way to identify the piety of the Athenians and suggest that the God he is about to proclaim is one that might be familiar to them.[9]

Having thus complimented them, Paul not only quickly changes the pronoun he has been using to refer to the "Unknown God" but also turns to the current practices of the Athenians to reveal the ways in which they have failed to understand who the true creator God is.[10] The criticism that he levels against the pagan practices comes in three parts, in accordance with common rhetorical practices of Hellenistic Judaism.[11] Both the change in pronoun and the leveling of criticism help provide theological separation between Paul and his audience.

Interwoven in his criticisms of the pagan practices are Paul's use of common theological and literary ground. The common theological ground is that of natural theology or "evidence from nature for the God who created it." Such theology takes what can be observed with the natural eye, that is, the "fixed and ordered seasons," and he uses it to reveal aspects of God (Acts 17:26). This type of reasoning would have been particularly persuasive for his audience of Epicurean and Stoic philosophers. The Epicureans focused their attention on natural reasoning because it was seen as the path to free people from that which enslaved them.[12] Stoics would have been attracted to Paul's description of the creator God because it complemented the teachings of Zeno, their founder.[13] Furthermore, Paul could make such references to the way of nature without compromising his own faith because natural theology is employed throughout the Hebrew Scriptures and therefore would have been seen as completely orthodox among both Jews and Christians.[14] Paul also employs his knowledge of Greek literature to give added weight to his own thoughts in verses 28–29 by using the words of the Greek poet Aratus of Soli or Tarsus, "For we too are his offspring."[15] It is this moment, in addition to his reference to the altar at the beginning of his speech, that most clearly raises the question of appropriation and therefore will be examined more closely later.

Defining Cultural Appropriation

The contemporary context of the Roman Catholic Church is defined in large part by its constant engagement with the world's cultures. Few cultures are now new to the Catholic Church, but in its mission to evangelize it is called to continue to meet and engage these cultures.[16] This process, however, is fraught with pitfalls where the church might degrade or harm the cultures it is trying to engage. Given this context, there is a need to turn to our models of evangelization, such as Paul's preaching in Athens, and ensure that they remain positive models that reflect our current understandings of culturally appropriate practices. Practically, what is revealed by this investigation will give the church guidance on how to act and what not to repeat. To begin this process, we must understand which actions are considered culturally degrading, or "appropriation," and which are not.

At first glance, deriving a definition for cultural appropriation might seem like a simple task. Cultural appropriation as most people understand it is "the taking—from a culture that is not one's own—of intellectual property, cultural expressions or artifacts, history and ways of knowledge."[17] When applied to individuals, this definition seems rather straightforward. Modern copyright laws seem to effectively police the inappropriate taking of an author's work without permission. As simple as this definition might be, however, it fails to fully illuminate the difference between appropriation and assimilation, and whether all cultural borrowing is to be avoided. It is one thing to determine appropriation between the works of two individuals, but a much more complicated task when dealing with entire cultures as the authors of certain ideas, works, or artifacts.[18] This task is made considerably clearer when we apply the lenses of power dynamics and of negative criteria for identifying appropriation to guide our assessment.

The difference between appropriation and assimilation comes down to a person's relationship to the group with which they are engaging. Both appropriation and assimilation are similar in that they are made possible by the separation of an in-group from an out-group.[19] A person must be a part of an "out-group" to either appropriate or assimilate the culture of the in-group. What separates appropriation and assimilation ultimately is the power dynamics between the in-group and the out-group. If the out-group exhibits dominance over and takes from a subordinate in-group, then it is appropriation. If the out-group exhibits subordination to and takes from a dominant in-group, then it is assimilation.[20] Therefore, the power dynamics are a key determining factor for whether an action is to be deemed appropriation. To complexify the relationship between assimilation and appropriation, a person in a dominant group could honestly desire to create something that is inspired by a group that is clearly subordinate to his or her own. In the face of such complexity, it seems wholly defensible to seek out further means of adjudicating what constitutes appropriation, so that cultural borrowing and the great boon it is to creativity might continue.[21] The work of scholars Bruce Ziff and Pratima V. Rao proves helpful in meeting this goal. They discuss four ways in which acts of appropriation can violate the culture being appropriated. Awareness—and, hence, avoidance—of these ways can ensure that appropriation does not take place.

The four possible forms of violation are (1) a disregard for damage done to the integrity of cultural groups; (2) a disregard for the damage done to the integrity of cultural artifacts; (3) the financial benefit to the dominant group over the subordinate group afforded to them by appropriation; and (4) a disregard for the sovereignty of the subordinate group.[22] The first of these is characterized by the degradation of a community's reputation or standing because of a misunderstanding that has been introduced by the act of appropriation.[23] A horrific example of this would be the damage the Third Reich perpetrated on numerous cultures around the world when they took the symbol of the swastika as their central symbol. Originally a symbol of good fortune in various Indian and Chinese cultures, it now symbolizes hatred and genocide because of its appropriation by the Nazi Party.[24] The second form of violation results in the specific degradation of a cultural artifact. This involves a lack of care for the uniqueness of artifacts and their relationship with the cultures that created them. This lack of care is on display, for example, when certain cultural narratives are romanticized by the dominant group, with the effect that their integrity is compromised.[25] The third form of violation pertains to the economic consequences of appropriation.[26] If a dominant group financially benefits over and/or against the subordinate group it took from, this is considered appropriation. An example is the financial success of authors who publish narratives from indigenous communities without compensating the indigenous communities.[27] Finally, the fourth form of violation is a disregard for the sovereignty or rules and customs of subordinate cultures. Appropriation takes place, for example, when those in dominant groups do not seek permission through the avenues established by subordinate groups for the use of their cultural artifacts. Delineating these forms of violation establishes helpful negative criteria for determining the boundaries between appropriate cultural borrowing and inappropriate cultural appropriation. These criteria will be helpful in assessing the impact of Paul's interactions with the members of Athenian society present at the Areopagus in Acts 17.

Was Paul Engaging in Cultural Appropriation?

Two lines of argument arise in claiming that Paul was not appropriating Athenian culture during his speech at the Areopagus. The first is based on an analysis of power dynamics and the second on applying the negative criteria discussed above.

Analysis of Power Dynamics

The primacy of Paul's Jewish identity makes it clear that he was not part of the Greek in-group.[28] As we have already established, though, simply being an outsider does not disqualify one from participating in cultural appropriation. What counts are the power dynamics.

Paul begins his ministry in Athens by preaching in the synagogues and therefore would have been known to the Greeks as a Jew (Acts 17:17). As indicated before, being a Jew in Macedonia afforded the individual no special rights and perhaps worked to disempower the individual (Acts 16:20). We should also recall that in the episode at Philippi, Paul used his Roman citizenship to gain some social leverage during his imprisonment; this reveals his ability, despite being a disempowered outsider, to position himself in some situations in such a way as to gain power over the Greeks (Acts 16:37). What makes our analysis of the power dynamics so complicated is the fact that the status that could change the weighting of the balances was something that could be concealed. Paul did not have to reveal that he was a Roman citizen, and it seems impossible to tell if his Greek audience would have known it if he did not mention it. At no point, though, in the eighteen verses dedicated to Paul's time in Athens is his Roman citizenship mentioned. Additionally, it seems relevant in a discussion of power dynamics that the speech given at the Areopagus was precipitated and facilitated by an invitation from the Greek philosophers (Acts 17:19). Paul was therefore speaking on terms established by the Greeks, which indicates that the Greeks maintained some dominance over Paul. According to this paradigm, Paul's reference to the altar to an "Unknown God" and use of the poet Aratus of Soli would fall more neatly under the heading of assimilation than appropriation. The strength of this claim, based solely on the power dynamics of the situation, is at least partially suspect. There are numerous factors, such as the intricacies of Greek, Jewish, and Roman relationships, which would need to be known to make a strong stand-alone argument. Therefore, if we want a clearer judgment on whether Paul was appropriating the Greeks' culture, it is best to turn next to the characterizations of appropriation provided by Ziff and Rao.

Applying Negative Criteria

When the four negative criteria for determining appropriation are considered alongside Paul's use of Greek culture, it becomes clear that he has not engaged in appropriation. Key to making this judgment is the reaction or lack thereof by the Greeks to his use of Greek culture. When Paul references the altar to the "Unknown God," there is no protest by the Greeks. In fact, it would be hard to find fault in the conclusion that Paul reaches through his reference. Unlike examples of appropriation given earlier, the reader does not walk away with some gross misunderstanding of the Athenian people, nor does the artifact itself seem misrepresented or taken out of context. With regard to the verse from the poet Aratus of Soli, Paul begins by giving credit to the poet, albeit not in name, which indicates care for the proper understanding of the passage. By giving credit he opens himself up to the audience to challenge him on the proper interpretation of the passage, which there is no record of their doing. This in and of itself does not seem sufficient evidence to rule out appropriation, considering the bias of the text.[29] However, Paul employs the poet's words in a setting that would have been wholly appropriate for such an artifact. By using a poetic line in such a setting, Paul reveals his conscious intention to build up rather than damage the culture from which it came. Therefore, it appears that the usage of both the altar and the poetry in his speech are cleared of the charge of misuse according to the first two negative criteria for determining appropriation.

Judging whether Paul was appropriating according to the first two criteria required a somewhat more nuanced investigation, but the evaluation according to the third and fourth principles is much simpler. There is no account of any financial gain by Paul through his use of Greek cultural artifacts, and the sovereignty of the Greeks to define their own culture appears to be completely intact. Evidence of Greek sovereignty appears in the Athenians' both calling for Paul's speech to begin (Acts 17:19) and calling for it to end (Acts 17:32). At no point in the text does the reader question who is setting the terms of Paul's speech. The reason the Athenians give for Paul to stop speaking is not a misuse of one of their cultural artifacts, but, rather, their objection to a notion proper to the Christian message being proclaimed, the resurrection of Jesus. Furthermore, in response to this abrupt call to stop, Paul does not invoke his Roman citizenship to prolong his proclamation, but abides by the terms set by the Athenians and walks away from the Areopagus (Acts 17:33). Therefore, Paul respects the sovereignty of the Athenian philosophical culture and leaves little room to assume he would not have, had he been challenged on his use of the Greek cultural artifacts.

Paul as a Model for Inculturation

This essay has shown that Paul's speech at the Areopagus in Acts 17 is worthy of the high regard in which it is held as a work of inculturation and not appropriation. Paul could have used a position of power to appropriate Greek culture, but he chose not to and thereby demonstrated respect for the integrity of that culture. The value of this analysis is to show that Paul's speech remains a model for modern evangelization in a global context. Paul's example helps clarify power dynamics in modern evangelization by providing us with a critical comparison necessary for culturally responsible evangelization. The church rarely is in the position of powerlessness that Paul found himself in and therefore must turn to his model to avoid the pitfalls of appropriation and to show respect for the cultures that Christianity meets and hopes to engage.

Notes

[1] Peter C. Phan, *In Our Own Tongues: Perspectives from Asia on Mission and Inculturation* (Maryknoll, NY: Orbis Books, 2003), 6.

[2] Jean Radermakers and Philippe Bossuyt, "Rencontre de l'incroyant et inculturation: Paul à Athènes (Acts 17:16–34)," *Nouvelle Revue Théologique* 117, no. 1 (1995): 42.

[3] Jacques Dupont, *The Salvation of the Gentiles: Essays on the Acts of the Apostles*, trans. John R. Keating (New York: Paulist Press, 1979), 30. For more on the connection between inculturation and evangelization, see Paul VI's *Evangelii Nuntiandi* (no. 29), and Phan, *In Our Own Tongues*, 5.

[4] See, for example, Hans Peter Hahn, "Diffusionism, Appropriation, and Globalization. Some Remarks on Current Debates in Anthropology," *Anthropos* 103, no. 1 (2008): 191–202. This article does not use the theological term "inculturation."

[5] Dupont, *Salvation of the Gentiles*, 31.

[6]Joseph A. Fitzmyer, "Paul," in *The Jerome Biblical Commentary*, ed. Raymond E. Brown, Joseph A. Fitzmyer, and Roland E. Murphy (Englewood Cliffs, NJ: Prentice Hall, 1968), 2:217.

[7]Dupont, *Salvation of the Gentiles*, 28.

[8]Radermakers and Bossuyt, "Rencontre de l'incroyant et inculturation," 28, 41.

[9]Richard J. Dillon and Joseph A. Fitzmyer, "Acts of the Apostles," in *The Jerome Biblical Commentary*, 2:200.

[10]Radermakers and Bossuyt, "Rencontre de l'incroyant et inculturation," 29.

[11]Dupont, *Salvation of the Gentiles*, 31.

[12]Dillon and Fitzmyer, "Acts of the Apostles," 199.

[13]Ibid., 200.

[14]William S. Kurz, "The Acts of the Apostles," in *The Collegeville Bible Commentary*, ed. Dianne Bergant and Robert J. Karris (Collegeville, MN: Liturgical Press, 1989), 1060.

[15]Dillon and Fitzmyer, "Acts of the Apostles," 200.

[16]Pope Paul VI, *Evangelii Nuntiandi*, no. 29, www.vatican.va.

[17]Bruce Ziff and Pratima V. Rao, eds., *Borrowed Power: Essays on Cultural Appropriation* (New Brunswick, NJ: Rutgers University Press, 1997), 1.

[18]Ibid., 3.

[19]Ibid.

[20]Ibid., 5.

[21]Michael F. Brown, "Can Culture Be Copyrighted?" *Current Anthropology* 39, no. 2 (April 1998): 204.

[22]Ziff and Rao, *Borrowed Power*, 8.

[23]David Waldron and Janice Newton, "Rethinking Appropriation of the Indigenous: A Critique of the Romanticist Approach," *Nova Religio: The Journal of Alternative and Emergent Religions* 16, no. 2 (November 2012): 65.

[24]Ziff and Rao, *Borrowed Power*, 12.

[25]Waldron and Newton, "Rethinking Appropriation," 78.

[26]Brown, "Can Culture Be Copyrighted?" 195.

[27]Waldron and Newton, "Rethinking Appropriation," 72.

[28]Fitzmyer, "Paul," 217.

[29]Dupont, *Salvation of the Gentiles*, 12.

West African Catechists

A Study of Ministerial Positionality and Border Navigation

Maureen R. O'Brien

Ever since Christian missionaries first entered sub-Saharan Africa, lay evangelizers, often known as catechists, have been integral to the spread of the gospel there. The missionaries, lacking understanding of local cultures and languages, needed local people to assist. The lay catechist accordingly served as the Catholic missionary's "interpreter, assistant, substitute," according to Adrian Hastings.[1] Pope John XXIII stated, "There was never a time when catechists were not excellent assistants to missionaries, sharing their labors and relieving them."[2] Catechists were usually men, typically well-respected leaders in their local communities. Driven by the imperative of rapid evangelization, missionaries set up small worship centers called "outstations" in villages, appointed catechists to maintain them, and visited only infrequently, primarily to offer the sacraments. Pope Pius XII opined that one missionary with six catechists could do more than seven missionaries.[3] Later, the Vatican II document *Ad Gentes* called catechists "true co-workers of the priestly order" (*AG* 17) and even advocated their ordination to the diaconate (*AG* 16).[4] In 1993, the Congregation for the Evangelization of Peoples (CEP) provided a full overview of their vocation, necessary formation, and ways to promote their ministry in the *Guide for Catechists*.[5] They also received respectful mention in the documents of the African Synod (e.g., *Ecclesia in Africa*, 91).[6]

Little in-depth literature on catechists' ministry exists, and those who write about catechists for official church purposes are almost never the catechists themselves. In this essay, then, I seek to lift the voices of contemporary catechists in a West African diocese as an affirmation of and contribution to their dignity and the importance of their ministry. I also expect that through learning from them, those interested in global Catholicism can find their theological perspectives helpfully enhanced and nuanced.

In what follows I provide a brief background on my qualitative research project in a diocese of West Africa and then engage in practical-theological reflection on my data. Two key thematic strands will be evident. First, catechists' ministry illustrates a distinctive challenge for theologically incorporating the experiences of nonordained ministers into viable models of "ordered" ministries that account for ordained and nonordained statuses relative to one another. Second, the catechists' words illuminate them as living examples of people being "about borders," to use Michele Saracino's evocative term.[7] In their continually shifting "border" relationships with ordained ministers and other laity in the congregations they serve, catechists must cultivate effective strategies for their interactions with others and spiritual practices to sustain them in their challenging vocation.

Study Background

In 2018, I spent four weeks in a West African diocese to gather data for this qualitative study of the theological and ministerial self-understandings and practices of catechists. Such projects typically are small-scale, aiming for "thick" descriptions of human phenomena rather than large-scale, generalizable, and replicable findings. In order to increase the validity and depth of a qualitative analysis, researchers often employ several methods, gathering data from several types of participants. Data are then "coded" (analyzed) for identification and interrelating of key themes. Researchers "deploy a wide range of interconnected interpretive practices" to surface important findings.[8]

For this study, I gathered data using the following research methods:

- An online questionnaire completed by over thirty individual catechists
- Individual and group interviews with over fifty catechists

- Focus groups with several dozen parishioners and parish lay leaders
- Attendance at the diocese's three-week residential catechist formation program
- Visits to ten parishes and outstations, observing liturgies led by catechists as well as some catechetical sessions with children and adults

I also incorporated a framework of practical theology in constructing the project. In this approach, the researcher/practitioner makes *theological* assumptions regarding the ways that in-depth, "thick" description and analysis of real-life "episodes, situations, or contexts" may be correlated with themes in the Christian tradition in order to yield new insights and strategies.[9] A team of British practical-theological researchers led by Helen Cameron has provided a helpful interpretive lens for my approach. In their Theological Action Research (TAR), they identify four theological "voices":

- *Espoused Theology*: "the theology embedded within a group's articulation of its beliefs"
- *Operant Theology*: "the theology embedded within the actual practices of a group"
- *Normative Theology*: theology expressed in authoritative sources such as Scripture, creeds, official teachings, and liturgies
- *Formal Theology*: encompassing "the theology of theologians" and "dialogue with other disciplines"[10]

The authors maintain that these voices come into fruitful and mutually critical conversation in TAR.

In this essay, I highlight the conversation between the espoused and operant voices of the African catechists along with selected normative and formal perspectives drawing on Christian themes. In the process I consider how contemporary "formal" theologies of ministerial "ordering" offer creative possibilities for situating the catechists' ministry and yet are challenged by the ambiguities of the catechists' lived ministerial realities. This tension is examined especially for the ways it highlights discrepancies between

the catechists' experiences and the prevailing, "normative" understandings of ordained and nonordained ministers. Drawing on
interviews with catechists, I also offer highlights of the "operant"
practices and "espoused" spiritual perspectives that sustain them
as they navigate what Saracino calls the affective, identity-focused
"borders" of their experiences and situations.

Ordered Ministries

Models of "ordered" and "relational" theologies of ministry,
such as those developed by Edward P. Hahnenberg, Richard
Gaillardetz, and others prove helpful for this study. In reading
the signs of the times of the growth of multiple new ministries
and ministers post–Vatican II, these models offer fresh ways of
configuring nonordained and ordained ministries relative to one
another, as well as viable approaches for forming, authorizing, and
liturgically commissioning nonordained ministers. They have been
frequently used in developing the nascent "normative" theology
of lay ecclesial ministry in the United States.[11]

As Gaillardetz puts it, "Ordered ministry refers to any and all
ministries that, once formally undertaken, draw one into a new
ecclesial relationship within the life of the church; in undertaking
an ordered ministry, one is ecclesially repositioned."[12] Hahnenberg, developing a model first proposed by Yves Congar, posits
that ministries should be ordered not as pyramidal—clergy on
top, laity below—but in concentric circles. The life of Christian
discipleship constitutes the outer, encompassing circle. Within it,
progressively narrowing circles indicate growing levels of formation, responsibility, and vocational commitment, with community
leadership at the center. Although Hahnenberg does not propose
a change in the structure of ministerial ordination, he believes
that many nonordained ministries are rightfully positioned in
inner circles and deserve their own forms of recognition. Thus,
ordination alone is not the only or best designator for ministerial "centrality"—rather, one's role within the overall relational
configuration becomes that indicator.[13]

Of course, this approach leaves ambiguities, notably in the
contrast between the high degree of universal clarity of normative
theological and canonical articulation of the status and functions

of the ordained, and the local and varied navigation of operant and espoused understandings of nonordained ministries. In my African research I have been struck by a particular manifestation of these dynamics in the ministry of the catechists, especially those in the small rural parish outstations, which I address below.

Some catechists in the diocese I studied have opportunities for formal training and ministerial recognition. If time and resources permit, they can receive intensive formation for their role while in residence at a catechetical center, with a festive liturgical commissioning at its completion. However, especially for outstation catechists, there is continual "depositioning and repositioning" in their ecclesial relationship with the parish priest and the outstation community.[14] Offering an operant challenge to Gaillardetz's and Hahnenberg's formal theological formulations, the catechist's status and function change noticeably between the typical, everyday situation in which one is leading the community—functioning in the innermost circle of Hahnenberg's model—and the sporadic occasions when one's priest shows up. This positional fluidity points to the "hybrid" nature of catechists' ministerial identity, to use Saracino's term.

In probing this further, I first note the list of catechists' responsibilities, articulated by my interview subjects and corresponding quite well to the official description used by the diocese. To use Cameron's terms, this list seems to show a congruence between espoused, operant, and normative theological voices:

- Catechizing all ages, especially for sacramental initiation
- Leading liturgies and prayer in the absence of clergy
- Visiting the sick and those otherwise absent from worship
- Collaborating with parish leadership and associations
- Preparing couples for marriage
- Conducting burial ceremonies
- Other responsibilities, including everything from mediating disputes among villagers to contributing alms to the poor (often from one's own pocket) to taking a shift in the construction of a new church building

It is evident that in the diocese where I did my research and generally across Africa, catechists—most of them unpaid—have varied and demanding pastoral responsibilities. In the outstations, the multiple duties of the catechists result in their serving, most of the time, as de facto church leaders. They are frequently ministering with people experiencing high levels of poverty, illness, lack of economic advancement opportunities, poor infrastructure, environmental degradation, and other ills. Thus, stress is intense, and strong personal and spiritual resources are important for fulfilling one's duties. (I address some of the catechists' prominent pastoral strategies and spiritual dispositions later in this essay.)

Navigating Ecclesial and Interpersonal Borders

To compound these challenges, in their everyday encounters, catechists must navigate multiple ecclesial and interpersonal "borders," to use Saracino's paradigm. Saracino states, "I imagine borders not in terms of a specific identity for any one specific group but rather more in regard to how they mark an encounter with difference, which creates an emotional response."[15] Catechists must continually negotiate the delicate and shifting border terrain of "otherness" in being a ministerial leader, yet not ordained; holding a certain amount of authority and fulfilling vital pastoral responsibilities, yet having neither clerical prerogatives nor the option of "fading into the crowd" of the general lay Catholic population in their small and often quite insular communities. Catechists, like other humans, have a range of emotional responses to their hybrid identities.

A striking illustration of both ministerial depositioning and affective response to a border situation occurs at the outstations. Having worked day after day to meet the needs of one's people, the catechist, like John the Baptist with Jesus, must "decrease" when the priest arrives and "increases." To use Hahnenberg's circles model, the catechist ordinarily ministers from an everyday central circle of community leadership until displaced by a visiting priest. In interviews, catechists reported having to scramble on short notice to accommodate priests' visits: informing parishioners of the date for liturgies and sacramental celebrations in order to ensure a good attendance, preparing the outstation church building, and sometimes offering one's own bed to the priest for an overnight stay. Yet they may find themselves frustratingly unappreciated by both priests and people, as attested in a lively interview I conducted with two catechists who serve together at an outstation. Their dialogue points to their experience of the difference in church attendance and size of the offertory collection when a priest presides at Sunday liturgy, as well as the priest's discretion in use of the collection.[16]

> MO: And you're also saying that unlike the priest, the catechist is with the people all the time [both catechists agreeing]. The priest is not with the people all the time.
>
> C22: And even when the priest comes . . . they come to church in their numbers. And they give bountifully. But when the priest goes, then they try to reduce. Their coming-to-church numbers are reduced and giving of collection, too, they try to reduce it. But when they hear that tomorrow the priest is here, Oh! Then we will come in numbers. With good—
>
> MO: With good collections. [Laughs]
>
> C23 and C22: Good offertories.
>
> C23: A bunch of bananas, plenty of cassava, fish. But when you—[laughs]—when the priest tells them, "Try to do something for your catechist," you have—[trails off]
>
> C22: We are suffering here. As catechists, we are suffering.
>
> C22: Our reward is from heaven. [MO laughs]
>
> C23: That's what they always tell us—the priests. They say our reward is from heaven. As they have got their offertory gift. Putting it at the back of their car. When we ask them to give us a little small [remuneration or gift], they say that our reward is coming from heaven. [C22 laughs]

Here the power differential in the border between catechist and priest is evident. Catechists are with the people "all the time." Yet the priest, able to offer the sacraments, draws greater numbers to worship on his visits, while simultaneously depositioning the catechist from the usual liturgical and communal leadership role. Having more attendees results in larger collections—which in Africa usually include both money and produce. The priest has discretion over all offertories and may or may not offer a portion to the unsalaried catechist. He then drives off in his car with the collection—a scenario that heightens the economic disparity, since I did not encounter a single catechist with a car, though a few had motorbikes. Thus, in my interviews, catechists could be both sincere and ironic in commenting that their own reward is in heaven.

In these situations, a conflict between what Cameron and associates would name as "normative" and "operant" theologies also becomes apparent. The CEP's *Guide for Catechists* distinguishes between catechists' "specific task of catechizing" and numerous other ways that they "collaborate in different forms of apostolate with ordained ministers, whose direction they willingly accept" (4). Most of the time, this normative distinction is invisible within the catechists' and parishioners' operant assumptions about their multifaceted ministerial tasks. When the priest appears, however, the distinction is thrown into sharp relief, and role disruption occurs. Thus, a smoothly functioning, concentric-circled, "formal" theology of ministerial ordering is also challenged.

Exercising "Border Vigilance"

In their shifting and hybrid relations with both priests and people, then, catechists continually must exercise what Saracino calls "border vigilance" to maintain their ministerial position and personal equanimity within an ambiguous ordering. Living at what we might call "the borders of orders," catechists have some well-developed pastoral strategies and assiduously cultivate their spiritual life. In what follows, I discuss two prominent pastoral strategies and one recurring spiritual disposition that were priorities for many catechists I interviewed.

Pastoral Strategy 1: Working for Cordial Relationships with Parishioners and Priests

When I asked catechists to describe the quality of their present relationships with these groups, virtually all of them used the same term—"cordial" or "very cordial." As we talked, their own efforts in fostering this cordiality became apparent. For example:

MO: So have your relationships been good with priests?

C5: Oh, yes.

MO: And what do you think has made that happen?

C5: Oh, eh—[clicks tongue] it seems—me, I don't see anything wrong with that. That if they [parishioners] talk about me or quarrel with me. Because when he [the priest] comes here, he sees me doing the work that I was sent to do.

MO: So, he has no quarrel with you. Because he sees you doing the work that you were sent to do. What about the people?

C5: Okay. The people too, the same thing. Because if I quarrel with them they will stop coming to the church. So I have to be cordial with them every day, social with them, too.

Others name their relationships with priests as cordial and collaborative due to the priest's willingness to delegate and, again in an echo of John the Baptist, the catechist's willingness to "prepare the way" effectively for his visits.

C8: Ah—the work that we are doing is quite collaborative. So whatever we want, we go to the priest. He also tries to help meet our requests. And most of the time he delegates— even some of his own duties to us to do. We do each report back and all that. And even the congregation too. Whatever they want—even from the priest—they come to us first. Then we lead them to the priest and so, whatever we are doing it's like—a collaborative way that we are doing. So, very cordial.[17]

Pastoral Strategy 2: Truth-Telling

While the first strategy's focus on fostering cordiality through one's own vigilant efforts might sound subservient and overly accommodating, catechists also insisted on the need for being honest in their interpersonal relationships—certainly with their parishioners, but also sometimes with their priest. They frequently connected this with the imperative to be fair in church life, for the sake of community harmony. One catechist, for example, described how he confronted a rich parishioner about offending a poor member, and successfully elicited an apology. Another offered the following statement, while discussing how he deals with the challenge of parishioners who criticize him behind his back:

> C21: Well, for now, what helps me most is sometimes when I tell the truth. When I hear [criticism], I don't pretend that I have not heard anything. . . . I try to encourage them and let them know the reasons why I did this or I did that. When they come to me then we move on. So always I try to voice out. When I voice out it helps me a lot.

In these instances, the catechist is functioning as a community leader and is feeling the responsibility for resolving disputes. Truth-telling to one's priest, however, can be considerably riskier, and catechists approach this with great care. Nevertheless, respectful confrontation at the border of authority does occur. One catechist, responsible for preparing an elderly woman for sacramental initiation, told a moving story:

> C3: We have some adults who have not been to school before. . . . A certain woman came for catechism for one or two years, three years. She hadn't been baptized. Because the priest there—was saying she had to say everything correctly. But that woman was sixty years! So one day I mustered courage and went to the priest. "Father, this woman every morning she has been at Mass. She didn't go to school. This woman cannot answer. So please, I'm pleading with you." So he did that for the woman. And the woman was very—she's a very, very active woman in the church. . . . [I] attested to the priest. And he agreed. He agreed.

Spiritual Disposition: Taking Refuge in the Suffering and Crucified Christ

As already noted, many catechists view their ministry as an opening to their heavenly reward. In the here and now, however, catechists often look to Jesus on the cross for solidarity, comfort, and protection in fulfilling their vocation. Thus Saracino's characterization of the Incarnation resonates with their border identity: "In becoming human, Jesus Christ *relinquishes the primacy of the one story*, kenotically surrendering himself to a hybrid existence that undercuts any absolute identity, creating room for the other."[18]

Many catechists strongly identified with the suffering Christ when I asked them to name a Scripture passage, symbol, prayer, or other touchstone that is important for them as a catechist. For example, several highlighted their devotion to praying the Stations of the Cross:

> C24: . . . the stations of the cross. Because during the minis-try, the catechists—as a catechist, there are more sufferings. . . . You see that some will be insulting you [laughs]. Due to some utterances that will come up from them. They may not be understanding. They will not understand you. So they will be insulting you. When you look at our Savior Jesus Christ, He suffered till death. . . . Our work is full of suffering. So we need to follow our Maker, as He did.

Another catechist elaborated on his devotion to the crucifix:

> C35: The picture I always look at is the crucifix. Most of the times when I look at the crucifix I watch it and it tells me a whole lot. . . . Because looking at the pedigree of Jesus Christ and the kind of humiliations he went through. Whenever I see that picture it tells me that, no, you should be humble. And you should also be obedient to the Lord. Because he was so obedient to the Father. That is why he went through all these things. . . . If anybody wants to attack you, just accept it . . . as it is, opening your arms widely. . . . So it tells me that, no, it's always emulating Jesus Christ. Always . . .

From our perspective, such a spirituality may seem to come uncomfortably close to accepting unjust humiliations. The catechists' highly pious and strongly devotional spirituality, inherited from the European missionaries who first evangelized them, does carry operant theological undertones of viewing earthly pain as a conduit to heavenly reward. However, it is clear from these catechists' espoused theological statements that they persevere amid suffering as a necessary consequence of their choice to follow their ministerial vocation amid shifting borders and multiple affective stressors. Personal hurts arising from daily embodiment of their ambiguous, hybrid calling—hurts arising from calumny and slights, lack of resources and remuneration, and so on—are transformed into kenotic offerings.

"Being Open to the Unexpected at the Borders"

Saracino comments on a Christian anthropology of "being about borders":

> Working toward a Christian understanding of being human must transcend holding on to what is familiar and encourage being open to the unexpected at the borders. In such an anthropology, Christians are chosen to mourn an idealized self with a pure singular story, in addition to the privilege that allows them to secure that sense of self and story in the first place. Borders become the site of the Christian's ethical obligation to relinquish and to mourn.[19]

Much remains for Catholic theologians from the global North to reflect on in order to learn, with respect, humility, and mutuality, how the faith tradition is embodied in a significantly different cultural setting. In this essay I have sought to contribute to such learning through suggesting that the lived realities of West African catechists can offer a model for being "open to the unexpected at the borders." Lacking the "pure singular story" of the ordained, they move between circles of ministry and borders of official and unofficial leadership, while serving at the borders of their people and those people's distinctive joys and griefs. It remains for those who are generally able to avoid these borders—perhaps including us in the Global North—to choose to engage there. In doing so, we can take up our own "ethical obligation to relinquish and to mourn" privileged status and a clear and comfortable identity. A commitment to global Catholicism demands no less of us.[20]

Notes

[1]Adrian Hastings, *Church and Mission in Modern Africa* (New York: Fordham University Press, 1967), 222.

[2]Pope John XXIII, *Princeps Pastorum*, "On the Missions, Native Clergy, and Lay Participation," 1959, www.vatican.va.

[3]As rendered by Raymond Hickey in "Ministry in Parallel Lines," *African Ecclesial Review* 23 (June 1981): 163, from Pius XII in *Acta Apostolicae Sedis* 49 (1957): 937.

[4]Vatican II, *Ad Gentes*, 1965, www.vatican.va.

[5]Congregation for the Evangelization of Peoples, *Guide for Catechists*, 1993, www.vatican.va.

[6]Pope John Paul II, *Ecclesia in Africa*, 1995, w2.vatican.va.

[7]Michele Saracino, *Being about Borders: A Christian Anthropology of Difference* (Collegeville, MN: Michael Glazier, 2011).

[8]Norman K. Denzin and Yvonna S. Lincoln, eds., *Handbook of Qualitative Research* (Thousand Oaks, CA: Sage, 2000), 4. My study also utilized aspects of the "grounded theory" version of qualitative research. A classic text expounding this methodology is Barney G. Glaser and Anselm L. Strauss, *The Discovery of Grounded Theory: Strategies for Qualitative Research* (Chicago: Aldine, 1967). In this approach, theory is developed as it emerges from the data, rather than beginning with a formal hypothesis and testing it.

[9]Richard R. Osmer, *Practical Theology: An Introduction* (Grand Rapids, MI: Eerdmans, 2008), 4.

[10]Helen Cameron, Deborah Bhatti, Catherine Duce, James Sweeney, and Clare Watkins, *Talking about God in Practice: Theological Action Research and Practical Theology* (London: SCM Press, 2010), 54.

[11]Edward Hahnenberg, for example, was a major contributor to the theology of lay ecclesial ministry presented in the seminal publication by the United States Conference of Catholic Bishops, *Co-Workers in the Vineyard of the Lord* (Washington, DC: USCCB, 2005).

[12]Richard Gaillardetz, "The Theological Foundations of Ministry within an Ordered Community," in *Ordering the Baptismal Priesthood: Theologies of Lay and Ordained Ministry*, ed. Susan Wood (Collegeville, MN: Liturgical Press, 2003), 36.

[13]Edward P. Hahnenberg, *Ministries: A Relational Approach* (New York: Herder and Herder, 2003), esp. 123–50.

[14]I could not address gender dimensions among catechists in my study, since the vast majority of catechists in the diocese I studied are men (over 97 percent) and all those quoted in this essay are male (and only two women catechists consented to interviews). Gender ratios are different in other parts of Africa, with women sometimes in the majority. I am conscious that the dominance of male voices in this study limits my representation of African ecclesial realities, and may contribute to reinforcing patriarchal and clerical paradigms—which are, of course, not exclusively held by clergy. My study

also does not address the cultural factors shaping men's and women's expected qualities and roles in West Africa, and those factors undoubtedly influenced the catechists and parishioners whom I interviewed.

[15]Saracino, *Being about Borders,* 5.

[16]Quotations from recorded interviews will be shown with "MO" indicating the author/interviewer and "C" used with numerals to label individual catechists.

[17]In practice, "leading" is two-way: while the catechist leads people to the priest, the catechist also leads the priest to the people. For example, catechists must physically guide priests through villages and neighborhoods to visit and confer sacraments for the sick, homebound, and others.

[18]Saracino, *Being about Borders,* 42; emphasis added.

[19]Ibid., 122.

[20]This study was funded by a grant from the Rev. Alphons Loogman, C.S.Sp., Faculty Research Grant, Duquesne University.

As Dewdrops on Indra's Web

Buddhism, Constitutive Relationships, and Care for Our Common Home

Paul J. Schutz

The writings of Jesuit astronomer William Stoeger (1943–2014) abound with analyses of "constitutive relationships"—the nested networks of particles, biotic and abiotic forces and systems, persons, communities, and so on—that make reality what it is.[1] Beyond describing these relationships, Stoeger sees them as a basis for ethical and theological reflection. To wit, he writes that the operation of constitutive relationships gives "incontrovertible support" to American naturalist Aldo Leopold's "land ethic" and provides "robust support to Buddhist and Hindu perspectives on the fundamental unity and interconnectedness of all things in the Universe."[2] Stoeger does little more than establish these intersections, but his claims invite theologians to consider how these perspectives might challenge, enrich, or transform Catholic theology—especially given historical links between empire, mission, colonization, and Christianity's treatment of the natural world as little more than a backdrop for the drama of human salvation.[3]

With Stoeger's claims in mind, I argue in this essay that Buddhist philosophy offers rich resources for correcting elements of Catholic theology that obstruct the vision of the "splendid universal communion" of *Laudato Si'* and perpetuate the legacy of empire in the myriad local contexts that constitute the global church.[4] To achieve this end, I place Stoeger's account of constitutive relationships into conversation with Aldo Leopold and Buddhist thought to imagine (1) how the correspondence between constitutive relationships and the Buddhist ideas of emptiness, dependent origination, and impermanence might challenge exploitative tendencies in Western thought; (2) how the operation of karma might clarify and enrich discussions of structural and social sin, moving toward mindful cultivation of just and sustainable socioecosystems; and (3) how mindfulness and Buddhism's "hierarchy of compassion" might foster greater action for the good of our common home. I conclude by reflecting on how embracing these ideas might constitute an act of atonement for Christianity's historical ties to empire and colonization, as we reflect on the mystery of God in a global church, on a threatened earth.

Two preliminary points bear mention here. First, my thesis is in large part grounded in James Cone's observation—also found in Rosemary Radford Ruether, Ivone Gebara, and Sallie McFague—that the logic of domination that propels imperial and colonial efforts to create civilizations "on which the sun never sets" also drives ecological exploitation, conquering lands and peoples in the name of Western ideas of civilization, progress, and salvation. Cone writes, "The logic that led to slavery and segregation in the Americas, colonization and Apartheid in Africa, and the rule of white supremacy throughout the world is the same one that leads to the exploitation of animals and the ravaging of nature."[5]

Second, the correlation of Buddhism and Christianity I undertake here does not aim at synthesis, nor does it aim to say anything about Buddhism in itself. It simply seeks to listen to Buddhist philosophy for resources that might—as Joseph Bracken puts it—foster "effective self-criticism in the light of other religious world views."[6] In taking up this approach, I was heartened to read Pope Francis's May 2019 homily on the debates over circumcision at the Council of Jerusalem. Francis states, "The outcome of that big dispute was not that of imposing something new, but of *letting go of something old.* . . . They arrived at having the courage of renunciation beginning with the *humility of listening.*"[7] With Cone's observation and Francis's exhortation as a "north star," I delve more deeply into the nature and function of constitutive relationships.

Science and Speaking of Faith:
Constitutive Relationships and Interreligious Dialogue

Constitutive relationships include the whole array of physical and social entities and forces that make reality what it is, including visible ones—like networks of waterways or great forest ecosystems—and invisible or hypothetical ones, like quarks, gravitons, or the processes and relationships that drive the macrophenomena of climate change. As Stoeger explains, "Everything we see, including ourselves, is made up of other things linked to one another in very special ways, according to the laws of nature."[8] Subatomic particles form atoms, which form molecules that enable the existence of matter, cells, mitochondria, rocks, trees, stars, and rock stars. These complex entities enable the existence of "nested" networks of relations, such as social and ecological communities, with higher-level relationships asserting top-down influence on lower-level relationships, and vice versa. This is relational ontology writ large.

Constitutive relationships are so pervasive that they also inform Stoeger's writings on epistemology and theological method.[9] He argues that knowledge is constituted by relationships, emerging from experience through creaturely interactions within shared socioecosystems. Thus, he writes, knowledge is conditioned by the circumstances in which acts of knowing occur, with different types of knowledge constantly and reciprocally modifying, enriching, challenging, and complementing each other.[10]

Stoeger's relational notion of knowing influences his writings on theological method in two key ways. First, because all knowledge—even knowledge of God—arises from experience in concrete contexts, he holds that theology must emphasize God's ongoing self-revelation over "philosophical assumptions or agendas" imposed from the top down.[11] Likewise, he argues that theology cannot be "determined by age-old truths that never change"—a point he states may come as a surprise to some.[12] With these qualifications in place, he posits an evolutionary theological method rooted in ongoing discernment:

The appropriation [of tradition] must always involve renewed personal and communal discernment in light of the new situ-

ations, contexts, understandings and experiences individuals
and communities encounter, including those triggered by new
scientific knowledge, and those emanating from new political, economic and social circumstances. For mixed in with
the tradition can be systematic blindnesses, misdiscernments
and socially and politically induced distortions.[13]

Thus, theology must embrace its place within the networks of
relations that constitute reality, taking stock of insights issuing
from other disciplines, other ways of knowing, and other realms
of experience, while maintaining a critical focus on the possibility
of tradition's "distortion" by sociopolitical and economic forces.
"This," Stoeger concludes, "is how we form notions of truth or
how we come to knowledge of God and God's self-revelation to
us, and about how we are to live our lives."[14] Therefore, while
religious traditions can make truth claims in harmony with revelation and the lived experience of their adherents, truth is for
Stoeger an emergent property that arises from the interaction
of various ways of knowing in concrete, particular contexts—a
point with great significance for generating a theology for a global
church that can address both Catholicism's imperial legacy and
the ecological threats facing our earth.

Buddhism's Challenge to Christianity:
A New View of Creation

Taking Stoeger's call for renewed discernment rooted in encounter as our starting point, I want to ponder how the Buddhist
principles of dependent origination, karma, and the "hierarchy of
compassion" might enable Christian theology to grow in harmony
with Stoeger's account of constitutive relationships and Leopold's
"land ethic," which "enlarges the boundaries of the community
to include soils, waters, plants, and animals, or collectively: the
land."[15] I have chosen Leopold, both because Stoeger invokes
him and because of his correspondence with Buddhist thought.

Emptiness, Dependent Origination, and Impermanence

As the Dalai Lama explains, Buddhist philosophy begins with
the recognition of a "fundamental disparity" between perception

and reality.[16] We perceive things as solid, stable wholes; yet on the Buddhist account, this is an illusion. In truth, the Dalai Lama states, all things are "empty"—"devoid of objective, independent existence."[17] This idea may baffle minds formed in the Cartesian notion of a rational individual who thinks *himself* into existence—"*Cogito, ergo sum*." Yet as Stoeger and the Dalai Lama both observe, there is strong scientific evidence for this disparity: in the radical indeterminacy that pertains at the quantum level—our models are at best probabilistic because of our inability to know a particle's velocity and position at the same time (the Heisenberg Uncertainty Principle), for example, and in our recognition that, as Leopold states, "The biotic mechanism is so complex that its workings may never be fully understood."[18] This disparity is, in fact, a function of the operation of constitutive relationships. Although we perceive phenomena as self-evident, vast networks of interacting systems are at work beneath the surface of all things.

The recognition of emptiness leads to the principle of "dependent origination"—or what Zen teacher Thich Nhat Hanh names "Interbeing."[19] For, to embrace emptiness is to see reality as a vast network of interdependent causal relations, wherein each cause has a cause, and effects both result from causes and are causes in themselves. Making a similar point, the Dalai Lama—like Stoeger—concludes that a thing exists only by virtue of "the total network of everything that has a possible or potential relation to it."[20] The *Samyutta Nikāya*, a text from the Pali Canon of Theravada Buddhism, illustrates the point:

> When this is present, that comes to be;
> From the arising of this, that arises.
> When this is absent, that does not come to be;
> On the cessation of this, that ceases.

Even more compelling is the image of the Jeweled Net of Indra. Indra's Net—which we might imagine as a spider web dotted with dewdrops—illustrates dependent origination, as each drop of dew is what it is only in relation to the beads that surround it. Moreover, light shines on each bead differently and is refracted according to the bead's place in the web. As the light moves from moment to moment, the whole web changes, until finally the dewdrops evaporate. Here we arrive at the Buddhist principle of impermanence. On the surface, impermanence simply indicates that "all good things must come to an end." But there is a more subtle dimension to this idea. For just as the sun's movement changes the web, phenomena come into being and cease to be in *momentary* interactions, like grains of sand swept by ocean waves or entangled particles dancing together over vast reaches of space. Or like you, reader, who—arising from moment-by-moment interactions with this text—are not the same now as you are . . . *now*. As the Dalai Lama puts it, "The moment [things] arise, the process of their disintegration has already begun."[21]

Together, the Buddhist notions of emptiness, dependent origination, and impermanence pose a critical challenge to the logic that undergirds the anthropocentric separation of humans and nature, offering an alternative, ecocentric view focused on the particular relationships that pertain in a given time and place. This ecocentric perspective succeeds, in my view, both on account of its correspondence with contemporary science and because of its potential to foster a robust, encompassing sense of the common good that arises from socioecological relations in particular, local contexts.[22] Thich Nhat Hanh illustrates the point. "If you are a poet, you will see clearly that there is a cloud floating in this sheet of paper. Without a cloud, there will be no rain; without rain, the trees cannot grow; and without trees, we cannot make paper."[23] So, too, for the logger, the miller, and the fields that feed them—and our minds, reading the page. The Buddhist view offers Christian theology fertile ground in which to cultivate an ecological ethics rooted in reflection on what Leopold names the "lines of dependency" that unite all things, breaking open traditional categories such as person and substance in keeping with their *functional significance within relational networks*—what they do, not what they are.[24] In this way, Buddhism counters the traditional Christian emphasis on individual relationship with God with an emphasis on how the encounter with God is mediated in concrete *socioecological* networks—providing a unique conversation partner for Rahner's notion of God's self-communication in the "categorical."[25]

In a different vein, the Buddhist principle of impermanence seems equipped to foster an attitude of humility and care for the socioecological networks we inhabit. For if things arise and fade from moment to moment, claims of human superiority and efforts to create eternal empires appear hollow, even false. Here, the *Diamond Sutra*'s perplexing claim that in the end, "there are no Buddhas and there are no teachings," may be a seedbed of wisdom that—in recognizing finitude—fosters joy of heart, a point Psalm 90 makes wonderfully clear:

> Seventy is the sum of our years,
> or eighty, if we are strong;
> Most of them are toil and sorrow;
> they pass quickly, and we are gone. . . .
> Teach us to count our days aright,
> that we may gain wisdom of heart.
> (Ps 90:10, 12)

Karma and Structural Sin

Mindful recognition of dependent origination and impermanence guides us to a second aspect of Buddhist philosophy: karma. Karma recognizes that by virtue of dependent origination, things arise within an "all-encompassing web of causal conditions."[26] Thus, karma extends far beyond the immediate outcomes of a causal interaction, considering the "ultimate effects" of a moral choice across space and time, linking past, present, and future in cycles of suffering and joy.[27] Consider how abuse—in families and churches—propagates itself over vast stretches of time, "echoing" beyond a victim's life into the lives of others, shaping attitudes and relationships over generations. Or think of a thriving garden, which in harmony with the sun, the rains, and the labor of the gardener bears fruit that feeds birds, bees, rabbits, and the gardener herself.

Pushing beyond transactional models of divine-human relations, karma prompts mindful reflection on the social and ecological implications of every moral action, as it arises within a network of relations that ultimately connects all reality. As such, no sin is just a personal affront to God; rather, karma tells us, sin has *effects*—many of which are invisible, even imperceptible. Karma thus invites Christian theology to reimagine the dynamics of sin and forgiveness in a broader way, with renewed emphasis on how sin resonates even after a sinner is forgiven, touching every socioecological community of which one is part, and affecting others for generations. Although they were not familiar with the principle of karma, perhaps this is what the ancient Israelites had in mind when they spoke of the positive and negative implications of parents' actions being visited upon their children for generations, as in Deuteronomy 5:9. Amid our church's present crises, and taking seriously the connections between empire, colonization, and ecological exploitation, karma provides a valuable resource for reflecting on the historical "echoes" of structural and social sin.

Further, karma highlights how fear, as a breeding ground for destructive suffering, arises from "grasping at independent existence"—of seeking to assert oneself against interrelatedness and impermanence.[28] As such, karma poses a challenge to the imposition of hierarchical dualisms, which as Elizabeth Johnson has shown, distinguish in order to dominate—spirit and matter, humans and nature, men and women—focusing instead on the suffering wrought by power and imparting a necessary pastoral orientation to theological reflection that is, as Pope Francis says, willing to listen and courageous enough to let go.[29]

Moreover, while natural cycles—weather, water, carbon—are not karmic in themselves, Buddhism's emphasis on cycles of recurrence provides a unique resource for seeing clearly how earth's present peril is a locus of both social and structural sin. To illustrate this claim, consider how feedback loops caused by anthropogenic resource depletion and warming operate: humans release greenhouse gases, causing the atmosphere to warm. Polar ice melts. Ice melt decreases albedo—the light and heat reflected by earth's surface—increasing ocean temperatures, releasing methane from permafrost, and causing the global temperature to increase once again. This melts more ice, which increases temperatures and decreases albedo—and so on. Today, this warming-melting-warming loop continues, irrespective of whether humans continue to emit greenhouse gases, and earth's poorest citizens suffer the consequences of a phenomenon not of their making. Now natural cycles appear as decidedly karmic—structures of sin—transformed by a logic of domination and exploitation that renders lands and people resources for consumption and denies our place within the networks of relations that constitute the reality we share with all creatures. In this sense, scientific accounts of the ecological crisis are accounts of structural sin, insofar as the feedback loops at work in our damaged socioecosystems mediate—independent of individual action—"echoes" of the imperial domination of nature, in parallel with the colonial domination of peoples—both in the name of a Western ideal of "progress."

On this level, mindfulness of karmic cycles actualizes Leopold's claim that to recognize the socioecological structure of reality is to accept a "limit on freedom" that counters our breathless, historical quest for economic and political expansion with an ethic that extends to the myriad biotic life-systems that constitute our being in the world, precisely as they are enmeshed within sociopolitical and economic systems.[30] In this sense, Buddhist thought sets up a world in which the traditional hierarchical dualisms of Western thought simply do not apply, providing an invaluable resource for linking social, historical, and ecological concerns in a global theology for a threatened planet.

The Hierarchy of Compassion and Solidarity with the Oppressed

Although Buddhist thought may challenge hierarchical dualisms, it would be an error to see Buddhism as completely anti-hierarchical. As Alan Sponberg observes, Buddhism possesses a clear "developmental dimension," whereby Buddhists ascend a hierarchy of mindfulness that corresponds with an increase in expressed interrelatedness and compassion. This "hierarchy of compassion," as Sponberg names it, constitutes the third and final principle of Buddhist thought I will take up.[31] Put simply, the more mindful a person becomes of "Interbeing"—of one's standing within a karmic network of constitutive relations—the more fully one can express one's relatedness in compassion to the whole. As the Dalai Lama puts it, "When you come across a situation in which you generate compassion, instead of becoming more detached from the object of compassion, your engagement will be deeper and fuller. This is because compassion is ultimately founded on a valid mode of thought and you will have gained a deeper insight into the nature of reality."[32] Put another way, detachment from claims to power over one's socioecological context increases the interior freedom necessary to live more fully *in the mode of compassion.*

According to Sponberg, the hierarchy of compassion opposes other hierarchies—such as the "hierarchy of oppression" he finds at work in much of Western thought. Driven by increasing power *over* things, the hierarchy of oppression progressively shrinks one's relatedness, until one has consolidated ultimate power to oneself—the emperor. Such is the logic that drives colonial expansion, resource exploitation, and the technocratic paradigm critiqued in *Laudato Si'*.[33] Yet the Buddhist hierarchy of compassion does not measure fulfillment in terms of the consolidation of a power on which the sun never sets. Rather, by accepting the rising and setting of the sun, it measures progress in terms of ascent to greater felt interconnectedness with all things, seeing the fulfillment of reality as something like Francis's "splendid universal communion."

This point illustrates the ethical thrust of Buddhism's challenge to Christian theology, in direct correspondence with Christ's call to love each other as he has loved us—yet with a cosmic orientation rarely found in Christian thought. For, when imagined through the lens of dependent origination, compassion extends the categories of experiencing and knowing to all creatures, by which and with which we humans live. Stoeger's exclamation, "We are in deep solidarity with all living things on this earth!" expresses the point well, driving discussions of ethics and solidarity to feel the realities present on *and in* the ground in the local, social, ecclesial, and ecological networks that constitute global reality.[34] Zen scholar Ruben Habito illustrates this point, noting that in mindfulness of dependent origination, "One is able to feel and see things *from the perspective* of the mountains, the rivers, the great wide earth, of everything else that lives and breathes—pelicans and dolphins, dragonflies and ladybugs, and of course, other human persons."[35] This, then, is Buddhism's challenge: to see ourselves in the universe, to express our interrelatedness in compassion, and to encourage the flourishing of every dewdrop on the web of creation—with which we arise and on which we depend in every moment of our existence.

Toward Atonement, for the Glory of Creation

To conclude, I offer one thought for further reflection. Honest, humble engagement with Buddhist thought—allowing it to foster renewed discernment in our tradition—can go a long way in clarifying the church's unique role in seeking justice around the world. This is simply because the Buddhist emphasis on dependent origination focuses attention on the relations that pertain in a given time and place; Buddhist mindfulness is mindful of a particular "now." This orientation defies top-down, monarchial solutions in a way that seems necessary, given the logic and Eurocentric legacy of empire that lies beneath the surface of racism, social and ecological exploitation, and the daily struggles of colonized peoples. In light of this legacy, relinquishing imperialistic claims to power and really listening to other traditions might constitute a much-needed act of atonement for Christianity's historical complicity in these sins, which goes unrecognized in official Catholic pronouncements on mission and interreligious dialogue.[36]

Moving in this direction would, I think, be a first step toward embracing Stoeger's joyous vision that "relishing the world as it really is—in all its richness, variety, and fragility, sometimes in its harshness, hostility and absurdity—is more consonant with true religion than any other defensive, reluctant or controlling stance we could have taken."[37] And in embracing this vision, we may foster God's reign of joy, peace, and gratitude for all our constitutive relations, held in being—as they surely are—by the Spirit who works in every corner of our world, in religions ancient and new, in every land and in every creature, great and small.

Notes

[1]For a detailed treatment of constitutive relationships, see William Stoeger, "The Mind-Brain Problem, the Laws of Nature, and Constitutive Relationships," in *Neuroscience and the Person*, ed. Robert John Russell, Nancey Murphy, Theo C. Meyering, and Michael A. Arbib (Vatican Observatory & Berkeley: Center for Theology and Natural Sciences, 1999), 129–46.

[2]William Stoeger, "Astrobiology and Ethics: From Science to Philosophy and Ethics," in *Encountering Life in the Universe*, ed. Chris Impey, Anna Spitz, and William Stoeger (Tucson: University of Arizona Press, 2013), 97–127.

[3]See Elizabeth Johnson, "Turn to the Heavens and the Earth: Retrieval of

the Cosmos in Theology," in *Proceedings of the Catholic Theological Society of America* 51 (1996): 1–14.

[4]Pope Francis, *Laudato Si': On Care for Our Common Home* (May 24, 2015), 220. http://w2.vatican.va.

[5]James H. Cone, "Whose Earth Is It, Anyway?" in *Earth Habitat: Eco-Injustice and the Church's Response*, ed. Dieter Hessel and Larry Rasmussen (Minneapolis: Fortress Press, 2001), 23.

[6]Joseph Bracken, *The Divine Matrix: Creativity as Link between East and West* (Maryknoll, NY: Orbis Books, 1995), 1–2.

[7]Pope Francis, "Holy Mass for the opening of the 21st General Assembly of 'Caritas Internationalis,' " May 23, 2019, https://press.vatican.va.

[8]William Stoeger, "Cosmology and a Theology of Creation," in *Interdisciplinary Perspectives on Cosmology and Biological Evolution*, ed. Hilary D. Regan and Mark Worthing (Adelaide: Australian Theological Forum, 2002), 2. I am working from Stoeger's original manuscript.

[9]See Stoeger, "Mind-Brain Problem," 136–44.

[10]See William Stoeger, "Our Experience of Knowing in Science and in Spirituality," in *The Laws of Nature, the Range of Human Knowledge, and Divine Action* (Tarnow, Poland: Biblos, 1996). I am working from Stoeger's original manuscript.

[11]William Stoeger, "God and Time: The Action and Life of the Triune God in the World," *Theology Today* 55, no. 3 (October 1998): 367.

[12]Stoeger, "Experience of Knowing," 13.

[13]William Stoeger, "Reflections on the Interaction of My Knowledge of Cosmology and My Christian Belief," *CTNS Bulletin* 21, no. 2 (March 1, 2001): 14.

[14]Stoeger, "God and Time," 369–70.

[15]Aldo Leopold, *A Sand County Almanac and Sketches Here and There* (Oxford: Oxford University Press, 1989), 203–4.

[16]Dalai Lama, *The Universe in a Single Atom: The Convergence of Science and Spirituality* (New York: Harmony Books, 2005), 46.

[17]Ibid., 46–47.

[18]Leopold, *Sand County Almanac*, 205. For Stoeger's account, see William Stoeger, "Contemporary Physics and the Ontological Status of the Laws of Nature," in *Quantum Cosmology and the Laws of Nature*, ed. Robert John Russell, Nancey Murphy, and C. J. Isham (Vatican Observatory & Berkeley: Center for Theology and Natural Sciences, 1993).

[19]See Thich Nhat Hanh, *Love Letter to the Earth* (Berkeley, CA: Parallax Press, 2013), and "The Sun in My Heart," in *World Ethics*, ed. Wanda Torres Gregory and Donna Giancola (Belmont, CA: Thomson Wadsworth, 2003).

[20]Dalai Lama, *Universe in a Single Atom*, 64.

[21]Dalai Lama, *The Essential Dalai Lama: His Important Teachings*, ed. Rajiv Mehrotra (New York: Penguin, 2006), 45.

[22]Daniel P. Scheid has taken steps toward such a vision. See Daniel Scheid, *The Cosmic Common Good: Religious Grounds for Ecological Ethics* (Oxford: Oxford University Press, 2016). Out of a concern for human uniqueness, *Laudato Si'* criticizes ecocentric and biocentric views. My position does not

deny human uniqueness, especially from an evolutionary standpoint. Instead, it intends to focus attention on how humanity, as a unique species, is *situated within* networks of socioecological relationships.

[23]Thich Nhat Hanh, *Peace Is Every Step: The Path of Mindfulness in Everyday Life* (New York: Bantam, 1991), 95–96.

[24]Leopold, *Sand County Almanac*, 216.

[25]See Karl Rahner, *Foundations of Christian Faith: An Introduction to the Idea of Christianity* (New York: Crossroad, 2010), esp. 31–38.

[26]Dalai Lama, *Essential Dalai Lama*, 95.

[27]Ibid., 236.

[28]Dalai Lama, *Universe in a Single Atom*, 51.

[29]See Elizabeth Johnson, *Women, Earth, and Creator Spirit* (New York: Paulist Press, 1993).

[30]Leopold, *Sand County Almanac*, 202.

[31]See Alan Sponberg, "Green Buddhism and the Hierarchy of Compassion," in *Buddhism and Ecology: The Interconnection of Dharma and Deeds*, ed. Marilyn Evelyn Tucker and Duncan Ryūken Williams (Cambridge, MA: Harvard University Press, 1998), esp. 366–71.

[32]Dalai Lama, *Essential Dalai Lama*, 115.

[33]See *Laudato Si'* 101–14 on the technocratic paradigm.

[34]William Stoeger, "Discerning God's Creative Action in Cosmic and Biological Evolution," *Mysterion: Rivista di Spiritualitá e Mistica* 1, no. 1 (2008): 72.

[35]Ruben L. F. Habito, "Mountains and Rivers and the Great Earth: Zen and Ecology," in *Buddhism and Ecology*, ed. Tucker and Williams, 170. Emphasis mine.

[36]Pope Paul VI's *Evangelii Nuntiandi* mentions colonization, but it does not link colonialism and missions. *Redemptoris Missio* praises missionaries and looks forward to "the five hundredth anniversary of the evangelization of the Americas." See Paul VI, *Evangelii Nuntiandi* (December 8, 1975); John Paul II, *Redemptoris Missio* (December 7, 1990), 22. http://w2.vatican.va.

[37]William Stoeger, "Contemporary Cosmology and Its Implications for the Contemporary Science-Religion Dialogue," in *Physics, Philosophy, and Theology: A Common Quest for Understanding*, ed. Robert J. Russell, William R. Stoeger, and George V. Coyne (Vatican City: Vatican Observatory, 1988), 242.

PART III

FOLLOWING THE FOOTPRINTS

OF GOD

Reform from the Margins

Pope Francis and the Renewal of Catholic Theology

Stan Chu Ilo

This essay is divided into three main sections. Each section develops one of three central ideas. The first section focuses particularly on a new historiography of world Christianity and its implications for doing theology. I argue that Christianity began as a movement in the margins and that the most enduring impact of Christianity in history has often emerged not from the centers of power and privilege, but from the margins. Joseph Ratzinger was prescient when he said that the time has come to say farewell to the idea of traditionally Catholic cultures and that we stand before a new epoch of church history in which Christianity will oppose evil intensely and bring good into the world.[1] It is important for today's church leaders and scholars to learn the lessons of history, to understand why the margins have been such a strong groundswell and mustard seed for Christian witnessing. I propose that today's church leaders and theologians follow the footprints of God in the people in the margins in order to find the reasons for the failed reform projects in the Catholic Church, particularly since the Second Vatican Council.

In the second section, I historicize current discussions on reform in the Catholic Church and on some of the key issues that are often raised in the conversation on reform since the Second Vatican Council. I do not think such issues are easy to resolve. Doctrinal and moral problems are not easily resolved through papal fiat. Such clear-cut answers as those found by many people with the publication of *Humanae Vitae* (1968) end up in polarization: dissenters versus loyalists. This approach does not often allow room for healthy dialogue in the search for consensus. Allowing for greater dialogue today would enable the church to walk humbly in the search for the truth, which continues to unfold before our limited human horizon as we enter more deeply into the divine and human mysteries. We cannot explore any fruitful and creative options if all conversations in our churches and in the theological academies are framed in absolute, oppositional categories driven by time-worn arguments that are repeated ad nauseam for and against every doctrinal or moral issue in today's church. What could be more fundamentalist than the extreme either/or positions on these issues—by both liberals and conservatives—in our churches and theologies? This stubborn clinging to unchanging positions by both liberals and conservatives has made it impossible for any theological progress to be made in the needed dialogue on how the churches can meet the yearnings of many today for an inclusive and welcoming church.

In the third section, I propose that the emergence of Catholicism in its Western cultural form should not be construed as God's preference for a static form of Christianity. Christianity will remain relevant in multiple contexts of history and diverse human conditions to the extent to which it is open to the surprises of the Holy Spirit. It is this openness to the promptings of the Holy Spirit that will enable Christianity to see the inner enrichments and footprints of God in both particular and universal contexts of faith. The West has given birth to a rich Catholic intellectual tradition, traditions of holiness and spirituality, practices of Christian charity, rich arts and music, and many other gifts that have enriched the history and traditions of the Catholic Church. However, the Christian movement is open to further cultural mediations as it continues to cross cultural and spiritual frontiers. The gospel is not to be enslaved to a particular cultural or sociological form, or else it will be emptied of its power to renew, revive, and re-create that which is circumscribed by history and the human propensity for distortion and sinfulness.

The proposal here, then, is that there is need for reform in the church today because its systems, laws, and structures are limited by their embodiment within a particular human culture and the particular historical circumstances in which they emerged. In order for this reform to occur, there is the need for a shift that can be achieved by looking at spiritual, ecclesial, and theological developments in the Global South—the so-called margins. Let me preface this, however, by stating outright that I am not claiming that the Global South offers us the perfect type for the realization of an idealized church of the future. It has its challenges and limitations with regard to faith and culture. Indeed, no human culture is capable of perfectly capturing the total ultimacy of the divine, which stretches beyond the human horizon as we come closer to the infinite horizon of God. However, in these sites in the Global South, one may find new pathways that the Holy Spirit is opening up for the World Church, away from the theological logjam and ecclesiological deadwood in the divisive cultural, political, and historical torrents continuing to rumble unrelentingly in the West.

I conclude with suggestions for reform in the church through a renewal of Catholic theology inspired by the teachings and practices of Pope Francis. Pope Francis offers a keen awareness of this character of the gospel to bring something new from what is old, decaying, contingent, and weak, as well as being conscious of the resplendence of the footprints of God in the margins of history. Pope Francis understands the need for a culture of encounter, a decentralized church, and a church that speaks more from the margins, that speaks more of Christ and of the poor and of sinners through a revolution of tenderness, than of itself, its institutions, and its structures. These new features and new faces in World Christianity represent, for some, a movement into uncharted waters that they are too afraid to enter. However, there is an invitation for us all to trust in the Lord and walk humbly with a God who tells us: "Do not be afraid, I am with you even to the end of time!" (Mt 28:30).

The Twentieth Century: The Christian Century?

According to Brian Stanley, "As the twentieth century dawned, many Christians anticipated that the coming decades would witness the birth of a new era. Their expectation was that the accelerating global diffusion of Christianity from its Western heartlands to the rest of the globe would usher in the final phase of human history—the climactic millennial age of international peace and harmony."[2] The project of bringing about the Christian century was to be marked by intense Western missionary activities to the non-Western world, to make the rest of the world Christian in the image and likeness of the West. The World Missionary Congress of 1910 was convoked to plan the strategies to achieve the "evangelization of the world in this generation."[3]

Among Protestants in Europe and North America, there was the prediction, Stanley noted, of the universal triumph of the Western civilizing creed of technological and scientific progress, democratic and liberal political values, and broad evangelical versions of the Christian religion. In 1905, Pope Pius X articulated the Catholic version of this euphoria in his encyclical *Il Fermo Proposito*:

> The civilization of the world is Christian. The more completely Christian it is, the more true, more lasting and more productive of genuine fruit it is. On the other hand, the further it draws away from the Christian ideal, the more seriously the social order is endangered. By the very nature of things, the Church has consequently become the guardian and protector of Christian society.[4]

But the pope went a step further in this document to also identify this civilization with the Catholic Church. According to him, the Catholic Church has received from God the mission of guarding the movement of human history and moderating cultural and political movements. This is why the Roman Church should strive, in Pope Pius's thinking, to take this civilizing and Christianizing project to the ends of the world.

At this point in time, "Christian" was understood by Pope Pius and many European ecclesial and political leaders as Western culture. This view was clearly reflected in Hilaire Belloc's now well-known quote: "Europe is the faith and the faith is Europe." David Goldman puts it this way: "Hilaire Belloc's famous quip—'Europe is the faith and the faith is Europe'—is precisely correct," because Europe came into being because of Christianity, and Christianity—in its form at the beginning of the twentieth century—was indeed European through and through. According to Goldman,

"Under the church and empire, nations owed fealty to a higher power by virtue of the authority of faith. Its common language was Latin, and its ultimate authority was the pope rather than the emperor."[5] Pius X rejected all forms of secular culture, proposed the subordination of all the laws of the state to the divine government of the gospel, and urged "regaining the losses in the kingdom already conquered" (*Il Fermo* 5), so as "to restore all things to Christ." Pius writes with great optimism in these glowing words (*Il Fermo* 5): "What prosperity and well-being, what peace and harmony, what respectful subjection to authority and what excellent government would be obtained and maintained in the world if one could see in practice the perfect ideal of Christian civilization" in the twentieth century.

By the beginning of the twenty-first century, not only has the world not become more Christian, but many in the defunct Western heartland of Christianity are now questioning the meaning of some of the key terms in its theological discourse: What is Christianity? Who is God? Who is Jesus Christ? What do terms such as church, mission, family, morality, spirituality, sacraments, ethics, politics, among others, mean today, as contrasted with what they meant at the beginning of the twentieth century? Another question therefore emerges: How did a century that began with so much hope of being a Christian century end up with such diverse histories, identities, and projects, partly diverging and partly converging behind the limited veil of a dominant Western Christian narrative of history?

It is clear that those who identified human civilization at the beginning of the twentieth century with Western culture and its imperialistic projects in politics, economics, education, and religion were mistaken. Particularly, those who advanced the Christianization of the non-Western world as a project in Westernization were struck then, as they are today, with the unexpected irruption of the work of the Holy Spirit in bringing to life a rich diversity of indigenous expressions and new narratives of Christian faith and life, beyond sometimes restrictive Western narratives of faith. These new and multiple forms of faith and life showed that the momentum of the gospel assumed its own cultural and local agencies in non-Western societies. They also gave birth to new forms and features of Christianity in the Global South that have become very strong and influential at the beginning of the twenty-first century. These new forms of Christianity do not resemble the monolithic sociological and ecclesial form of the cultural plot designed by Western missionaries and colonialists at the dawn of the twentieth century.

To understand the reasons for the failed attempt to make the twentieth century a Christian century, and the failure of associated Western political and cultural projects and international development designs for a greater convergence of a global economy in the non-Western world, one must appreciate the changing and intersecting cultural, political, and social histories of the last century. One must also appreciate the relationship between present tensions in the world and in the church and the failed Western Christianizing and civilizing projects of the last century. Some of the issues we face today in the world—nativism, wars, immigration crises, racism, Islamophobia, the resurgence of the abortion debate, rising nationalism, growing religious intolerance, rising poverty, and clerical sexual abuse, to mention only a few—have their roots in the failed Western cultural and "Christian" projects of the twentieth century.

The twentieth century witnessed giant leaps in human innovation and creativity. However, it was also the century of rising poverty, genocides, wars, environmental degradation and climate change, and increasing isolationism and nationalism. This is why a great disease began to spread across humanity, for which humans seem powerless to find a cure. This incurable disease, to use the characterization of Mother Teresa, is the fact that there are millions of people in our world today who feel unwanted and unloved. They may be poor people who feel alienated and abandoned in our cities; vulnerable migrants who are rejected and treated as threats at many borders; and those who are drowning in the seas and dying in the torturous and perilous journeys across deserts and muddy waters. They also include our brothers and sisters who feel rejected and abandoned by the churches because they are divorced or because of their sexual identity or because of their mistakes, and the many silent victims of abuse by representatives of the church.

In the face of these changing and complex political, religious, and cultural forces, Lamin Sanneh proposes that historians must "move beyond Christianity as a 'universal religion' . . . to Christianity in its local expressions, in the forms in which the people of the world have clothed the religion as recognizably their own."[6] Christianity grew among marginal communities as the followers of Christ began to disperse with the message of the gospel of love. Indeed, as Christians dispersed from the margins, the strongest impulse emerging from their communities, which helped them transform their culture, was the quality of their love and commitment to one another, especially those in need. They were propelled by "love which crosses boundaries, which includes the outsider and the marginalized, proves itself in particular by recognizing outsiders as those who show love. Here the equality in principle contained in the love of neighbor establishes itself in the face of actual differences."[7] What the early Christians sought was not a dominant culture or a hegemonic religious system, or a universal civilizational project. The early Christians desired a way of life that was inspired by the priorities and practices of Jesus Christ—caring for everyone, especially the poor and the marginalized, and helping to bear the pains of one another through selfless love. The mission of proclaiming the gospel to the ends of the earth, given to the followers of Jesus, was to be modeled on the priorities and practices of Jesus Christ through the triumph of the Cross and the path of humility. It was never to be realized through power, politics, wealth, and violence, all of which we can identify in different phases of the projects of Christendom, both at its highest and lowest points in history. The values and virtues to which these early Christians witnessed would ultimately trigger a tectonic cultural shift and balance of power in the Roman Empire.

The question arises: How could this scattered group of men and women emerge from the margins to the center?[8] What is obvious from both Old and New Testament histories is that there is a constant double pull from the margins to the center (centripetal force) and from the center to the margins (centrifugal force). It is a kind of *metaxy*, an in-between existence, which helps to relativize all historical mediations in which the faith appears, while constantly stretching humanity and cultures to expand in the direction of the infinite horizon of the God of love and the God of surprises.

Appreciating the coherence in the tension between the centrifugal and centripetal dimensions of Christian mission is necessary for understanding the limitations in Christian expansion across history. It will also help today's theologians deepen their understanding and insight beyond received theological and epistemological canons on how to follow the footprints of God in the new sites of faith and life in the Global South. Today's World Christianity teaches us that, unlike in the past when Christianity identified itself with cultural, political, and economic privilege, domination, and influence, today the mission of God calls us to move away from the desire to preserve the earthly dominion that threatens to empty the gospel of its truth and force. It also calls for exploring the rich possibilities of developing a humble and expansive theological engagement, which can birth intercultural and theological border-crossings in the beauty, diversity, and cultural pluralism of World Christianity.

This new approach challenges us to a more comprehensive and diffuse narrative, leveraging multiple voices on where God is at work in the church and in history, beyond the dominant, restrictive Western account. It transgresses the universalizing dominance of historical canons that often have marginalized the voices of minorities; it also challenges the essentialized sociological form of institutional Catholicism that continues to hamper the flourishing of the charisms of individuals and cultures in diverse contexts of faith and life. It calls for an open-structured empirical approach that privileges the narrative of living-faith-in-action of ordinary, everyday Christians at the multiple frontiers of proclamation, witnessing, martyrdom, worship, and service. In this regard, one cannot claim that there is an original Christianity, by which other forms will be judged. Nor can one claim that there is a traditional language of Christianity, or give preference to any particular historical form in which Christianity has appeared as an ideal model that has to be retained, reformed, restored, replicated, or rejected. Attempts to absolutize particular cultural mediations of the faith could be forms of either cultural romanticism or cultural idolatry, both of which threaten the ever-renewing impulse of the gospel to speak from within and beyond human culture. In addition, one cannot insist on a transcendental ecclesiology or an ecclesiological archetype that has to be replicated root, stock, and branches from Rome to the margins.

Three points summarize what I have attempted to accomplish in this first section. First, I am arguing that a new Christian historiography will help articulate better the need for reform in the church today. This new account of history will actually show that reform is taking place in World Christianity outside of the West. Allan Anderson, for instance, has called African Pentecostalism a new reformation.[9] Some of these reforms are taking place without receiving much attention because they are happening in the margins and on the new frontiers of faith. Some of the signs of reform identified by Lamin Sanneh include the ecumenical, cross-cultural, and intercultural nature of Christian expansion in many societies in the Global South; the variety and diversity of its expressions; the structural and antistructural nature of the changes taking place in organization, worship, and social engagements; the familiar and nonfamiliar manifestations of spiritual experiences among new Christians in these areas; the wide spectrum of theological views and ecclesiastical traditions represented; the diffuse and inclusive nature and style of authority and leadership; and the process of acute indigenization that fosters liturgical renewal, the production of religious art, music, hymns, songs, and prayers, which has given Christianity in the non-Western world a stunningly diverse and changing profile.[10]

These cultural processes and the "modern-day indigenous formative process" in the Global South, Sanneh argues, may not fit into established canons of orthodoxy or canon law in the institutional narrative of Catholicism. As a result, they are not accounted for as reforms within the old historiography of Christianity, which is still dominant globally.

Second, there is the need for liberation historiography that recognizes and reverences the voices of peoples, social classes, groups, and races whose embrace of the gospel has been badly affected by cultural erasure, violence, and narratives of contamination mediated through some of the older versions of Christianity. As Wilbert R. Shenk proposes, "In the quest to embrace authentic Christian identity, no one culture is privileged over other cultures. Within the economy of the new humanity, all cultures are valued equally and are worthy of respect. Cultural and ethnic diversity becomes the means by which the richness and glory of God's grace is more perfectly revealed to us."[11] Liberation historiography challenges us to write a different kind of history and to embrace conversion from the cultural hubris that claims that Western Christian traditions, sacramental systems, theologies, and church structures are original traditions. It summons us to abandon the idea that a particular gender and sexuality is God's preferred mode of mediating God's work, or the claim that because we believe that certain beliefs and practices are revealed, they are not open to further revision or future interpretation—perhaps they even need to die, so that something new can be born from the ashes. We should dare to imagine different kinds of Christianities and different kinds of churches that reflect fully the meaning of catholicity. This is because, as Andrew Walls rightly proposes, any observer of World Christianity today will notice that despite the diversities within it, there are some family traits that show

> continuity of thought about the final significance of Jesus, continuity of a certain consciousness about history, continuity in the use of the Scriptures, of bread and wine, of water. But he [our observer] also recognizes that these continuities are cloaked with such heavy veils belonging to their environment that Christians of different times and places must often be unrecognizable to others, or indeed even to themselves, as manifestations of a single phenomenon.[12]

World Christianity thus challenges every generation of Christians from every language, race, and nation to use their own cultural and spiritual resources, guided by the wisdom and creative gifts of the Spirit, to enrich the ever-expanding Christian religious tradition.

Third, in order to understand and think differently about reform in the church we may need to think outside the box, that is, outside the preoccupation with the remnants of empire and power in the old Christian historiography. Theologians and scholars ought to "break out of their preoccupation with the European heartland and its structures of power, and look to the frontier, scarce in institutional assets but with a teeming diversity that attests to the religion's genius for fostering a spirit of unity along with a variety of styles and idioms."[13]

When this shift in thinking occurs, we can conceive of reform as the antistructural and unofficial renewal of the church, as in the Christian witness, spirituality, and ethics of the great movements in Christian history such as the rise of monasticism in Egypt.[14] Although we need institutions to ritualize practices in the church, the history of our church and of society have proven again and again that institutional authorization or approval is driven mainly by the protection of institutional privilege and power. This is why a central impulse of reform today from the margins concerns how the movement of the Spirit in history could proceed in the direction of the eschatological fulfillment of the mission of God enabled by these institutions, rather than being predicated on institutional predilections that may not always correspond with the overall goal of the Reign of God.

Conversations on Reform in the Roman Catholic Church

Reform has been a preoccupation of the Catholic Church of the West.[15] The focus of reform in the past has been narrowed to a particular cultural tradition and worldview that gave birth to the kinds of sociological forms in modern Catholicism that have to be constantly defended or contested. These theological battles have not been nourished by the reform initiatives seen in the Global South today. This is also true in the present papacy—the push of Pope Francis for a poor and merciful church, with its implications for the larger conversations of the day, has been stymied by cultural and ideological wars in the West. These conversations have polarized the so-called progressives and traditionalists, as we saw in the two synods on the family in Rome in 2014 and 2015.[16] I propose that there is a need to widen the conversation about reform in the church beyond the kind that is taking place today in the West.

There are at least five reasons why reform based on the old historiography of Christianity has been unsuccessful and has continued to polarize the church since Vatican II. First, reform based on this old historiography proceeds from a presumption that there is some uniform or essentialized form of the church, an idealized archetype that is often corrupted by cultural and historical forces that are sinful and unworthy of God. Second, as

John O'Malley and other Catholic historians point out, in most councils—including Vatican II—the powers of the pope and how they are exercised have always been a sticking point. Even though *Lumen Gentium* (no. 23) attempted to delegate more powers to local bishops, it is obvious, at least in Africa, that local bishops in the Catholic Church are still like legates of Rome. The dependence of the multicultural masses of the faithful on the predilection and ideological leaning of any pope that comes to office continues to make it impossible for any effective and fundamental reform to occur in Catholicism. Third, the assumption that a council, synod, or law is capable of bringing about change still ignores the voices of the margins—the heartbeat for the emergence and renewal of the fruits of the gospel and the mission of God in history. The decisiveness of "reception" in local churches, small Christian communities, spiritual communities such as Focolare, and among the lay faithful is considered a key factor in most councils, including Vatican II. To a great extent, however, conversation about reform in the Catholic Church has been clerical, elitist, and often legalistic. Fourth, reform in the old Christianity proceeds from a notion of reform built around the two plagues of clericalism and centrism in the church (*Evangelii Gaudium* [*EG*], no. 3). Fifth, such reform has always been moderated and mediated by Rome. This proceeds from the general belief that once the center (that is, Rome) is reformed, the local churches will automatically follow the same path, and that the reform of the life of the clergy will automatically bring about the reform of the life of the laity.

When I use the term "reform" here, I employ the description given by Hans Urs von Balthasar. He argues that the reform of the church is not an introduction of a new element into the church, because the central idea of the church is love, which alone is credible. This love has become incarnate in the Lord Jesus Christ and is continued in the church and in its members in the world through word, sacrament, and witnessing. Reform, according to him, involves two aspects. The first is "a broadening of the horizon, a translation of the Christian message in language understandable by the modern world." The second is the specifically Christian aspect, or the internal dimension of reform: "a purification, a deepening, a centering of its idea, which alone renders us capable of representing its idea, radiating it, translating it believably in the world." Indeed, the touchstone of reform in Balthasar's proposal for mission "is the greatest possible radiance in the world by virtue of the closest possible following of Christ."[17] So, according to Balthasar, any successful reform of the church is to be judged by the extent to which it brings about a greater fidelity to enacting in history and to Christian witnessing of the priorities and practices of the Lord Jesus Christ. This should happen in the inner life of the church, in the lives of its members, and in its evangelizing mission in the world.

The approach to reform that Pope Francis represents in a significant way is one that dares to ask new questions; an approach that courageously seeks to think of another possible church; a more ecumenical, intercultural, interfaith, and intercivilizational Christianity that works with all humanity, all religions, and all peoples, to bring about the conditions for human and cosmic flourishing. Pope Francis is calling for a humble and open church that searches for the face of God, rather than a church that hijacks the God-narrative as uniquely and only its own. This approach represents a vision and a mission to bring about a creative destruction, to borrow the term from economist Joseph Schumpeter regarding how to bring about innovation by dismantling long-standing practices.[18] This would allow the God of newness to bring to birth, in us and through us, something beyond our present church—something that no eyes have seen, as the new signs of a new heaven and a new earth.

In concluding this second section, I contend that when we look at the Global South and the burgeoning Latino, African, and Asian Catholic communities in North America and Europe, what we see are popular Catholic devotions, new spiritual movements and spiritualities, Pentecostal and Charismatic Christianity, Catholic pro-life movements, and concern for the ethics of marriage and family life. What we see is a growing concern for solidarity in dealing with the complex challenges of human security. We are seeing in the Global South new martyrs who are dying for standing up for human rights, human solidarity, and the virtues and values of the Christian faith.

These martyrs and giants of faith and life do not understand the language of curial reform or the Latin Mass, nor are they concerned about papal primacy or who is going to be the next bishop or cardinal. They are fighting for survival from diseases and epidemics; they are fighting against dictatorship, poverty, crimes, and violence. These Christians are dealing with religious conflicts and persecutions, all of which were worsened by Western colonialism and the ongoing economic exploitation of the poor. They are fighting to stay alive. This kind of reform begins from the grassroots and challenges church leaders to listen to the margins, to accompany them by being present with them in their places of pain and fear. It will require transgressing boundaries of clericalism and curial culture toward a more dynamic involvement in richer conversations at all levels of Catholic life, without privileging one particular mode of being in the church. It demands of theologians and church leaders to be present to God's people in these marginal sites and allow their experience to become the phenomenological foundation of our theologies and pastoral practices for the renewal of the church, faith, and life.

Lessons from Pope Francis on Reform and Renewal of Catholic Theology

Pope Francis captures the heart of his agenda for the renewal of Catholic theology in his 2018 Apostolic Constitution *Veritatis Gaudium* on Ecclesiastical Universities and Faculties. He proposes that theologians could contribute to the missionary reform of the church through a renewed Catholic theology. He captures this central idea in these words:

> Against this vast horizon now opening before us, what must be the fundamental criteria for a renewal and revival of the contribution of ecclesiastical studies to a Church of missionary outreach? ... This then is a good occasion to promote with thoughtful and prophetic determination the renewal of ecclesiastical studies at every level, as part of a new phase of the Church's mission, marked by witness to the joy born of encountering Jesus and proclaiming the Gospel, that I set before the whole people of God as a program in *Evangelii Gaudium*. (Nos. 4, 1)

For Pope Francis, the kind of theology that can accompany the church on the path of reform is a theology constantly renewed "through the practice of discernment and through a dialogical way of proceeding capable of creating a corresponding spiritual environment and intellectual practice. It is a dialogue both in the understanding of the problems and in the search for ways to resolve them."[19] Such a theology has the following features: theology as a spiritual ethnography; doing theology in a spirit of humility, freedom, and worship; and pastoral life and the margins as the laboratory of theology. I discuss each in turn.

Theology as a Spiritual Ethnography

In *Veritatis Gaudium,* Pope Francis writes that one of the criteria for doing theology is "a culture, we might say, of encounter between all the authentic and vital cultures, thanks to a reciprocal exchange of the gifts of each in the luminous space opened up by God's love for all God's creatures" (*Veritatis Gaudium* [*VG*], 4.b). This culture of encounter is the starting point of a dialogical embrace that for theologians is primordially foregrounded in the assent of faith made through a deep encounter with the form and concrete revelation of God in history, Jesus Christ. This encounter makes possible and specifies our conversation with God and all things seen in the light of faith. This dialogical disposition invites theologians to plunge into history and to recognize the footprints of God in personal and group histories, especially in unfamiliar sites. Theologians are invited by Pope Francis to become spiritual ethnographers who are able to engage in "a hermeneutical integration" through an encounter with others from within their own cultures, histories, and religious contexts. A hermeneutical integration begins from above with the stance of faith, received as a gift from God, which moves the mind and the intellect to God in humble attention to God's voice in all things. This is followed by hearing God's voice from below through a critical engagement with all things and discerning the will of God in history. Both approaches take account of the breadth of the human condition, on one hand, while, on the other hand, identifying the signs of the Kingdom, through the paschal logic of the Lord, in what disfigures humanity, and how it can be transformed in "the Spirit of the Risen and Crucified One."[20]

This stance, which invites theologians to be immersed in history, enables them to be "inwardly touched by the oppressed life many live, by the forms of slavery present today, by the social wounds, the violence, the wars and the enormous injustices suffered by so many poor people." It is through this immersion in history that theologians can do their work "in solidarity with all the 'shipwrecked' of history."[21] This means that a renewed theology capable of sustaining a reforming church will move away from a disembodied theology that grows from the uncritical quest for, and defense of, institutional claims and practices. Such a disembodied theology seeks only to preserve and protect an idealized sociological form of the *ekklesia* and its embodiment of an idealized notion of truth and culture. The shift being proposed here moves theological reflection away from the normativity of some of the church's historically conditioned Eurocentric traditions of thought, epistemological structure, beliefs, and practices. It locates the heart of the church, not in Rome, but in the margins. It seeks the heart of truth and beauty, not simply by memorizing and reproducing catechetical tracts and magisterial documents, but in deep connection, reflective practice, and recognition of the footprints of God in intimate communication with the other.

Doing Theology in a Spirit of Humility, Freedom, and Worship

According to Pope Francis, "Theological freedom is necessary. Without the possibility of experimenting with new paths, nothing new is created, and there is no room for the newness of the Spirit of the Risen One."[22] This invitation was first proposed in his speech to the Italian Theological Association, where Pope Francis speaks of theology as "a free and responsible reflection" while at the same time asking theologians to undertake the task of theology as part of the missionary work of the church, with sensitivity to a changed world and in "creative fidelity." He speaks of Catholic theology as being driven by "the perennial novelty of the Gospel and in dialogue with the world and as a communal encounter which must be done together."

This stance invites Catholic theologians to abandon what Pope Francis calls "rigid schemes" and the "tendency to provide pre-packaged answers and ready-made solutions" without allowing the real questions of everyday Christians to emerge from their living context of faith and life (see *Christus Vivit*, no. 65). Rather, theologians are encouraged to engage in a bold, courageous, and creative reflection on the mysteries of faith born of love, faith, and fidelity, on bended knees. The fear of error seemed, for the church prior to Pope Francis, to be the beginning of wisdom. However, Pope Francis speaks differently about where wisdom is to be found and how wisdom can be found, through a "welcoming theology": "To go out as ones sent. It is not enough simply to open the door in welcome because they come, but we must go out through that door to seek and meet the people!"[23]

This new spirit of searching for the footprints of God in people's daily experiences has made possible greater dialogue in the Catholic academy and between Catholic scholars and their colleagues from other faiths and nonfaith traditions. The nature of this kind of dialogue that Pope Francis wishes to see in the Catholic academy could be gleaned from his speech at the beginning of the synod on the family in 2014. He was quoted as saying, "Open and fraternal debate makes theological and pastoral thought grow. . . . That doesn't frighten me. What's more, I look for it." Elsewhere, Pope Francis says to the synod participants, "You need to say all that you feel with parrhesia" (boldly, candidly, and without fear). "And at the same time, you should listen with humility and accept with an open heart what your brothers [and sisters] say." He invites all to open-mindedness, because "we cannot dialogue with people if we already know all the answers to their problems."[24]

There are some who are uncomfortable with this approach to doing a theology, which, as Pope Francis writes, "risks and remains faithful on the borderline" (*VG 5*). This kind of healthy dialogue would engender creative theologizing and the deepening of the understanding of the mysteries of God, so that what Italian Archbishop Zani refers to as the "anthropological perspective of faith" could become more evident in our theologies and ecclesial life.[25] This should move theologians to more creative engagement with each other and even with those who disagree with them, so that the Holy Spirit can inspire us to seed in our ecclesial and theological soils new insights and perspectives on what we believe, live, celebrate, and hope for.

Pastoral Life and the Margins as the Laboratory of Theology

Pope Francis is renewing Catholic theology by locating the center of Catholic theology at the frontiers, that is, in the pastoral life that is the laboratory of theology, rather than in libraries. In a letter to the chancellor of the Pontifical Catholic University of Argentina in 2015, Pope Francis said that to do theology is "to live on a frontier," and that "every good theologian, like good shepherds, has the odor of the people and of the street." He proposed that theologians, by their reflection, can develop reflective practices that "pour oil and wine onto the wounds of humanity." Pope Francis gives this definition of theology in his letter: "Theology is an expression of a Church which is a 'field hospital', which lives her mission of salvation and healing in the world."[26] He rejects any form of reflection that he calls "desktop theology" that is comfortable with settled answers and afraid to meet headlong the big questions and new complexities of our times. Pope Francis is helping to build bridges in encouraging the church and theologians to seek new answers from the cries and hopes of people on the margins, away from the corrupting and deceptive centers of power, wealth, violence, and politics; to look for God in the in ghettoes and slums, in prisons and hospitals, in the killing fields of our war-torn world, on our national borders, in the Mediterranean waters where thousands of people are drowning, and in the isolated and painful lives of those who feel abandoned and unwanted in our churches. This challenges theologians to also search for God in the bleeding earth and in the cries emerging from the Amazon, among other places in the world where creation is waiting for liberation from anthropogenic factors and forces.

Indeed, unlike previous papacies, which often presented the theological enterprise simply as a service to them, Pope Francis makes two very important revolutionary statements. First, theology is at the service of the whole people of God and not only the magisterium; the magisterium, along with theology, is one of the many ways in which the Holy Spirit enriches the people of

God. Second, both theology and magisterium are placed on the same level with the *sensus fidelium* and charism of the prophets of the church, and all are placed, not above each other, or above the people of God, but as being on the same path of discernment, purification, and reform to meet the needs of the whole people of God.

What Pope Francis is doing is showing that theology is not a second-order act that happens outside of the context of ecclesial faith and life. Rather, theology is a paradigm for action and thought (*VG 5*, para. 1), that must simultaneously accompany social and cultural processes as the faith crosses different faith and cultural frontiers. Pope Francis calls this new pathway for theology "a radical paradigm shift" and a "bold cultural revolution" (*VG 5*). This is because it forces theology not simply to be content with explication of the intelligibility of doctrine, but to engage with the daily realities of people by showing the light and leaven of the gospel in pastoral approaches that meet new situations with new ideas (*VG 3*, penultimate paragraph). Such a theology is capable of seeing new events of revelation in history and of embracing the vocation of theology as a continuation of the worship of God.

Two Propositions

How can this kind of theology emerge in our churches and from the margins? I offer two broad propositions.

An Openness to Wonder and to Being Surprised by God: A Theology of Recognition

Pope Francis calls on theologians "not to lose the ability to wonder, to practice theology in wonder," to practice theology on their knees, and to do theology with and for the people who, he says, have "the nose for faith." There is the need for humility and devotion to the God who reveals, so that we can see clearly the footprints of God and the "beauty of the varied faces of the Church" in diverse histories (*VG 4.d*). This humble attitude is also necessary particularly in the way Catholic theologies are framed. I am referring here to the language of discourse, to the kinds of claims theologians make about God and humans, how we construct our systems of thought, and how we teach theology. Sometimes our theologies are not only inaccessible but also do not move hearts or minds in the direction of God, nor do they inspire conversion and transformation in daily action. They also create a wedge between theologians and our faith communities. Often, theologians speak from the ivory tower, while their writings lack grounding in concrete history and the phenomenological basis of theology, the Word of God.

A sense of mystery invites us to celebrate differences and the beauty of diversity. This is why Pope Francis invites us with the image of a great orchestra, which he uses to describe the catholicity of the church and which should form the impetus for theological plurality in the one church:

> This is a beautiful image illustrating that the church is like a great orchestra in which there is a great variety. We are not all the same, and we do not all have to be the same. We are all different, varied, each of us with our own special qualities. And this is the beauty of the church: everyone brings their own gifts, which God has given, for the sake of enriching others. And between the various components there is diversity; however, it is a diversity that does not enter into conflict and opposition. It is a variety that allows the Holy Spirit to blend it into harmony.[27]

Pope Francis calls for the acceptance in the church of "differing currents of thought in philosophy, theology, and pastoral practice," which are reconciled "by the spirit of respect and love" and which help the church grow in its understanding and application of the "riches of God's Word" (*EG* 41). People should recognize themselves and their cultures in our liturgy, in the faces of our church officials, in our church language, and in the prophetic nature of our institutions and laws. People should be able to see God and our symbols of God through their own cultural lens, and to see and love in the images of God what they would like to see and love in themselves and in their culture, because it invites them to a beautiful embrace, beyond the limitations of culture, of what is true, good, beautiful, and harmonious, transcending space and time.

The Theology of Action and Transformation

All theologies, like every experience of faith, must bring about a new reality and a deeper understanding of the mysteries of God in relation to the deepest human concerns and people's daily experiences. Any theological reflection that is grounded in the phenomenology of the Word of life is very concrete. This is because it draws its source from the Incarnation and the Paschal mysteries, whose connection to the act of faith and witnessing in the social context of the followers of Christ brings about a faithful and transformative living out of the message of the gospel in history. The gospel always brings a great reversal in the history of those who make an assent of faith: it brings down the mighty, raises the lowly, and makes a preferential option for the poor and the weak.

Theologies help followers of Christ see clearly how their personal and communal stories today and in the past are adding together in the consummation of all things, as concrete signs of the irruption of the eschatological fruits of God's Reign. Theologians can shed light on how following the way of the Lord in our human and cosmic contexts leads believers to enter into deeper communion with God. They can help God's people and the entire church embrace and enact God's will in history and remove anything that is opposed to God's Reign in the ambiguity and complexities of our earthly pilgrimage and in the life of the church.

This kind of theology is seeded in the heart of theologians who have a deep faith in God. This is why I pray for theologies and theologians who are seeking new answers to the new contexts and questions which the faith of God's people presents to us today. Catholic theologies have always been a source of guidance and illumination for God's people. I am convinced that in our times, faithful and creative theological productions can emerge to accompany the church in the missionary conversion proposed by Pope Francis as the path to the reform of the church. Christians are craving such theologies, which move their hearts to believe and to witness to the faith. They are looking for beautiful theologies, which inspire hope, and theologies of transformation, which make God's people believe in better days so that they can look beyond limited human and sociocultural horizons toward the infinite mysteries of God, which are beyond our human and cultural imaginings.

Finally, creative and transformative theologies that nourish the spiritual and moral life should be born from present challenges and opportunities beyond theological activism, careerism, moralism, and neo-fundamentalism. The question of whether one is a good theologian should not be about whether one is progressive or conservative, or whether she or he looks like me or studied at a certain university—restrictive categories that have limited the ability of today's theologians to set their sights on the infinite horizon of God. The judgment of whether one is a good theologian should be based on the extent to which one is in love with God, with God's people, God's church, God's creation, and all things because of God. It is a vocation to embrace the wisdom of God, born out of deep faith and love, and to be a bearer of a message of hope and newness to the church and the world.

Notes

[1] Joseph Ratzinger, *Salt of the Earth: The Church at the End of the Millennium*, trans. Adrian Walker (San Francisco, CA: Ignatius Press, 1997), 16.

[2] Brian Stanley, *Christianity in the Twentieth Century: A World History* (Princeton, NJ: Princeton University Press, 2018), 1.

[3] Brian Stanley, "Africa through European Christian Eyes: The World Missionary Conference, Edinburgh 1910," in *African Identities and World Christianity in the Twentieth Century*, ed. Klaus Koschorke (Wiesbaden: Harrassowitz Verlag, 2005), 116–80.

[4] Pope Pius X, *Il Fermo Proposito* (2005), no. 4, w2.vatican.va.

[5] David P. Goldman, *It's Not the End of the World: It's Just the End of You* (New York: RVP Publishers, 2011), 353–54.

[6] Lamin Sanneh, "World Christianity and the New Historiography: History and Global Interconnections," in *Enlarging the Story: Perspectives on Writing World Christian History*, ed. Wilbert R. Shenk (Eugene, OR: Wipf and Stock, 2011), 95.

[7] Gerd Theissen, *The Religion of the Earliest Churches: Creating a Symbolic World*, trans. John Bowden (Minneapolis: Fortress Press, 1999), 68.

[8] Larry W. Hurtado, *Destroyer of the Gods: Early Christian Distinctiveness in the Roman World* (Waco, TX: Baylor University Press, 2016), 20–21.

[9] Allan Anderson, *An Introduction to Pentecostalism* (Cambridge: Cambridge University Press, 2004), 104.

[10] Lamin Sanneh, *Disciples of All Nations: Pillars of World Christianity* (Oxford: Oxford University Press, 2008), xix.

[11] Wilbert R. Shenk, "Recasting Theology of Mission: Impulses from the Non-Western World," in *Landmark Essays in Mission and World Christian-*

ity, ed. Robert L. Gallagher and Paul Hertig (Maryknoll, NY: Orbis Books, 2009), 120.

[12]Andrew F. Walls, *The Missionary Movement in Christian History: Studies in the Transmission of Faith* (Maryknoll, NY: Orbis Books, 1996), 7.

[13]Sanneh, *Disciples of All Nations*, 55.

[14]Ibid.

[15]See John W. O'Malley, "Reform in the Life of the Church: The Council of Trent and Vatican II," in *For a Missionary Reform of the Church: The Civiltà Cattolica Seminar* (Mahwah, NJ: Paulist Press, 2016), 77–100.

[16]See Marco Politi, *Pope Francis among the Wolves: The Inside Story of a Revolution*, trans. William McCuaig (New York: Columbia University Press, 2015); Gianluigi Nuzzi, *Merchants in the Temple: Inside Pope Francis's Secret Battle against Corruption in the Vatican*, trans. Michael F. Moore (New York: Henry Holt, 2015). Perhaps the strongest of such rejections of Pope Francis is a work that challenges the validity of his election as pope; see Antonio Socci, *Non é Francesco: La Chiesa nella grande tempesta* (Milan: Arnoldo Mondadori Editore, 2014); see also Christopher A. Ferrara and Thomas E. Woods Jr., *The Great Façade: The Regime of Novelty in the Catholic Church from Vatican II to the Francis Revolution*, 2nd ed. (Kettering, OH: Angelico Press, 2015); Robert M. Whaples, ed., *Pope Francis and the Caring Community* (Oakland, CA: Independent Institute, 2017).

[17]Hans Urs von Balthasar, *My Work in Retrospect* (San Francisco, CA: Ignatius Press, 1993), 51.

[18]See Joseph A. Schumpeter, *Capitalism, Socialism, and Democracy* (London: Routledge, 1976).

[19]Address of His Holiness Pope Francis at the meeting on the theme, "Theology after *Veritatis Gaudium* in the Context of the Mediterranean," promoted by the Pontifical Theological Faculty of Southern Italy—San Luigi Section—Naples, w2.vatican.va.

[20]Ibid.

[21]Ibid.

[22]Ibid.

[23]Homily at the XXVIII World Youth Day, July 27, 2013.

[24]Greetings of Pope Francis to the Synod Fathers during the First General Congregation of the Third General Assembly of the Synod of Bishops, October 4, 2014, w2.vatican.va.

[25]"L'arcivescovo Zani, 'Evitare la teologia da tavolino,' " www.avvenire-dicalabria.it.

[26]See Greetings of Pope Francis to the Synod Fathers.

[27]Pope Francis, *The Church of Mercy: A Vision for the Church* (Chicago: Loyola University Press), 34.

Mystical yet Political

A Liberative Encounter with God through Popular Piety

Wilson Angelo Espiritu

In *Religion in the Secular City*, Harvey Cox describes his encounter with the prominent liberation theologian Juan Luis Segundo in 1969. When Cox asked Segundo to accompany him to the shrine of the Virgin of Guadalupe, Segundo sternly disagreed and was dismayed that Cox would even consider visiting a devotion that deceives a great multitude of innocent people.[1] Contrary to Segundo's disapproving stance, I argue that popular piety should not be easily dismissed, for it can serve as a legitimate point of encounter with God, notwithstanding its need to be pastorally guided, purified, and even corrected in some cases.

According to Damayanthi Niles, there can be two opposite approaches in dealing with popular piety, namely prejudgment or romanticization.[2] Both are equally dangerous overgeneralizations. On the one hand, it is not right to judge, criticize, or oppose something that one does not understand properly. On the other, one must not lose sight of the dangers of alienating practices. Like any other human action, popular piety can be either liberative or oppressive. One should, then, foster what is liberative and reject what is oppressive.[3] A theologian must make room for a respectful yet critical assessment of popular piety. It is not right to make hasty judgments on the piety of the masses, who are often the poor and uneducated, without carefully considering what this could mean for them and for their spirituality.

In this essay I set forth three aspects of popular piety that are positive: an embodied spirituality, an epistemology of trust, and a catalyst for liberation. I describe these while refuting some common objections to popular piety. In each case, I argue for the liberative potential of this significant dimension of global Catholic faith. Following Edward Schillebeeckx's soteriological framework, I propose an understanding of popular piety as a mystical-political activity in which a liberative encounter with God can be discerned. This notion asserts that, from a Christian viewpoint, practices that deal with the sacred have political implications, while political praxes must be grounded in and animated by mystical practices. Schillebeeckx's often-quoted statement captures this proposition perfectly: "Without prayer or mysticism politics soon becomes cruel and barbaric; without political love, prayer or mysticism soon becomes sentimental or uncommitted interiority."[4]

An Embodied Spirituality

One objection to popular piety arises from a misunderstanding of its use of symbols and rituals. Critics argue that devotional practices are superstitious and pagan.[5] Others see them as efforts to manipulate God, so as to gain divine favors.[6]

I do not discount the possibility that such distortions may arise within the practice of popular piety. People can perform pious rituals without interiority, from force of habit or in passive compliance to tradition. Others may even really think that performing religious rituals gains them merit toward obtaining God's favor. But does this accurately describe the entire picture of what is going on in the practice of popular piety?

Albert Alejo argues that popular piety involves a "spirituality of the body." He claims that the experiences of the body are mediations by which a contact with the sacred happens. There can be no interiority without the body, for the body serves as an external structure for one's interiority.[7] Similarly, Clemente Ignacio calls this quality of popular piety a form of "incarnational spirituality," in which people use their senses to encounter God.[8] Following these views, I suggest calling it an "embodied spirituality," in order to point to the bodily encounter between the human spirit that yearns for God and God's Spirit whose presence permeates the world. The symbols, gestures, and sensibilities involved in popular faith practices are ways in which people attempt to touch the Sacred or, better yet, are ways for people to be touched by the Sacred. Therefore, the use of symbols, gestures, and rituals in popular devotions is the embodiment of people's encounters with the sacred.[9] Symbols are necessary insofar as humans need symbolic representations to perceive God's presence.[10] After all, every encounter with God must be embodied or mediated. Schillebeeckx rightly refers to this reality as "mediated immediacy."[11] This means that, from the perspective of humans, encounter with God is always an encounter with something corporeal, a tangible reality. The bodiliness is the point of contact where God's immediacy is apprehended.

Regarding the objection that ritual actions are efforts to manipulate God, perhaps a more fundamental question should be asked: Can God be manipulated, in the first place? Can humans direct God how to act? For Alejo, ritual acts are not means for manipulating God. He refers, rather, to this aspect of popular piety as a "spirituality of negotiation."[12] He claims that people do not instruct God compulsorily to do what they want. Based on their interpersonal understanding of their faith, they express their petitions through negotiation. This arises from the natural tendency of people to express their requests to God in a human manner, much like a child requesting something of his or her parents. Ernest Henau suggests, furthermore, that the Christian use of symbols is not intended to manipulate God, but to serve as a means of allowing oneself to be led by God.[13]

It is easy to judge popular piety without really understanding what its devotees go through in their lives. Their experiences and struggles mark their faith expressions. The church reminds us that the symbols and rituals involved in popular piety are the externalization of people's deep personal relationship with God and their Christian commitment.[14] When popular piety is rooted in one's personal relationship with God, the symbols become a "sacramentalization" of God's presence and of the human receptivity to it.[15] It should, then, lead the faithful to the liturgy.[16] Genuine devotions are, indeed, fruits of the Holy Spirit and expressions of the church's own piety.[17]

In sum, popular piety's use of the senses, of symbols, gestures, and rituals—its embodied spirituality—expresses the interrelationship of the mystical and the political dimensions of Christian life. Devotional practices may be understood as liberative, in the sense that they are reminders that one relates with the sacred not in an otherworldly manner, but in a very tangible and corporeal way. This runs counter to the disembodying error of neo-gnosticism, against which Pope Francis warns Christians in his Apostolic Exhortation *Gaudete et Exsultate*.[18] In the practice of popular piety, people are reminded that communion with God does not mean departing from the world, but instead embodying the divine presence in the world.[19] Thus, it entails not only the performance of pious rituals, but also a responsible engagement in the political sphere to "sacramentalize" God's ongoing work of liberation.

An Epistemology of Trust

A second objection characterizes popular piety as mere "sentimentalism, externalism, and subjectivism," and this is thought to keep people infantile in their faith.[20] Feelings are said to take precedence over rationality.[21] Devotees are called fanatics, who do not even understand that what they are doing is idolatry.[22]

It is true that popular piety involves, to a great extent, the emotions and sentiments of the people. But their motives for these pious practices cannot be reduced to mere sentimentality and subjectivity. The people who practice popular devotions may be inarticulate about doctrinal matters, but this does not mean they do not have any intellectual grasp of what they are doing. They have their own way, simple and direct, of theologizing.[23] Humans as they are, these people have the capacity to think, to make choices, and to safeguard their intellectual integrity.[24] While there is indeed a need to continue to grow in the knowledge of the Christian faith, the lack of sophisticated doctrinal or theological aptitude does not imply immaturity or shallowness of faith. These people would not engage in spiritual activities requiring their time, effort, and sacrifice if they did not have sincere reasons for doing so. These reasons are founded on a personal relationship of trust that goes beyond mere rational grounds.

Henau contends that rationality cannot be the only criterion for assessing expressions of faith, and it is not an absolute assurance that misconceptions of faith will be prevented. Both emotion and reason are important, and they can enrich each other.[25] Nevertheless, in popular piety it is the relational aspect that takes precedence over the rational. Relationship with God is the priority, and the rationality of the acts may not be the immediate concern of the devotees. Henau further states that popular faith is not something expressed in creedal or doctrinal formulations. It is transmitted through other forms that cannot be reduced to intellectual formulations. This makes it easy to dismiss them as subjective or sentimental.[26] For Luis Maldonado, people who engage in popular piety are searching for a simpler relationship with God. Rather than approaching God in a cerebral, dogmatic, and abstract manner, they prefer intuitive and imaginative forms.[27] How else can relationship be better expressed? For most people, it is not by words of the intellect, which tend to be dry, sophisticated, and prosaic, but by the words of the heart, which are direct, simple, and poetic.[28] The priority of the heart over the mind actually enables people to engage with the sacred in a way that is both familiar and sensible to them.[29]

Hence, it is not all that profitable to approach popular piety from a standpoint of mere rationality. It would be difficult to understand the deep trust that is engendered among devotees if one measures the maturity of their faith by the criterion of proficiency in doctrinal matters. The trustworthiness of God, who is acknowledged in their devotion as love, is the underlying reason and source of these people's hope. This is a different kind of knowledge, one that is based on trust and not on demonstrable proofs or arguments.[30] This kind of reasonableness can only be deciphered within a framework of relationality. Popular piety, therefore, has an inherent depth that is rooted in a personal relationship of trust in God.[31]

The sincere attitude of trust behind popular piety liberates people from their self-sufficiency. What is more liberative than to know that God is the most trustworthy of all? It is the very same trust that enables devotees to believe that God is actively working in their lives and in the world. Through this trust, they can be empowered to participate in God's ongoing saving action in the world today. Their devotion to God can find its corollary expression in dedication to God's creation. In this way, popular piety can be understood as a mystical-political activity.

A Catalyst for Liberation

The last objection that I would like to address concerns the use of the old Marxist critique of religion as "the opium of the people" to vilify popular piety.[32] Critics claim that it keeps people in a spiritual realm divorced from the pressing realities of this world. It distracts them from what truly needs to be done in the here and now, and they become conditioned to accept the toils and sufferings of this life in view of salvation in an afterlife. Popular piety is accused of having nothing to do with sociopolitical transformation.[33]

Popular piety can, indeed, have an oppressive side.[34] It is true that it can be utilized as an opiate for the sufferings of the people, an instrument for domination, and a distraction from the urgent realities of life. For example, Tony Conway claims that in the Philippines, Christian symbols have been misused for the concealment and justification of violence, injustice, and class warfare.[35] And Enrique Dussel points out that in Latin America, popular religion has been manipulated as an ideology used to control the dominated people.[36] This happens when symbols and practices are misused by the oppressors and as a result lose their real value and become tools of subjugation, serving to maintain the alienating status quo.[37] Michael Candelaria conjectures that there are instances when popular piety has created an attitude of escapism from the realities of this world.[38] It has produced a "substitute satisfaction" for the needed historical transformations.[39]

Nevertheless, popular piety also has a liberative side.[40] It is reputed to have kindled sociopolitical emancipative movements. While popular piety has, indeed, been misused for oppressive purposes, it has also been instrumental for liberation. For example, returning to the context of the examples cited above, in the Philippines, the popular devotional practice of the passion play was once used by Spanish colonizers to keep the Filipinos subservient. But it has subsequently become a force for awakening the social consciousness and patriotism of the people. It eventually instigated the Filipino resistance movement against Spain.[41] This instance has an equivalent example in Latin America. There, popular piety has created a synthesis between faith and liberation.[42] It has also served as a symbol for resistance against oppression, a force for transformation, and an inspiration for liberation.[43]

In response to the criticism that religion, because it (allegedly) serves as the opiate of the people, should be abolished altogether in order that liberation may take place, Andrew McKinnon argues that Marx's critique of religion cannot be generally applied to every instance of faith or religion. Each must be considered in relation to its own uniqueness, complexities, and social implications. The critique of Marx must be understood as a call for vigilance regarding what is oppressive and what is liberative within each specific faith practice.[44] Michael Welton points out that, in Marx's view, religion is an indicator of the oppressed condition of humanity. It enables people to endure until injustices are ameliorated and they are able to realize their role as active agents in history. Ironically, Marx's point has even served as an opportunity for further exploring the liberative potential of religion, which has been taken seriously by critical theorists and liberation theology.[45]

Therefore, the question is not whether religion in general, or certain popular faith expressions in particular, should be eradicated, but whether they can be of service to God's Reign by being a sign and instrument of God's liberating action in the world. The hope that popular piety engenders in the people has proven to have the potential to lead to liberation.[46] Besides being a personal expression of devotion, popular piety also includes a communal liberative dimension. There are devotional practices that are performed in solidarity with the other devotees.[47] Even some private devotions are performed not exclusively for the benefit of the individual devotee, but also for the welfare of others.[48] Of course, to be truly liberative, the intended beneficiaries must be extended to a larger circle than only the in-group of the devotees.

Seen as a mystical-political activity, popular piety can be understood as a catalyst for liberation.[49] To say that it is a catalyst must at the same time emphasize that it is not the ultimate source of liberation: that source is God alone. However, it plays an important role in allowing God's liberative activity to be realized and revealed in the world. It bears liberative value in bridging the gap between what is sacred and what is secular, and what is individual and what is communal. If liberation is effected in the interaction of the mystical and the political, sociopolitical emancipative movements can be grounded in and nourished by "the people's mysticism." In turn, "the people's mysticism" may inspire liberative praxis.[50] Both can, therefore, be understood as manifestations of God's continuing act of salvation in history. Thus, popular piety is not a mere "spiritual" practice that is isolated from the political. Rather, it is through its relationship with the political that it bears witness to its authentic spirituality.

Popular Piety as a Mystical-Political Activity

Pierre de Charentenay claims that if popular devotions are to take part in positive sociopolitical transformation, their theological significance must be kept alive and strengthened. People must be able to make the connection between their expressions of faith and the command to love one another. Love of neighbor can then be externalized as sociopolitical action.[51]

When popular piety is understood as a mystical-political activity, its connection with sociopolitical emancipative praxis becomes evident. As embodiments of a living faith, symbols and rituals may serve the common good if they are not separated from the social, political, and economic aspects of people's lives.[52] Engagement in these areas of life can be rooted in and nourished by one's piety, which engenders a deep relationship of trust in God. Hence, popular piety does not serve merely as an opiate that desensitizes people toward their suffering, nor a distraction from the real work that must be done, but as a springboard for action. Being a catalyst of liberation and transformation, it becomes a trustworthy sign of God's abiding presence amid life's challenges and difficulties, and a reminder of the Christian disciple's mandate to embody God's Reign, making it more visible in this world.[53]

Notes

This essay is a reworking of a previously published paper, "Popular Piety as a Locus of Salvation: Towards a Mystical-Political Hermeneutic of Liberation," *Pamisulu: An Interdisciplinary Journal of Theology and Philosophy* 6, no. 1 (November 2018): 56–96. Used with permission.

[1]Harvey Cox, *Religion in the Secular City: Toward a Postmodern Theology* (New York: Simon and Schuster, 1984), 243–44.

[2]Damayanthi Niles, "How the Study of Popular Religion Can Help Us in Our Theological Task," *International Review of Mission* 93, no. 369 (April 2004): 215.

[3]Ibid., 216.

[4]Edward Schillebeeckx, *Jesus in Our Western Culture: Mysticism, Ethics and Politics*, trans. John Bowden (New York: Crossroad, 1987), 75.

[5]See Michael Candelaria, *Popular Religion and Liberation: The Dilemma of Liberation Theology* (Albany: State University of New York Press, 1990), 20. Fr. Arnie Catalan points out that the fervor of the people is often misunderstood as fanaticism, and some criticize the religious practices as a form of idolatry or paganism. See "Popular Religiosity Called Potent Source of Evangelization," *UCA News*, October 11, 1994, https://www.ucanews.com.

[6]See Enrique Dussel, "Popular Religion as Oppression and Liberation: Hypothesis on Its Past and Present in Latin America," *Concilium* 186 (August 1986): 86–87; Bernhard Raas, *Popular Devotions: Making Popular Religious Practices More Potent Vehicles of Spiritual Growth* (Manila: Logos Publications, 2014 [1992]), 26–27; Paul Hiebert, Daniel Shaw, and Tite Tienou, "Responding to Split-Level Christianity and Folk Religion," *International Journal of Frontier Missions* 16, no. 4 (Winter 1999/2000): 174.

[7]Albert Alejo, "Religion and Secularization: Some Challenges in the Philippines," in *Religions in Society in Asia: Conflict and Convergence*, ed. Michael Amaladoss (Bangalore: Claretian Publications, 2017), 190.

[8]Jose Clemente F. Ignacio, "Understanding the Devotion to the Black Nazarene," paper presented at the National Liturgical Congress, Loyola School of Theology, Quezon City, January 19, 2011.

[9]See Edward Schillebeeckx, *Christ the Sacrament of the Encounter with God*, trans. Paul Barret and Lawrence Bright, vol.1 of *The Collected Works of Edward Schillebeeckx* (London: Bloomsbury T&T Clark, 2014), 45 [76–77].

[10]See Edward Schillebeeckx, *Church: The Human Story of God*, trans. John Bowden, vol. 10 of *The Collected Works of Edward Schillebeeckx* (London: Bloomsbury T&T Clark, 2014), 74 [76], 98 [101].

[11]Ibid., 68 [70].

[12]Alejo, "Religion and Secularization," 193.

[13]See Ernest Henau, "Popular Religiosity and Christian Faith," *Concilium* 186 (August 1986): 77.

[14]Congregation for Divine Worship and the Discipline of the Sacraments, "Directory on Popular Piety and the Liturgy: Principles and Guidelines," para. 15, last modified December 2001, http://www.vatican.va.

[15]See Schillebeeckx, *Christ the Sacrament of the Encounter with God*, 159 [269–70].

[16]See Second Vatican Council, "Sacrosanctum Concilium," para. 13, http://www.vatican.va.

[17]Congregation for Divine Worship and the Discipline of the Sacraments, "Directory on Popular Piety and the Liturgy: Principles and Guidelines," para. 83.

[18]See Pope Francis, *Gaudete et Exsultate*: Apostolic Exhortation on the Call to Holiness in Today's World, paras. 36–37.

[19]See Schillebeeckx, *Jesus in Our Western Culture*, 69.

[20]See Raas, *Popular Devotions*, 26–27.

[21]Henau, "Popular Religiosity and Christian Faith," 79.

[22]See David Lozada, "Idolatry Is a Sin, Preachers Tell Nazareno Devotees," *Rappler,* January 9, 2015, http://www.rappler.com.

[23]See Luis Maldonado, "Popular Religion: Its Dimensions, Levels and Types," *Concilium* 186 (August 1986): 6.

[24]See Benigno Beltran, *The Christology of the Inarticulate: An Inquiry into the Filipino Understanding of Jesus Christ* (Manila: Divine Word Publications, 1987), 135.

[25]Henau, "Popular Religiosity and Christian Faith," 79.

[26]Ibid.

[27]Maldonado, "Popular Religion," 6.

[28]See Michael Paul Gallagher, "Escaping from the Wrong Question," in *Free to Believe: Ten Steps to Faith* (Chicago: Loyola University Press, 1987), 42–50.

[29]Salvador Ryan, "Some Reflections on Theology and Popular Piety: A Fruitful or Fraught Relationship?" *Heythrop Journal* 53 (2012): 964.

[30]See Nicholas Thomas Wright, *Surprised by Hope: Rethinking Heaven, Resurrection, and the Mission of the Church* (New York: Harper Collins, 2008), 71–74.

[31]Pope Francis, *Evangelii Gaudium*: Apostoli Exhortation on the Proclamation of the Gospel in Today's World, para. 125.

[32]See Karl Marx, "A Contribution to the Critique of Hegel's *Philosophy of Right,* " 1844, https://www.marxists.org.

[33]Pierre de Charentenay, "Popular Religion and Social Change," *Ateneo de Manila University Blue Board*, November 14, 2013, http://www.ateneo.edu.

[34]As a matter of fact, some liberation theologians have highlighted and criticized these alienating tendencies of popular piety. See Candelaria, *Popular Religion and Liberation*, 4–7.

[35]Tony Conway, "Christian Signs and Symbols," in *Culture and Force for Change* (Manila: Socio-Pastoral Institute, 1988), 46. Cited in Jaime Belita, *And God Said: Hala!: Studies in Popular Religiosity in the Philippines* (Manila: De La Salle University Press, 1991), 57.

[36]Dussel, "Popular Religion as Oppression and Liberation," 90–91.

[37]Paulo Suess, "The Creative and Normative Role of Popular Religion in the Church," *Concilium* 186 (August 1986): 124–25.

[38]Candelaria, *Popular Religion and Liberation*, 2.

[39]Ibid., 3.

[40]Although there are liberation theologians who focused on the alienating tendencies of popular piety, there are those who opted to highlight its liberative capacities. See ibid., 7–9.

[41]Niceta Vargas, *Word and Witness: An Introduction to the Gospel of John* (Quezon City: Ateneo de Manila University Press, 2013), 297–98. See also Reynaldo Ileto, *Pasyon and Revolution: Popular Movements in the Philippines: 1840–1910* (Quezon City: Ateneo de Manila Press, 1979), 15–16.

[42]See Dussel, "Popular Religion as Oppression and Liberation," 92–93.

[43]Christian Parker, "Popular Religion and Protest against Oppression: The Chilean Example," *Concilium* 186 (August 1986): 34–35. Dussel claims that the Virgin of Guadalupe became an inspiration for various resistance movements in Latin America. He also cites the Sandinistas as an example of how Christians, moved by their faith, can engage in revolutionary activity. Dussel, "Popular Religion as Oppression and Liberation," 88, 92.

[44]Andrew M. McKinnon, "Opium as Dialectics of Religion: Metaphor, Expression and Protest," *Critical Sociology* 31, no. 1/2 (2005): 15–38.

[45]Michael Welton, "Opium of the People? The Religious Heritage of Karl Marx and the Frankfurt School," *Counterpunch*, September 11, 2015, https://www.counterpunch.org.

[46]See Henau, "Popular Religiosity and Christian Faith," 77.

[47]See Robert Schreiter, *Constructing Local Theologies* (Maryknoll, NY: Orbis Books, 1985), 129–30.

[48]Some examples of devotions that I can immediately point to as communitarian are the public recitation of the rosary, pilgrimages, processions, and novenas. It must also be noted that the prayers recited in these devotional practices indicate a strong communitarian aspect.

[49]See Belita, *And God Said: Hala!* 51–60.

[50]"The People's Mysticism" is a term used by Pope Francis in *Evangelii Gaudium* to refer to popular piety. See *EG* 124.

[51]de Charentenay, "Popular Religion and Social Change."

[52]Belita, *And God Said: Hala!* 59.

[53]See Stephan van Erp and Karim Schelkens, eds., *Conversion and Church: The Challenge of Ecclesial Renewal* (Leiden: Koninklijke Brill, 2016), 84–85.

Global Faith and African Eco-Cultic Spirituality

Charting a New Path to a Global Catholic Ecological Spirituality

Gregory Aabaa

There are varieties of spirituality in the Catholic Church. Within the context of an upsurge in global awareness of the ecological crisis, it is important that our spiritualities take into consideration a serious concern for environmental sanity.[1] Situating environmental concerns within the purview of Catholicism or any Catholic spirituality that is essentially global is not unwarranted.

Furthermore, the spirituality of a faith that is essentially Catholic must be open to the polyphony of voices around the globe: voices that attempt to contribute from the repertoire of their own indigenous and spiritual resources to address issues of global concern such as the ecological crisis. This is precisely where I locate the African voice, particularly, that of the Akans of Ghana, in this discussion.

This essay argues that there are certain bodies of organized wisdom informed by an indigenous Weltanschauung of the Akan ethnic group that shape the cultic behavior and spirituality of Akans in relation to the natural environment. The Akan spirituality, like those of most traditional ethnic communities in Africa, contains "ecocentric" values and practices that are derived from environmental considerations.[2] Ecologically oriented taboo systems and Akans' understanding of ontology, cosmology, biocentric axiology, and psychical interaction give coloration to an eco-cultic spirituality that must not be obviated in tackling the menace of the current *oikocide* that humans have unfortunately begun.

For the sake of methodological clarity, although this discussion is derived from the wider context of Africa, the focus is on the Akan ethnic group in Ghana and its relation to the subject of global Catholicism in their common concern for the environment. Examples may occasionally be drawn from other traditions within Ghana and West Africa.

Brief Notes on the Akans of Ghana

The Akan people constitute the largest ethnic group in Ghana (about 49.1 percent of Ghana's population)[3] and one of the largest ethnic groups in West Africa. The Akans also occupy the larger part of the southern sector of Ghana. The Akans are further divided into many groups based on dialect, although the main dialect of the Akans remains the Asante Twi language, which is widely spoken in Ghana. Despite further divisions based on dialect, Akan ethnic unity is arguably unparalleled in West Africa. In terms of religion, their chief religion remains the Traditional African Religion, although many have embraced Christianity.

Traditional African Spirituality within Global Faith: A Case for Pluriversality

Global faith, as used in this essay, is a semiotic construct or a linguistic symbol that stands for the diverse forms of creedal expressions according to the numerous faith communities around the world. With global faith, we are talking not just of a faith but of faiths.[4] Global faith is a canopy term that excludes no faith tradition. It is universal in its all-embracing sense and also pluriversal[5] in its inclusive outreach. The Christian faith, Islamic faith, Buddhist faith, Traditional African Religious faith, and so on, are individually necessary and collectively required in our understanding of global faith. The presence of the plurality of faiths[6] captured by the essence of global faith makes it possible to locate Traditional African Religious ethos, cultic praxis, and spirituality within this pluriversality of faith. Global faith thus allows us to listen to the voices of other faith traditions available in the world, and the pluriversal quality of global faith provides justificatory leeway for bringing into the discussion the voice of the Akan traditional community as a co-participant with the Christian faith and Catholic spiritualities in common dialogue concerning the environment.

The Cosmovision of the Traditional Akan Religion

The Akans, like any other African society, are guided by a certain understanding of the world in which they live, their relationship with the creator, and all natural and supernatural phenomena.[7] This basic understanding is what informs the worldview of the Akan ethnic group, from which conceptual premises are derived that constitute the guiding principles of their social organization, religion, culture, and spirituality.[8]

The first point to note is that the basic view of reality from an Akan perspective is what is termed "ontological holism,"[9] the view that reality is a whole.[10] The dualism pervasive in Western metaphysical thought has no place in Akan cosmovision, and although Akan thought yields to duality, it is always a duality in complementarity, the totality of which forms a whole: hence, ontological holism.

Second, the Akan cosmology is premised on an ontology that partitions the universe into what we shall call "planes of being." There is an onto-binary categorization of the world into the visible and the invisible worlds,[11] yet it is one world indivisible with one sphere touching on the other.[12] In addition, the universe is inhabited by an onto-triadic calibration of being: the living, the living-dead, and the unborn.[13] All of these form a single community of beings.

Third, the spiritual world is inhabited by the Supreme Being (*Odomankoma*), the ancestors, and nature gods or spirits, while the material or the visible world houses human beings, animals, plants, and inanimate beings.[14] The Akans also believe that the ancestors and spirits, though of a spiritual existence, also reside in trees, rivers, mountains, and animals.[15]

In any case, the Akan does not conceive of the physical world without the spiritual world; neither does she or he conceive of the spiritual world apart from the physical world. Although Akans maintain a spiritual and physical world, the duo are, nevertheless, in a constant flux of interaction,[16] a kind of "cosmological *koinonia.*"[17] There is no discontinuity between the material and the spiritual worlds.

Fourth, Akan cosmology, like most cosmologies in West Africa, is also premised on a felt hierarchy of being, with the Supreme Being (whose reality is an ontological given) at the apex, followed by the lesser gods, the ancestors, humans, and nonhuman creatures.[18]

This summary of the Akan worldview is not exhaustive, but it does provide the required lens through which we can see and appreciate Akan spirituality and the role that spirituality plays in Akan environmental conservation.

Akan Spirituality

Akan spirituality can be defined as the cultic expressions of the Akans' openness to the divine. These cultic expressions, as a way of affirming the connectedness of Akan indigenes with the divine, are captured in their rituals and belief systems and their devotional practices—such as the offering of sacrifices and libations—and taboo systems. For the Akans, spirituality is not just what they do, it is what they are. The Akan woman or man looks up at the sky and sees God; they look at the tree and they find a spirit; they look down at the land and see a goddess. At the very root of Akan spirituality is their belief in the sacredness of the whole of reality or the cosmos. For them, the universe is not merely a cosmological space: it is a religious space, because they encounter the sacred in it.[19]

Akan spirituality is characterized by a deep sense of devotion to God. It is a religious requirement that traditional Akan societies erect special altars dedicated to the worship of God. For instance, in Akan traditional homes, an altar in the form of a tree or forked stick with a pot held by the fork branches is erected in the middle of the compound or in front of the house. Occasionally, libation is offered to *Onyankopon* (God) at the base of the tree (altar) to worship him and ask for his protection.

Ancestor veneration is a common cultic expression of Akan spirituality. The ancestors, unlike God, are not worshipped; they are venerated. They are believed to reside in trees, animals, bodies of water, mountains, and forests. Akans also believe that the ancestors are capable of hierophanic appearances to humans through natural phenomena.

Eco-Cultic Practices and Beliefs of the Akans

In this section, I discuss three Akan environmental conservation techniques that reflect the ecological wisdom and spirituality of the African peoples in general: sacred groves, totemism, and the taboo system.

Sacred Groves

Sacred groves are also known as ancestral forests or sometimes evil forests. These are usually large forest reserves in which any form of human activity is prohibited. Various communities in Ghana have these forests set aside as sacred groves. These forests are seen as the dwelling of the ancestors. Some are also royal burial grounds. In some communities, these forests are seen as evil forests because they believe that countless numbers of malicious spirits (*mmoatia* and *sasabonsam*) reside there.[20] Because human activities such as farming, hunting, and logging are prohibited in such areas, these forests support countless species of plant and animal life, thereby sustaining biodiversity.

Totemism

Totemism is the belief system that holds that some spirits reside in some animals and plants, which thus are to be revered. Oftentimes, such animals or plants are deified. Totemism is a common religious belief in Ghana, where totemic animals, plants, and birds are connected to clans or families. Such families see in their totems the immanence of their spiritual guides. As such, members of that family are forbidden to kill (in the case of animals and birds) or cut down (in the case of plants) the totemic creatures for any reason. For instance, the Benyine clan of the Dagaaba ethnic group in the Upper West Region of Northern Ghana holds the porcupine, hedgehog, and dove as their totems. Members of this clan are forbidden to either kill or eat any of these animals. Those who flout this cultural rule suffer untold hardships, including incurable sicknesses and untimely death. The keeping of totems has proven to be one of the major traditional conservation tools that have helped to conserve many wildlife and plant species in Ghana.

The Taboo System

Closely associated with totemism is the system of taboos, some of which are equally ecologically friendly. Here, I refer strictly to environmental taboos intended by traditional authorities to ensure ethical use of the environment. Munamato Chemhuru and Dennis Masaka define taboos as "'avoidance rules' that forbid members of the human community from performing certain actions, such as eating some kinds of food, walking on or visiting some sites that are regarded as sacred, cruelty to nonhuman animals, and using nature's resources in an unsustainable manner."[21] Some of these environmental taboos can be gleaned from the different cultures on the African continent. For instance, among the Akans of Ghana, it is a taboo to clear any part of the sacred forest; it is a taboo to go fishing or hunting or farming on some specific days that are termed sacred days; and it is a taboo to eat certain kinds of animals or cut certain kinds of trees. Often, the Akans would argue that violation of any of these taboos could incur the severe wrath of the gods, including the goddess of the earth, known as *Asaase Yaa*. It is true that the basic motive for such taboos was to avoid the anger of the gods and ancestors. However, traditional African peasants knew that cutting all or most of the available forests would not only deprive the future generations of rare plants and animals; it would also affect the delicate balance between plants, animals, and humans—with their needs for food, medicine, space, clean water, and clean air. The point to note then is that long before environmental consciousness began to have a grip on the Western mind, it was already part and parcel of the traditional African mind.

Charting a New Path to a Global Catholic Ecological Spirituality through African (Akan) Conservation Techniques

In the preceding sections, we have seen that some of the traditional cultic practices and beliefs of the Akans, such as the keeping of sacred forests, veneration of trees and mountains, totemism, and taboos, are ecologically beneficial. We must, however, admit that the fundamental spiritual and theological underpinnings of these traditional practices and beliefs are greatly unlike the Christian theological explicatory model for earth care. However, theology, cast in the matrix of a global context, particularly African theology in its inculturation dimension, can reinterpret the African eco-cultic spiritual practices in the light of the Christian gospel that is global in its universal and pluriversal outlook. In this way, African theology shall bring its own solution to the round-table of the global dialogue concerning our common home, in which Pope Francis is calling all to be involved.[22] For this reason, a reinterpretation and a retheologizing of these African eco-cultic spiritual systems and beliefs would be useful. The project of our African theologies should be to arrive at, among other goals, a new understanding of the indigenous eco-cultic practices of African traditional communities. This can be achieved through the tedious and careful task of reinterpreting and retheologizing the motives for these traditional practices in light of the Christian faith.[23]

For instance, most African societies keep sacred forests because they believe that the spirits of the ancestors dwell there. For some communities, these forests are homes to malicious spirits. Hence, they refer to the sacred forests as "evil forests." For these traditional communities, the "evil forests" also serve a punitive purpose. They are places of exile to which notorious deviants who have committed a sacrilege are banished and left to wander and die. They also once served as places of slaughter, especially, the slaughter of twins and albinos, who were thought to be signs of a curse or an abomination. Evidence of the existence of evil forests for such murderous purposes among the Yoruba of Nigeria can be found in Ola Rotimi's classical play *The Gods Are Not to Blame*.[24] This is evidence that the religious motives for the "forest reserve" in some traditional communities still stand in need of evangelization. Although the act of forest keeping in itself is good and ecologically valuable, the traditional African communities may be made to see a new reason for keeping sacred groves. This is where theology and spirituality within a global Catholic context must come in.

There is no harm in encouraging indigenous communities in Africa to retain the name and practice of keeping "sacred forests." However, the forest is sacred not because the spirits of ancestors dwell there. The spirits of the ancestors are in the hands of the

Supreme Being, that is, God, from whom they came. The forest is sacred precisely because God manifests Godself in these forests and, indeed, in the whole of nature.[25] The sacred forests, therefore, become what I call "sacramental catchment points." The forest becomes the sacrament of God's creative power. All creation speaks a divine language that proclaims the fear and the veneration of God.

Furthermore, the Akans have over the years preserved their natural environment through taboos. Although taboos, especially ecological taboos, are primarily ethical codes of right relationship with all the levels of being in the cosmos, fundamentally taboos have a spiritual orientation. For instance, the taboos prohibiting farming activities on the land on certain days during the week are justified, especially among the Akans of Ghana, by the reason that the goddess of the earth (*Asaase Yaa*) is venerated on those days or that the goddess of the earth takes her rest on one of those specific days. In our estimation, such ecological taboos practiced all over the world would be helpful in engendering a culture of respect for the land. However, the reason for such a culture of respect for the land would not be tenable to other people beyond the borders of Africa until we fashion a new spirituality for such a culture of respect for the land. Therefore, to facilitate the project of Catholic ecological spiritualities that are in tune with African conservation techniques, we need a new spirituality for earth care that can inspire global adherence, and, for this, I propose a "spirituality of rest." The spirituality of rest respects the natural rhythm of the land to "till" and "still," so that the intermittent interjection of days of "no tilling" reduces the impact of human activities on a piece of land, allowing the land to rest, for the sake of renewed productivity.

Unfortunately, the spirituality of rest in our time has been heavily conceived in anthropocentric terms. For instance, while Pope Francis articulated a spirituality of rest in his encyclical *Laudato Si'*, he sees rest as contemplative rest, something that only humans do. Rest, for Pope Francis, prevents human labor from degenerating into mere activism (*LS* 237). Ultimately, it is humans who rest so that the environment can also rest. Although he does not deny the need for rest for nonhuman creation, it is certainly not looked at from the earth perspective, but from an anthropocentric perspective. However, Africans' practice of earth care (especially, the Akan practice of having a day's rest for the land and water bodies in each week)[26] shows the world that a spirituality of rest viewed from the earth perspective is necessary for maintaining the integrity of nature for ecological balance and harmony. Any Catholic ecological spirituality, to be catholic (global), must incorporate a global and multiperspectival view of ecological spirituality, from the perspectives of both human and nonhuman creation. Africa seems to be leading the way as an example from which the global community and the Catholic Church can learn a robust spirituality of earth care.

Akan Environmentalism as a Contribution to Global Efforts

This essay is an experiment in articulating a concept of global faith that has ears for the polyphony of voices from indigenous communities around the globe—with emphasis on the Akan religiocultural life—on an issue of global concern, the ecological crisis. The Akan culture harbors an immortal sagacity in its indigenous traditional and spiritual systems that have augured well for ecological sanity. The eco-cultic spirituality of the Akans has contributed in no small measure to maintaining ecological harmony and biodiversity in the southern part of Ghana. Today, inspired by a global approach within the context of global faiths to seek holistic solutions to issues of global concern, we have every reason to turn to the spiritual wisdom of Africa, particularly, the Akans of Ghana. This discussion has examined various conservation techniques used to preserve balance and harmony in nature: the articulation of their cosmology (ontological holism) and the "land ethic" entailing the cultic practices of totemism, taboo systems, and the keeping of sacred forests. In the wake of the global awareness of the monstrous crisis faced by the environment, the project of Catholic ecological spiritualities, among other ends, could be to adopt these indigenous eco-cultic practices prevalent in Africa and to find new spiritual and theological bases for preserving them and making them globally relevant.

In a time when the global community is on the verge of ecological collapse, Africa, with all its poverty, serves as a powerful reminder to the industrialized rich nations that "only when the last tree has been cut, the last river poisoned, and the last fish caught, only then you will realize that one cannot eat money."[27]

Notes

[1]Salah M. Taylor, *Green Sisters: A Spirituality of Ecology* (Cambridge, MA: Harvard University Press, 2007). Taylor demonstrates in a highly practical manner what can be termed eco-spirituality in praxis and emphasizes the strong link between Christian spirituality and ecology as a matter of necessity.

[2]Edwin Etieyibo, "Anthropocentrism, African Metaphysical Worldview, and Animal Practices: A Reply to Kai Horsthemke," *Journal of Animal Ethics* 7, no. 2 (Fall 2017): 145–62. See also Monica Gratani et al., "Indigenous Environmental Values as Human Values," *Cogent Social Science* 2, no. 1 (article 1185811) (2016): 1–17; Diana-Abasi Ibanga, "Is Deep Ecology Applicable in African Context? A Conversation with Fainos Mangena," *Journal of African Philosophy, Culture and Religions* 6, no. 2 (July–December 2017): 101–19.

[3]Kofi Agyekum, "The Sociolinguistic of Akan Personal Names," *Nordic Journal of African Studies* 15, no. 2 (2006): 206.

[4]Faith, here, is understood not just as the creedal assent to the transcendent but the very expressions of creedal confessions of different faith communities.

[5]Walter Mignolo writes, "Pluriversality is not cultural relativism, but entanglement of several cosmologies connected today in a power differential," in "On Pluriversality," October 20, 2013, http://waltermignolo.com.

[6]Robert Schreiter validates the plurality of faith based on Christological considerations of the universal Lordship of Christ over all peoples, irrespective of their faith confession. See Robert J. Schreiter, "The Anonymous Christian and Christology," *Occasional Bulletin of Missionary Research* (January 1978): 2.

[7]M. Asante, *The Afrocentric Idea* (Philadelphia: Temple University Press, 1987); A. B. Chima, *Communication, Culture and Community* (Nairobi: Pauline Press, 1999), 35.

[8]C. H. Kraft, *Anthropology for Christian Witness* (Maryknoll, NY: Orbis Books, 2000), 21.

[9]Edwin Etieyibo, "Ubuntu and the Environment," in *The Palgrave Handbook of African Philosophy*, ed. Adeshina Afolayan and Toyin Falola (New York: Springer Nature, 2017), 636.

[10]Ayuya Caroline et al., "African Worldview: An Integrated Psychological Perspective," *International Journal of Humanities Social Sciences and Education (IJHSSE)* 2, no. 5 (May 2015): 56.

[11]Kola Abimbola, *Yoruba Culture: A Philosophical Account* (Birmingham: Iroko Academic, 2006), 52.

[12]Joram Tarusarira, "African Religion, Climate Change and Knowledge Systems," *Ecumenical Review* 69, no. 3 (October 2017): 400.

[13]Mogebe B. Ramose, "The Philosophy of *Ubuntu* and *Ubuntu* as a Phi-

losophy," in *The African Philosophy Reader*, ed. P. H. Coetzee and A. P. J. Roux, 2nd ed. (London: Routledge, 2003), 278.

[14]Sivave Mashingaidze, "Cosmovision and African Conservation Philosophy: Indigenous Knowledge System Perspective," *Environmental Economics* 7, no. 4 (2016): 27.

[15]Francis Etim, "African Metaphysics," *Journal of Asian Scientific Research* 3, no. 1 (2013): 13. See also John S. Mbiti, *African Religions and Philosophy* (London: Heinemann, 1969), 79; Adebola B. Ekanola, "Yorùbá Conception of Peace," in *The Palgrave Handbook of African Philosophy*, ed. Afolayan and Falola, 675.

[16]A. A. Berinyuu, *Pastoral Care to the Sick in Africa* (Frankfurt am Main: Peter Lang, 1988), 5.

[17]J. McDonnell, "Challenging the Euro-Western Epistemological Dominance of Development through African Cosmovision," in *Emerging Perspectives on "African Development,"* ed. George J. Sefa Dei and Paul Banahene Adjei (New York: Peter Lang, 2014), 98–116.

[18]Abiola Irele, Introduction to *African Philosophy: Myth and Reality*, ed. Paulin Hountondji, trans. Henri Evans and Jonathan Rée (Bloomington: Indiana University Press, 1996), 16.

[19]As Nwachukwu wisely observed, "Africans are deeply spiritual." See D. N. Nwachukwu, "Rituals and Symbols in the Healing of Infertility in Africa," in *The Church and Healing: Echoes from Africa*, ed. E. Lartey et al. (Frankfurt am Main: Peter Lang, 1994), 81; Anthony Kanu Ikechukwu, "The Dimensions of African Cosmology," *Filosofia Theoretica: Journal of African Philosophy, Culture and Religion* 2, no. 2 (July–December 2013): 552; Mbiti, *African Religions and Philosophy*, 256.

[20]B. Davidson, "The Motives of Mau," *London Review of Books*, February 24, 1994, 12.

[21]Munamato Chemhuru and Dennis Masaka, "Taboos as Sources of Shona People's Environmental Ethics," *Journal of Sustainable Development in Africa* 12, no. 7 (2010): 123.

[22]Pope Francis, Encyclical Letter *Laudato Si'* (May 24, 2015), 13, 14. Hereinafter referred to as *LS*.

[23]I have used the expression "tedious and careful task" because such an attempt at "reinterpretation and retheologizing" of some elements of an indigenous culture could easily run the risk of cultural appropriation. Christianity's encounter with other cultures should not take the form of cultural apartheid in which cultural elements of a minority group are adopted and twisted out of original context for a disparaging intent. Rather, Christianity respects the context of the cultural elements or practices of an indigenous group and gives them deeper meaning for enhancement in a manner that the indigenous cultures can still embrace as their own while appreciating the deeper context and meaning our Christian theologies suggest.

[24]See Ola Rotimi, *The Gods Are Not to Blame* (Ife: University Press PLC, 1971).

[25]See *LS* 85, 87.

[26]Each community has a day set apart for the land to rest. Based on tradition and customary practice, each community chooses the day to dedicate to the land's rest. For instance, the people of Ejisu observe this day on Sunday, while the people of Bonwire and Kwamo observe it on Wednesday and Friday, respectively.

[27]Margot Kassmann, "Covenant, Praise and Justice in Creation," in *Ecotheology: Voices from South and North*, ed. David Hallman (Geneva: World Council of Churches Publications, 1994), 49.

Decolonizing Ourselves

Looking toward the Gospel and the Margins

Linda Land-Closson

I write this piece for those of us[1] in the Global North committed to working for more just systems and societies. Whether we do this work through our personal lives, in the classroom, from the pulpit, or via nonprofits, we strive to expose and change unjust systems that prevent certain people from thriving. This is necessary work, long and tiring, frustrating, yet sacred work; however, because of personal, occupational, and educational experiences, I argue that we unknowingly and dangerously undermine this important work through a lack of awareness about the anthropology permeating how we live, work, relate, and attempt to create change in the Global North. My argument centers on the assertion that our prominent beliefs and dominant narratives about what it means to be human remain embedded in colonialist[2] ideologies presuming the primacy of the individual, individualized notions of freedom, and protection from suffering.[3] Through our efforts to create justice, we perpetuate this colonialist anthropology and thereby paradoxically contribute to suffering by upholding the ideal of individual freedom, an ideal that carries with it experiences of disconnection and exclusion. Therefore, in order to do the deep and transformative work of justice, we need to develop the awareness, courage, and humility required to decolonize ourselves and our work by seeing the gospel and the margins as beckoning us to interdependence.

Methodology

In part to help concretize the relevance of my argument, I begin my explanation with personal reflection and context. I also begin in this manner to model some of the changes for which I advocate in this essay. By doing so, I aim to subvert the academy's tendency to offer theories unmoored from the realities of the margins and its privileging of prescription over description. Moreover, with this modeling, I strive to embody different, more authentic standards for those of us engaged in justice work. To be clear, these standards ought not to require *more* work—since, of course, few of us have more time to offer—but they will likely require deeper and more courageous work, specifically the work of decolonization, work that is long overdue.

Following my personal reflection, I shift to a more traditional academic methodology to expose the role and impact of a colonized anthropology. To do so, I employ feminist and postcolonial[4] scholarship to identify and interrogate core Global North presumptions about what it means to be human. Through this interrogation, I critique our understanding of independence in order to expose its less-visible experiences of disconnection and exclusion. I then turn toward the margins in hopes of learning different, gospel-based ways of being that invite us out of colonization and into interdependence.

Reflection and Context

Although my interest in many of the questions generating this essay began in graduate school, my sense of frustration and urgency to find answers developed through my role as an adoptive parent.[5] Being an adoptive parent is like being an ethnographic researcher. I participate in the world of parenting, but I am also an observer of this world because many of the parenting techniques, expectations, and, more foundationally, ideologies, seem off the mark. As ethnographers know, this observer's vantage offers a perspective often unavailable to those who are participants only. And this observer's vantage gifts me—as an adoptive mom, a scholar, and an educator—with experiences propelling me to seek anthropologies that authentically represent and support my family.

The dominant parenting narrative in the Global North tends to run along these lines: "Care for your children in ways that create secure attachments and minimize suffering, and then help them develop into strong, self-sufficient, and independent adults you hope will find life partners with whom they will have mutually fulfilling relationships." The first indicator of a problem with this narrative rests in the hope that two independent adults are capable of forming mutually fulfilling relationships without sacrificing their independence. A second, more obscure and complex problem resides in the goal of minimizing suffering.

Every child and every parent struggles deeply, meaningfully, and painfully, and I do not intend to discount or diminish those experiences in what follows. From my perspective as an adoptive mom, however, I argue that the developmental journey of adopted children and the roles of parenting those on that journey differ qualitatively from the dominant narrative, particularly because of the function and misunderstanding of suffering caused by disconnection, as well as our beliefs about independence and interdependence. When life starts with experiences of disconnection caused by abandonment, neglect, abuse, or "simply" stress and chaos, the journey cannot be the same. When the realities of disconnection create gaps in prenatal or early experiences, and when disconnection erases family physical and mental health histories and family trees, the journey is not the same. In short, suffering caused by disconnection becomes an integral part of the developmental and familial journeys as adoptive families meander through relational pain, confusion, and fear. I have yet to find a parenting book up to the entirety of this challenge and instead have found some of the most relevant "parenting" support in the writings of people living in the margins, to which I return later. In the meantime, however, I turn to postcolonial and feminist scholars for critical consideration of the anthropology informing the dominant parenting narrative.

Living through a Colonized Anthropology

In *Interdependence: A Postcolonial Feminist Practical Theology*, HyeRan Kim-Cragg identifies the European Enlightenment as the foundation of the modern notion of self—of the independent individual—and pinpoints colonialism as solidifying the association between this independent individual and freedom.[6] To support this association, she draws on the work of Frantz Fanon: "Fanon argues how European individual freedom was used as a colonial strategy to divide colonized groups. . . . This sugar-coated idea of freedom forms the basis of Europe's pretensions to being a universal standard of culture and civilization while dismissing the culture of the colonized and labeling it as uncivilized."[7] Accordingly, in a colonizer's worldview, independence and individual freedom are equated with power. To be powerful—to be the colonizer—is to be free and independent. Conversely, to be without access to power—to be colonized, oppressed, or marginalized—is to lack freedom and independence. This colonized way of seeing and being functions as a source of suffering in two primary ways: it discredits interdependent and communal ways of being, which are normative for most of humanity, including many in the Global North; and it promotes the denial and dismissal of relational disconnection.

For a more complex understanding of the relationship between our colonized anthropology and suffering, I turn to relational-cultural theory (RCT), a feminist model of psychological development that counters this colonized and prescriptive anthropology in traditional models by offering a descriptive and more inclusive model.

At its core, RCT, founded by Jean Baker Miller and Irene P. Stiver, offers a basic reorientation regarding the purpose of human development. According to traditional, prescriptive—and colonial—models, one exists as an independent, separate self and engages in relationships with other separate selves.[8] In contrast, RCT claims that one develops "the increasing ability to build and enlarge mutually enhancing relationships in which each person can feel an increased sense of well-being through being in touch with others and finding ways to act on her or his thoughts and feelings."[9] As Miller and Stiver point out, this understanding represents a paradigm shift in the focus of development from "static states of the individual . . . to the dynamics of relationships."[10] Janet Surrey, another RCT theorist, articulates this shift as follows: "*Connection* has replaced *self* as the core element or the locus of the creative energy of development."[11] One does not, RCT argues, develop a self; instead one participates in the development of relationships that provide a context through which one acts with increasing agency and mutuality. In other words, we develop in and through relationship and connection in an interdependent manner.

Yet this interdependent quality of human development struggles for recognition, let alone value, within a colonized anthropology centered on individual freedom. Instead, through binary constructs typical of this anthropology,[12] we discredit interdependence by mislabeling it dependence and associating this "lesser" way of being with life in the margins and the lives of the oppressed.[13] Moreover, instead of recognizing and valuing interdependence, we strive to save ourselves and those in the margins from what we believe are lives of dependence by promoting independence in the form of individual freedom and self-sufficiency. Accordingly, many of our efforts to help others result in discrediting communal and relational ways of being and encouraging people to separate themselves from (or not establish in the first place) interdependent relationships and communities of support. We are colonizing through the imposition of our colonized anthropology. In doing so, we contribute directly to suffering when we attempt to "save" people from the margins by promoting the independence and self-sufficiency characteristic of our privileged lives, feigned though these characteristics may be.

Our colonized anthropology also contributes to suffering in more subtle and complex ways through experiences of relational and communal disconnection. Because of our standard of individual freedom, we tend to misunderstand and misconstrue experiences of disconnection. I return to RCT to explain this misconstruction and how it adds to suffering.

Miller and Stiver define disconnection as "a break in connection accompanied by a sense of being cut off from the other person(s)," and they claim, "Disconnections occur whenever a relationship is not mutually empathic and mutually empowering."[14] Yet even the most empathic and empowering relationships involve experiences of disconnection, of exclusion; none of us exists in a state of uninterrupted connection.

Even though we all experience disconnection, neuroscience

research suggests our nervous systems do not register disconnection as benign. Karen Craddock and Amy Banks credit the
work of Naomi Eisenberger and Matthew Lieberman in support
of their statement that "the same alarm (the dorsal anterior cin-
gulate cortex) [registers] the danger and distress of physical pain
or injury AND social exclusion."[15] In other words, even though
experiences of disconnection or exclusion occur periodically for
all humans, our nervous systems, which exist primarily to support
our chances of survival, are activated by disconnection.

This reality resonates deeply with my experiences as an adoptive mom, and RCT assists me in understanding this dimension
of my family dynamics. Judith Jordan explains, "Disconnections
[resulting from] empathically failing and non-responsive relationships early in life get encoded as relational images which shape our
expectations for current relationships."[16] I suspect that the early
experiences of disconnection for my children were profound and
threatening enough that their alarm systems are more finely tuned
and more reactive to disconnection than is typical. And yet I do
not suspect that their alarm systems operate *differently* from those
of us without early relational trauma. Perhaps the same alarm
system, when triggered by disconnection or exclusion, screams at
a few, while only whispering to most of us. Perhaps most of our
alarm systems only whisper because our colonized anthropology
suppresses, or tells us to ignore, the much louder responses. What
if my children's more extreme responses to disconnection might
function as a wake-up call to those of us who dismiss (or do not
even hear) the whispers?

Living with goals of independence and self-sufficiency necessitates and normalizes experiences of disconnection. This nor-
malization, however, does not undo the reality that experiences
of disconnection result in "real, demonstrable neurobiological
pain,"[17] so our colonized anthropology of independence brings
with it pain and suffering caused by disconnection. Yet since our
anthropology continues to demand independence and disconnection, we must downplay or ignore this suffering enough to
continue striving for self-sufficiency; we must experience disconnection as normal and desirable to quiet our alarm systems.

It seems we have found ourselves in a self-perpetuating loop
of independence leading to feelings of disconnection, which lead

to suffering, which then necessitates the suppression of suffering in support of the ideology of independence and freedom, which requires disconnection. In other words, through our desire to minimize suffering caused by disconnection, we live out our ideals of independence and self-sufficiency in a manner that both feeds off and creates suffering caused by disconnection. Moreover, by living as independently as possible, we normalize and avoid small disconnections and deprive ourselves of opportunities to reconnect, to learn, and to grow relationally. We are allowing our relational muscles to atrophy.

According to Kim-Cragg, these ways of being are not only problematic but are also the exception, especially in a global context. Through her discussion of various marginalized and vulnerable populations—people with disabilities, queer people, children, members of faith communities other than Christianity, immigrants, and animals—Kim-Cragg demonstrates that our colonized anthropology belies the experiences of most living beings. In other words, our colonized anthropology, with its expectation of independence, freedom, and the protection from suffering, is not experientially normative and, I argue, is not sustainable as a way of life. Therefore, we need to begin looking critically at this anthropology and stop assuming its universal normativity and desirability. Concomitantly, we need to consider openly other ways of being.

To convey the importance of opening ourselves to other anthropologies, I turn to Audre Lorde's metaphor of the Master's tools.[18] In 1984 Lorde called out feminists within the academy for a lack of inclusion and interdependence in their efforts to create change in higher education. Specifically, she accused feminists of retaining certain patriarchal practices in the academy and thereby perpetuating the exclusion of people of color and members of the LGBTQ community. Lorde coined the phrase "Master's tools" as a metaphor for strategies of oppression such as racism, homophobia, and independence, asserting that feminists were using these tools of the Master while attempting change. Of particular importance for my argument is her critique of the refusal among feminists to draw on interdependent ways of being that were more typical among people of color and members of the LGBTQ community.

Thirty-five years later, none of us has a valid excuse for our reluctance to respond to Lorde's call, except perhaps that we are attempting to dismantle colonial structures with colonized ways of being. We cannot undo or unlearn a colonized anthropology of independence by maintaining the expectations of independence and the avoidance of suffering caused by disconnection. We have to learn how to be human differently, yet we cannot teach this to ourselves. Therefore, an important first step requires that we *see* differently in order to open our eyes to the teachers in our midst; we need to lose the Master's lens and gaze at what and who is in front of us with new, humble, and courageous eyes.

Looking toward the Gospel and the Margins

In *Galilean Journey*,[19] Virgilio Elizondo shows us the transformative possibilities of seeing differently. He uses the marginalized lives of Mexican Americans as an impetus to revisit the historico-cultural context and significance of Jesus from a marginalized Galilee. In doing so, Elizondo persistently reminds us that the gospel centers and privileges the marginalized and that the global church ought to do likewise. While most Christians are familiar with this general message, Elizondo's work deepens the integrity and broadens the implications of this message by focusing our sight *through* a marginalized lens.

Specifically, by showing us the journey of a twice-colonized people and their responses to the gospel, Elizondo illustrates how an anthropology centered on a gospel of the margins might lead to profoundly new ways of being. Through the story of rejection that surrounds Mexican Americans, whom Elizondo refers to as *mestizo* (mixed or hybrid),[20] we see another, more communal way of orienting ourselves toward one another within the global church:

> Out of this suffering of rejection should logically come an attitude of fatalism, hatred, resentment, anger, and vengeance. Yet in their Christian faith a *mestizo* people can see another alternative, which alone can break the hellish cycle of violence; because their suffering has been intense, even more intense must be their desire to initiate something

new so that others will not have to suffer what they have
had to suffer. It is the translation of this desire into practice
that ushers in the new creation, the process of liberation
for everyone.[21]

In other words, these rejected people understand the Christian
message as a call to transform their own suffering, which results in part from rejection, into a model for the liberation of
all—including those who rejected them. From the perspective
of a colonized anthropology, rejected people working for the
liberation of oppressors may seem naïve or foolish, particularly
given their continued marginalization. From the perspective of a
gospel-informed anthropology, however, these same people appear humble, selfless, and interdependent.

On Easter Monday of 2019 the Ignatian Solidarity Network
published a reflection written by Jocelyn Sideco that reaffirms
Elizondo's portrayal of the Mexican American response to the
gospel. Sideco directs the Community Service and Social Justice
Office at St. Ignatius College Preparatory in San Francisco, and she
offers the following advice for living into the Easter season: "Live
into vulnerability and follow women of color, not because we
are perfect, but because we have the most desire to thrive within
a society that dismisses us. We are quick to go to the suffering
because we know this all too well. Go there with us. Go there
often. . . . Go to the people who have been most hurt, damaged,
destroyed by society."[22] Sideco calls us to accompany and learn
from—not lead—those who regularly navigate relational suffering. If we accept Sideco's invitation, this profoundly relational
way of being, which resists a colonized anthropology, might assist
us in building relational resilience and muscle that allow us to
continue the work of our own decolonization.

Accepting the models of and invitations toward the margins
will also affect how we attempt to create a more just world, in part
because our sense of who we are and where we fit in the world
will change. Making such foundational changes to our ways of
being will not be easy, for, in Elizondo's words, "The 'law' that
the ways of the powerful . . . are the norm for all is so deeply
engrained that it takes a kind of dying to oneself to be able to
break through the cultural enslavements that keep the dominant

from appreciating the inner beauty, the values, the wisdom, the worth and dignity of a subjugated people."[23] Yet this type of dying—the shedding of our colonized ways of being that contribute to suffering—will free us of the burden of feigned independence and the isolation that accompanies disconnection. Additionally, we will be freed to engage justice work in a manner centered on interdependent and mutually salvific relationships instead of on a desire to save others.

Acknowledging Suffering as We Accompany One Another

Shortly after Jean Vanier's recent death, I listened to Krista Tippett's interview with him and was struck by his claim, "We don't want a God hidden in the dirt or hidden in dirty people or in smelly people or disfigured people, or in those people who are in the refugee camps throughout the world."[24] To this, I would add that we do not want a God hidden in human suffering, *and* we do not want a God who created a world in which suffering exists. In a quixotic manner, those of us in the Global North brandish our colonized ways of being in attempts to ward off (inevitable) suffering. Equally quixotic is our tendency to assume that God blesses our lives of privilege because of and/or through our privilege. This, however, is not what the gospel tells us, as witnessed by Elizondo, Sideco, and Vanier.

Suffering defies logic and reason, the Global North tools for explaining life; we cannot adequately comprehend suffering in a way that justifies the "undeserving" nature of so much pain. What my children are teaching me over and over again, though, is that suffering is very real and that it needs to be acknowledged. Even more than acknowledged, though, suffering needs to be experienced. By avoiding suffering, we are denying ourselves a vital dimension of human existence, a dimension that all but requires that we accompany one another and that we live interdependently with each other and with our God.

Notes

Sections of this article were previously published in Linda Land-Closson, "The Paradox of Privilege: Fr. Gregory Boyle, S.J., Relational-Cultural

Theory, and the Expansion of the Margins," *Jesuit Higher Education: A Journal* 6, no. 2 (2017): article 21. Used with permission.

[1]Unless otherwise specified, when I use first person plural, I am referring to predominantly White people of above average education and economic means in the Global North.

[2]For the purpose of readability and clarity, I use "colonialism" (and its various forms) when discussing both colonialism and neocolonialism. By doing so, I do not intend to ignore or minimize important differences in the tools (e.g., physical violence) used by colonizers and neocolonizers.

[3]I explain and discuss suffering later. For now I need to point out that I am not suggesting all types and levels of suffering are equal or that suffering is noble, only that suffering, particularly suffering caused by disconnection, is a universal human experience.

[4]I use the term "postcolonial" to align myself with the field; however, as this article demonstrates, I also assert we are not living in a postcolonial world.

[5]In using this term, I realize I am not speaking for all families created by adoption.

[6]HyeRan Kim-Cragg, *Interdependence: A Postcolonial Feminist Practical Theology*, with forewords by Mary Elizabeth Moore and Musa W. Dube (Eugene, OR: Pickwick, 2018).

[7]Ibid., 9.

[8]Jean Baker Miller and Irene Pierce Stiver, *The Healing Connection* (Boston: Beacon Press, 1997), 42–62.

[9]Ibid., 47.

[10]Ibid., 53.

[11]Ibid.

[12]See, for example, Kim-Cragg, *Interdependence*.

[13]Although I cannot engage this distinction in the confines of this article, I need to point out that I recognize a clear difference between interdependent and oppressive relationships and communities. Although many in the margins live interdependently, some also, unfortunately, live in oppressive circumstances. For the context of this article, I am limiting my work to the former group because I want to highlight interdependence as an asset and resource.

[14]Miller and Stiver, *Healing Connection*, 51.

[15]Karen Craddock and Amy Banks, "Stopping the Pain of Social Exclusion: Using Relational Neuroscience as an Approach for Social Action," in *Transforming Community: Stories of Connection through the Lens of Relational-Cultural Theory*, ed. Connie Gunderson, Dorothy Graff, and Karen Craddock (Duluth, MN: WholePerson Mental Health and Wellness, 2018), 42. Emphasis in original.

[16]Judith Jordan, Introduction to *Transforming Community*, xii.

[17]Ibid., xiii.

[18]Audre Lorde, *Sister Outsider: Essays and Speeches by Audre Lorde* (Trumansburg, NY: Crossing Press, 1984), 110–13.

[19]Virgilio Elizondo, *Galilean Journey: The Mexican-American Promise* (Maryknoll, NY: Orbis Books, 1983).

[20]Ibid., 5.

[21]Ibid., 99.

[22]Jocelyn Sideco, "Easter Monday/Easter Challenges" Broken Lent 2019 (blog), Ignatian Solidarity Network, April 22, 2019, www.ignatiansolidarity.net.

[23]Elizondo, *Galilean Journey*, 17.

[24]Krista Tippett, host, "Jean Vanier: The Wisdom of Tenderness," *Speaking of Faith* (podcast), December 20, 2007, www.onbeing.org.

Ethnography and Theology in the World Church

Reflecting on Vocation, Liturgy, and Ethics with Selva J. Raj

Introduction to the Panel on Selva J. Raj
Reid B. Locklin

In his now-famous "fundamental theological interpretation" of the Second Vatican Council, Karl Rahner adduced a "genuine caesura" between Hellenistic or European Christianity and what he perceived as an incipient "world Church":[1]

> I venture to affirm that the difference between the historical situation of Jewish Christianity and the situation into which Paul transplanted Christianity as a radically new creation is not greater than the difference between Western culture and the contemporary cultures of all Asia and Africa into which Christianity must inculturate itself if it is now to be, as it has begun to be, genuinely a world Church.[2]

Full realization of the catholicity of the church, on Rahner's reading, entails a process of becoming new, in the world and in its many diverse cultures and contexts.

The influence and prescience of Rahner as a theologian of the council is widely recognized.[3] But Rahner articulated his vision of a "world Church," and the new possibilities opened for it in Asia and Africa, more or less in the abstract. In the three short essays that follow, we explore this claim by focusing on the particular and concrete. Specifically, we engage the ethnographic studies of

Tamil Catholicism by Selva J. Raj (1952–2008). These studies form the core of a recently published collection, titled *Vernacular Catholicism, Vernacular Saints: Selva J. Raj on "Being Catholic the Tamil Way."*[4]

Raj was one of the most important anthropologists of popular Indian Christianity and South Asian religion at the turn of the twenty-first century. A native of Tamil Nadu in India and a Catholic priest for most of his scholarly career, Raj's research focused on popular ritual practices at four Catholic shrines in rural Tamil Nadu, two dedicated to St. Anthony of Padua and two associated with the missionary martyr St. John de Britto. He observed that the popular religiosity at these sites, though ostensibly dedicated to European figures, revealed a much more profound indigenization of Christianity than the self-conscious attempts by priests and other religious elites to sponsor Christian ashrams or inculturate the liturgy. At the shrine of St. Anthony in the coastal village of Uvari, for example, Raj observed a variety of rituals that drew Hindus and Catholics together in a shared pursuit of healing and health. Such rites, he argued, implicated Hindu villagers in distinctively Catholic practices, while also drawing the shrine itself into the distinctively "indigenous worldview and epistemology" of Tamil Hinduism.[5]

Raj was not unique in drawing attention to elements of religious hybridity in popular practice. This is common in ethnographic studies of religion, in North America and Europe no less than in South Asia. What distinguishes Raj's work is his subsequent critique of what he called "institutional indigenization," in favor of the spontaneous, grassroots "popular indigenization" revealed by his ethnographic work.[6] Raj introduced three binaries to differentiate the two forms of indigenization. The first of these is interior and exterior: whereas priests and theologians focus on the cultivation of "interior, enlightened faith," the popular devotions focus on "supernatural manifestations and irruptions into the mundane."[7] A second binary is elite and popular, which Raj also codes as the tension of "center and periphery" in the Tamil church. In many of the rites he studies, for example, religious elites are reduced to a strictly marginal role, as when a priest offers an initial blessing before being "whisked away" to his residence or otherwise excluded from the central ritual performance.[8] A third binary is between conceptualism and embodied practice. Commenting on rituals of pilgrimage, animal sacrifice, and shared commensality at Uvari, Raj notes that such rites directly implicate devotees' bodies in a lived encounter with the "religious other," rather than engaging at an abstract, theoretical level. Thus, popular indigenization also emerges as an authentic form of interreligious exchange, rooted in "the world of rituals rather than the sophisticated world of theological concepts and categories."[9]

Selva J. Raj offers one rich ethnographic window into what might be termed, following Rahner, a "radically new creation" of Catholic faith and life in the context of South Asia. At the same time, perhaps because he died suddenly of a heart attack in 2008, Raj never took a possible next step. That is, he never developed the full consequences of his critique not only for an anthropological understanding of Tamil Catholic practice, but also for a theology of the world church.[10] The following essays attempt to take this next step—or, at least, to offer several explorations that move in the direction of such a next step.

Much of Raj's work focused on transgressing boundaries and crossing borders, and we hope to demonstrate that his significance transgresses the boundaries of South Asia and of the Hindu-Catholic dialogue that was the particular focus of his work. Specifically, each of these essays draws on Raj to complicate or to add nuance to substantive debates in the contemporary North American academy. Annie Selak suggests that, as a scholar, Raj models a distinctive, prophetic vision of the theological vocation. As a theorist, he helps us think more carefully about liturgy, solidarity, and ecclesial communion, as Susan Bigelow Reynolds brings out in her essay. Finally, Mary Beth Yount argues that, as a dialogue partner, Raj intensifies the summons of some US Latinx theologians to situate particularity and place at the heart of our ethical discernment. In every case, we contend, Raj presents an opportunity for contemporary theologians, in any context, to raise new questions—and to deepen old ones—in conversation with the church as a complex, global reality.

Selva J. Raj and the Theological Vocation
Annie Selak

How can I be a theologian in a church marked by scandal? What does it look like to speak to the presence of God in our midst while I am in a church where that presence seems elsewhere, where the abuse of children is silenced to protect the abuser, where white supremacy results in silence regarding racism, where women are marginalized? Over the past year, these questions have become all the more pressing. Although I do not have answers to these questions, I have found in Selva J. Raj a new conversation partner. In this essay, I identify the most salient aspects of Raj's theology and his own unique way of being a scholar. In particular, I look to experience, liminality, and the prophetic role of the theologian.

Experience

Raj's work is permeated with lived experience, both his own and the experience of Hindus and Tamil Catholics. While it is not surprising to have ethnography filled with the experience of others, Raj extends his incorporation of experience into his own life. He routinely draws on his own life, infusing his own stories seamlessly into his work. In his editorial introduction to *Vernacular Catholicism, Vernacular Saints,* Reid Locklin describes this as Raj's "beautiful humanity that characterized his person and permeated his scholarship."[11]

Raj's theological method is not simply an "add experience and stir" approach, where experience is an external category that serves as a point of departure or final touch. Rather, experience permeates his entire scholarly method. In the foreword to the volume, Bindu Madhok explains that themes such as "the crossing of boundaries, the experience of liminality, and communitas were not merely intellectual concepts of great significance in Selva's scholarship; they were lived realities for Selva."[12] This articulates the witness of Raj's work for contemporary theologians: it is a challenge not simply to include experience, but rather, to live and breathe theology in such a way that everything is theological.

This is all the more striking in light of the conversation in the United States about the silencing of parenthood. Emily Oster, an economist who researches parenthood, recently wrote on what she calls "the plague of secret parenting." She explains that "the general sense is that everyone should adopt the polite fiction that after the first several months of leave, the child disappears into a void from which he or she emerges for viewing and discussing only during nonworking hours."[13] Oster draws on anecdotes of women not putting pictures of their children in their office for fear of not being taken seriously enough as a scholar and not getting promoted as a result. In the midst of this and my own experience of growing into my identity as a scholar and a mother and a Catholic who struggles with the failures of the church hierarchy, Raj's unabashed incorporation of his own lived experience is significant. There is not a division for Raj between his scholarly life, his ministerial life, and his life outside of these two things; they are all connected for him. And they are connected because they *must* be connected. There is no theology apart from our own role as a theologian, and there is no "me" as a theologian without "me" as a person. In one scene early in the volume, Raj describes being a teenager and watching his neighbors make offerings of coconuts and limes to the Hindu deity Muniandi, resulting in a stampede of people scrambling for pieces of coconut on a hot afternoon.[14] For him, this experience is as essential a source of theological reflection as would be more traditionally recognized sources.

Raj's example is also an important challenge for the hierarchically arranged academic system that values output above all else, and orders theoretical theology above practical theology, as though there is any theology that is disconnected from practice and practical implications. It is a challenge not only not to hide or quarantine off certain aspects of our lives from the vocation of the theologian, but rather, to integrate our lives in such a fashion that all is theology. This is a prophetic challenge to the theological guild today.

Liminality

Raj's embodiment of liminality furthers his prophetic witness. In a politically and religiously polarized context, such as the

United States in 2019, there is a tendency to gravitate toward absolutes. "My side is right and yours is wrong, and we are divided by X, Y, and Z," or so the thinking goes on issues ranging from clericalism to female altar servers to abortion. Raj's life and work resists such absolutes, inviting us instead into a middle ground of complexity. The "both/and spirit"[15] that Raj discerns as a defining characteristic of Tamil Catholicism in its Hindu context is a spirit that affirms that many truths can be true. He describes it as "the interactive and assimilative spirit—some might say transgressive spirit."[16] This spirit is indeed transgressive, leading us away from our fixed positions of certainty and into the unknown and oftentimes uncomfortable world of experiencing new things.

In his opening essay, titled "Being Catholic the Tamil Way," Raj comments, "The ritual life of Tamil Catholics in South India defies tidy, conventional categories like assimilation, differentiation, and othering, since the complex negotiations characteristic of this lived tradition often involve both assimilation and differentiation."[17] In many ways, Raj's work speaks back to the categories of theology that seek to create defined categories and tidy boxes, offering instead a multitude of images of both/and theology.

We see this, especially, with regard to the shrine of John de Britto in Oriyur, a site to which Raj devotes significant attention. The Oriyur pilgrimage associated with this site transcends many boundaries and identities, bringing together Catholics and Hindus, people from various backgrounds, and people of differing castes. Further, Tamil Catholics experience a type of liminality themselves, because of their "dual identity as Tamils and Catholics . . . existing in a state of permanent liminality."[18] In many ways, it is possible to look at the rituals associated with the Oriyur pilgrimage and see them as rituals that foster liminality and erase distinctions.

At the same time, these rituals can function to bring about a hyperawareness of division. Raj observes, "Although as Catholics these pilgrims are expected to transcend caste and social boundaries and demonstrate their catholicity in faith, Catholic pilgrims at Oriyur are deeply conscious of and committed to caste identities and distinctions."[19] Crossing boundaries and bridging identities can reinscribe differences. This is built into Turnerian theory, which Raj draws on as well as critiques, for a Turnerian theory underscores that "role reversal and status elevation rituals help reinforce hierarchy and order insofar as participants return to their socially defined position with a renewed fervor and commitment to upholding structure."[20] In effect, liminality only goes so far. Yet it is wise to remain with questions surrounding liminality, seeing the benefits it offers while also taking seriously the limitations of this category. Ultimately, the spirit of liminality invites us to relish the mystery of God.

Prophetic Role of the Theologian

Raj's witness to theologians today can be summarized by examining the prophetic role of the theologian. Although Raj may not have articulated this himself, it serves as an overarching theme of his witness for theologians today. Pope Francis's 2013 address to the International Theological Commission underscores the location of the theologian:

> Theologians, then, are "pioneers" . . . in the Church's dialogue with cultures. But being pioneers is important also because sometimes we think they stay back, stay in the barracks. . . . No, they are on the frontier! This dialogue of the Church with cultures is a dialogue at once critical and benevolent, which must foster the reception of the Word of God by people "from every nation, from all tribes and peoples and tongues." (Rev 7:9)[21]

The problematic imagery utilized by Pope Francis notwithstanding, the image of being on the frontiers rather than in the safety of barracks is an important one. Raj lived his life in dialogue with cultures. He lived a both/and approach in the midst of a borderland. In living in the vibrant interchange of cultures and systems, Raj sought to make meaning through new, living exchanges. In this way, he lived into the reality of the prophetic role of the theologian.

Sandra Schneiders notably describes a prophet as "a mediator of the ongoing three-way interaction among God, people, and culture. Because culture is continually developing, the prophetic task will never be completed."[22] The ongoing nature of the prophetic role lends itself to the role of the theologian, for theology cannot be exhausted, due to the continually evolving cultural context and expansive mystery of God. Through this lens, we can see Raj as living into the prophetic role of the theologian. If the prophet articulates meaning in the interaction between God, people, and culture, there may be no better lived example of this than Raj. Raj took seriously each of these categories distinctly, yet also looked to the relationship between God, people, and culture. These were not divergent categories, but all-important ways of entering deeper into the mystery of God.

Being an Authentic, Faithful Witness

I conclude by returning to the questions with which I opened this essay: How can we be theologians in the midst of scandal, in a church that too often fails to live into the Reign of God? Raj does not provide easy answers for these questions, but his life does provide an example of what it looks like to be an authentic, faithful scholar. Raj's witness is one of being present. It is one of thoroughly engaging the world. It is one of living, truly living—an example all the more heartbreaking in the wake of his premature death. It is finding richness in the "both/and," not being satisfied with tidy resolutions, but rejoicing in the complexity of cultural interchange. It is coming to know a God who reveals Godself to us in cultural diversity, a God whose mystery is always deeper than our attempts to neatly categorize.

The witness of Selva Raj for today is an example of how to live a life dedicated to experiencing God revealed in diverse ways. What a prophetic challenge for the world church and for each of us today.

Selva J. Raj, Solidarity, and the Language of Ritual
Susan Bigelow Reynolds

In contexts of profound diversity, is solidarity possible? This is a question that forms an undercurrent through the work of the late ethnographer Selva Raj. It is also one interlaced within my own work in ecclesiology and ethnography. This essay considers Raj's work, and particularly his concept of "dialogue on the ground," as a resource for examining, on a broader scale, the possibilities and limits of ritual in evoking solidarity across difference. I contend, with Raj, that understanding ritual as a kind of dialogue, as the embodied "language" of community, helps recast solidarity in practical terms.

In his analyses of Indian Catholic practice, Raj draws a stark distinction between the institutionalized faith of religious elites and the hybrid, grassroots faith practices of ordinary people. Although I take issue with the adequacy of this binary to capture the complexity of the relationship between "religion from above" and "religion from below," it nevertheless serves to frame with a certain urgency Raj's preferential option for religion as lived. Thus, in the spirit of his work, I begin by emphasizing that the question at the heart of this inquiry is not a "mere" theoretical one. The question of the possibility of solidarity is one that lies at the heart of even our most ordinary attempts at community in a pluralistic society. In this way, I believe it to be a faithful theological extension of Raj's thought.

Ritual and Social Division

Ritual makes space for both the transgression and the affirmation of boundaries, rendering the relationship between ritual and social solidarity a complex one. These competing forces can be illustrated by briefly considering the interplay of unity and difference in three rituals: an American holiday, a Catholic liturgy, and a pilgrimage in Tamil Nadu.

First, let us consider Thanksgiving, that late-autumn ritual of homecoming, kinship, and national identity. Few other well-known rituals possess such a clear, double-edged capacity to gather together and to magnify divisions among those so gathered. The ritual reunion, meal, religious celebrations, sporting events, and various other practices associated with Thanksgiving together evoke a sense of kinship among those immediately present while simultaneously incorporating participants into a larger mythos of American history, identity, and social unity.[23] Yet the Norman Rockwell portrait of familial harmony evoked by traditional portrayals of Thanksgiving cannot escape the influence of social division. The spatial intimacy occasioned by the shared meal heightens the capacity for contentious political and ideological differences to surface—a dynamic so widely acknowledged, particularly after the 2016 presidential election, that it has become a modern trope. Thanksgiving dinner brings people together around a common table, but it does not erase the acute and consequential social divisions that may exist among the people seated there. Nor, for that matter, does it redress the history of conquest and violence that marks the actual historical encounter between European settlers and indigenous peoples. It can temporarily alleviate or even subvert the grip of such divisions, making space for togetherness and empathy. But it can just as easily magnify them.

This double-edged character applies to religious rituals as well as civic ones. Consider next a bilingual Sunday liturgy at a multiethnic parish where bilingual masses and intercultural engagement are not otherwise the norm. Does the celebration help bridge divisions between, say, the parish's Spanish- and English-speaking communities, or does it merely lay bare to parishioners the extent of their separation? Does the mass subvert or reinscribe power asymmetries among ethnic groups? Does the sense of appreciation that the liturgy perhaps evokes for the fellowship of cultural "others" bear fruit in real relationships and changed practices once people leave the four walls of the church?

An analogous sense of ambiguity is observable in Selva Raj's account of pilgrimage practices among Catholic and Hindu worshippers at the shrine of the Jesuit martyr Saint John de Britto at Oriyur. The classic ritual theory of Victor and Edith Turner serves as a key conceptual framework in many of Raj's writings, a framework that his conclusions both affirm and critique. In their analysis of Christian pilgrimage, the Turners describe the relationship between ritual liminality and what they term *communitas*. In the liminal, in-between state, social boundaries are temporarily transgressed, upended, and even reversed. This boundary transgression creates the conditions for *communitas*, a strong feeling of egalitarian kinship and unity across once unbreachable divisions. In the case of a pilgrimage, this dissolution of social boundaries is felt both during the ritual journey and at the destination shrine.[24]

Yet among pilgrims to Oriyur, as Raj observes and Annie Selak has discussed briefly above, social divisions and caste boundaries are *not* transcended, but rather reinforced. Both the particularities of the pilgrimage journey and the social dynamics at the shrine itself reinscribe rather than defy familial, village, and caste differences.[25] Framed in positive terms, when it comes to class and caste, the pilgrimage more readily promotes intragroup bonding than intergroup bonding. Any chance transcendence of social boundaries is temporary at best and does not carry over in any meaningful way beyond the ritual itself. Raj acerbically terms this superficial solidarity "cocktail *communitas.*"[26]

However, other boundaries *are* transgressed during the Oriyur pilgrimage, and quite meaningfully. Of particular note are the religious boundaries between Catholics and Hindus. This crossing occurs in the fluid and mutual borrowing of religious symbols and practices among members of these two religious groups. Most vitally, it occurs in the transposition of the life of Saint John de Britto himself into a Hindu cultural and devotional vernacular, giving the Jesuit martyr currency as a powerful holy figure and healer for Tamil Catholics and Hindus alike.[27] Unlike the non-transgression of caste distinctions, the ritual transgression of religious boundaries *does* shape devotees' lives, relationships, and faith practices well beyond the space and time of the pilgrimage. This devotional sharing enables Tamil Catholics to exist as both Tamil and Catholic in a religiously pluralistic society.

As these three cases demonstrate, ritual practice is not insulated from social reality or from the complex multiplicity of identities that participants carry with them into the ritual space. In considering the bridge-building potential of ritual, then, solidarity should be understood not as a feeling but as a practice, a kind of ongoing project. In this way, it should be distinguished from *communitas*. While the experience of *communitas* may serve in some cases to evoke a kind of solidarity, within the Turners' theoretical framework it functions ultimately to maintain social equilibrium after the ritual has concluded rather than as a catalyst for the renegotiation of power relationships. It is the latter—the reimagination and sustained transformation of the way in which power circulates among different groups and individuals within a society—that the notion of solidarity seeks and demands. Each of the above examples, and Raj's account of the Oriyur pilgrimage in particular, prompts attention to the multiplicity of boundaries— social, ideological, religious, economic, cultural, ethnic—present in any situation of joining, and thus the inevitable incompleteness of the solidaristic project. At the same time, acknowledging this ambiguity compels us to attend more patiently and perhaps creatively to the embodied intricacies and dialogical form of ritual practice in contexts of difference.

"Dialogue on the Ground"

Given ritual's double-edged capacity to unite and divide, how do we understand the role that it plays in the work of forging solidarity across difference? Theologically, Raj's conclusions offer a practical rebuke of certain trajectories of thought (postliberal and otherwise) that regard the sacraments, and particularly the Eucharist, as efficacious social equalizers and the church as a unified counterculture.[28] There is an unfortunate tendency among ecclesiologists to idealize the unitive aspect of sacramental practice, and thus to overstate its potential for fostering social communion in local communities. A more robust consideration of insights from the fields of ethnography and ritual studies would help theologians discern the boundary crossing that ritual (including liturgical and sacramental ritual) occasions without succumbing to ahistorical idealism or theological fantasy-fulfillment. The remainder of my essay applies Raj's concept of "dialogue on the ground" toward this task.

Raj defines "dialogue on the ground" as the "intimate, subtle, and spontaneous ritual exchange and dialogue between ordinary Hindus and Catholics occurring in the arena of popular piety and rituals at the grassroots level—often in opposition to institutional norms and directives."[29] He looks critically upon top-down models of dialogue facilitated by those whom he terms religious elites. These "contrived institutional initiatives"[30] privilege religions' texts and written theologies, and as such often remain mere intellectual exercises, divorced from the lived realities, acute concerns, and faith practices of lay people. Within this exclusive, elite-driven paradigm, dialogue occurs primarily through verbal forms of communication, requiring linguistic sophistication and often necessitating translation, making the process stilted and halting. In contrast to modes of dialogue from above, Raj argues that ritual, particularly grassroots popular ritual, creates space for an organic, evolving sort of dialogue-in-action. For Raj, the everyday ritual exchange that occurs among Catholics and Hindus is the site of a fluid and authentic crossing of boundaries precipitated by unsystematic, embodied acts of cooking together, practicing ritual hospitality, and sharing religious objects and saints and stories.

I wish to note two dimensions of this ritual dialogue. First, what is central in the act of boundary negotiation is not first and foremost the exchange of ideas but rather the exchange of relationships. In other words, ritual is dialogically meaningful insofar as it facilitates the embodied act of encounter. In Raj's analysis, "dialogue on the ground" serves the practical end of enabling neighbors of different faiths to live together peacefully. In my own work, which examines liturgical and ritual practice in highly racially and culturally diverse US Catholic parishes, I contend that ritual is the language of community. In these spaces, ritual—particularly popular ritual—functions as an embodied "script" through which people who may share little else in common are nevertheless able to practice (in the literal sense of the word) the work of community.[31]

Second, the goal of ritual dialogue is not consensus, nor is it the dissolution of difference. Far from consolidating group identity or communicating a unified set of cultural beliefs or values, the embodied "language" of ritual enables us to dwell in ambiguity rather than to resolve or even merely tolerate it. For theologians, understanding the church as a ritualizing community in this sense helps remedy certain ecclesiological misperceptions about the extent to which liturgical participation breaks down social boundaries. The work of communion ecclesiologist J. M. R. Tillard is representative of this position. Eucharistic participation, he contends, "renders null and void any distinction of race, dignity, or social status."[32] Liturgical participation is often portrayed as the momentary in-breaking of an eschatological future in which human difference is rendered temporarily inconsequential, even nonexistent—a sign of the equality of all persons in the eyes of Christ.[33]

By contrast, Raj's case studies of Catholic practice in contexts of pluralism underscore that shared participation in ritual—whether civic, liturgical, and/or popular—does not erase difference, nor should we want it to. Neither does it miraculously alleviate social divisions or power asymmetries. Rather, more pragmatically, it allows participants to construct a shared life with one another, to make their ecclesial home on the borderlines—to "stay liminal." This should not be understood as a dismissal of its power or sacred character. Indeed, at its best, ritual makes space for embodied encounters that transform relational imaginations. It is this transformation that renders solidarity across difference conceivable, that makes possible the sort of conversion to the other that the work of solidarity demands. In this way, Raj's ethnography can open new possibilities for rethinking our lived practices of liturgy, community, and solidarity in North America, no less than in Tamil Nadu.

Privilege, Power Dynamics, and Radical Particularity

Mary Beth Yount

Selva J. Raj's examination of the ritual practices of lay Indian Catholics—with its attendant notions of ritual exchange, dialogue, and the importance of presence and experience—surfaces several important themes. This essay focuses on questions of identity and relationality and draws out some implications in the realms of practical theology and ethics. Several of Raj's points regarding power relations, especially religious hierarchies and status, authority, social location, and the distance between the concerns of the religious elites and the regular folk are put into dialogue with Miguel A. De La Torre's work on the development and application of an *ethics of place*. The result is the beginning of a theory of *radical particularity* in decision-making structures, one that, if implemented further, can help respect indigenous voices and organic practices while avoiding paternalistic and missionary approaches.

Privilege and Identity-Forming Rituals

During the fieldwork of his ethnographic project, Raj is more than an observer or participant-observer; he reflects deeply on ways that specific rituals affect relationships. Of considerable concern is who gets the privilege of determining which identity-forming rituals are performed, honored, and allowed to occur. This should not be determined by the ordained and academic elites, who, according to Raj, prioritize the perpetuation of power and interior adherence to doctrines above the concerns of those at the margins and their embodied practice. Raj maintains that both ordained hierarchical leaders and theologians of the Catholic Church stand at the centers of power structures and, being out of touch with those at the peripheries of such structures, overlook the practical concerns of regular people: "Topics of concern for scholars of Christianity seem to be inversely related to religious concerns of the majority of its practitioners."[34]

Raj's own approach attempts to privilege experience and particularity, such that real folk priorities are made visible. Ethnographic studies can help bridge the gap between official and popular Catholicism, a distance reinforced by "the *ecclesial model*, the attempt by the institutional church to indigenize the official liturgical rites and life."[35] Raj calls us to pay attention to naturally occurring, organic beliefs, rituals, and identities rather than impute official teachings and liturgies, "developed by liberal theologians and mandated and imposed on the laity by ecclesiastical authorities, frequently amid protest and under duress."[36]

Power Dynamics and Boundary Crossing

Much more than merely advocating for what is commonly called a *bottom-up* rather than a *top-down* approach to official church teaching and practices, Raj examines questions of identity, power, and boundary-crossing. Asserting well-taken points on the necessity of examining particularity and lived experience, he attempts to avoid reinforcing underexamined assumptions about folk Hinduism and indigenous traditions, the practitioners, and the community members. He references—although perhaps not often enough—his privilege as an ethnographer and its impact on his experience. The important work of vernacular Catholicism can be seen as a *rupture* or as a *combining*, or both. Rituals, he insists, can help rearrange set boundaries and foster multiple layers of belonging, as well as bridging and affirming differences.

He does, however, highlight that not all rituals are transgressive, as some actually uphold preferred power narratives.[37] His work on ritual as interreligious and intercultural dialogue is an example of the positive. Transgressive rituals can upend power structures, although resistance to this can be strong. For example, when clerical leaders are preoccupied with power and laity concern themselves with the efficacious—thus developing and participating in rituals that address mundane concerns—a priest who supports inclusive rather than exclusive and power-preserving rituals could have such support dismissed by leadership as a gap in the spiritual formation of that priest.

Challenging Missionary and Paternalistic Approaches

Allowing for grassroots ritual practices to emerge among the practitioners of the Catholic traditions, often called "vernacular Catholics" by Raj, can help mitigate the perpetuation of power structures by those in authority. It can also allow for the organic development of Catholic identity and for its emergence in all of its fluidity with cultural and other aspects interwoven throughout. Raj points to grassroots religious identities "in sharp contrast to one framed—some might say contrived—by the religious elite."[38] He details situations such as miraculous healings at a shrine that, not having been mediated or approved by institutional and academic authorities, bring challenges to those authorities. For Raj, "the locus for dialogue is the world of rituals rather than the world of theological concepts and categories."[39]

Top-down imputations of identity-forming practices combined with missionary motivations can be destructive in many ways. Raj details examples of institutional inculturation within the establishment that can become offensive cultural appropriation; he calls it a form of "indigenization from above"[40] when clerics become involved in inculturation and it becomes cultural appropriation. He notes that "many orthodox Hindus resent and protest the contrived Catholic appropriation of symbols, rituals, myths, and institutions from Sanskritic Hinduism," but they demonstrate no such discomfort with "spontaneous appropriation by the Catholic laity of symbols and practices from popular Hinduism."[41]

Contexts that allow for a fluid Catholic identity, Raj continues, can help overcome—or begin to overcome—missionary and paternalistic approaches, cultural appropriation, and conquest discourse and allow for an understanding that religions might have commonalities and beliefs that people can appreciate across boundaries. Raj's friend and peer anthropologist Eliza Kent, discussing the impact of his work on multi- and interreligious approaches of lay Indian Catholicism, comments that it

> unsettles those who hold the modernist view of religion dominant in the higher reaches of ecclesiastical hierarchy, according to which religions are coherent, internally consistent "belief systems" with clear boundaries that distinguish them from other religions. According to this view of religions as mutually exclusive wholes, one can only properly adhere to one of them at a time.[42]

Place and Transformation

Selva J. Raj makes clear the significant attitudinal, behavioral, relational, and perspectival shifts, both permanent and substantive, that rituals can bring about. Ritual can help militate against unjust structures and slowly transform them, or, in the negative case, uphold and perpetuate them. Raj's notions of practice and presence can assist in addressing some of the struggles and tensions between the center and the periphery, between "elites" and regular folk. The positions of prominent ethicist Miguel De La Torre can help extend Raj's thought to consider the integration of ethics of place and the scholar-activist.

These two thinkers, Raj and De La Torre, are natural complements for each other because they raise similar issues and solutions. Raj spends more time discussing religious power structures than he does the politico-social structures that are De La Torre's main concern, but both advocate for particularity as an antidote to (official and scholastic) oppressive and out-of-touch centers of power. Both write about the importance of allowing grassroots development and of *being present*. De La Torre takes this so far as to say that without being actually, physically present at the site of injustice one is not an ethicist ("An ethics of place is what makes me an ethicist") or, at the very least, that those not physically present cannot be *relevant* ethicists. "The only hope that an ethicist can have of their work holding relevance among those who structurally are suffering," he writes, "is to be present."[43]

In De La Torre's ethical methodology, as expressed in his *ethics of place*, orthodoxy should flow from orthopraxis. Traditionally, ethics has been seen as beginning with ethical contemplation, which leads to a truth claim or theory, revealing the morally correct course of action. In alignment with Raj, De La Torre rejects such claims, saying that everything must begin with practice. Even case studies, De La Torre says, are insufficient and "useless to those residing on the margins of society" because the case study approach creates "spectator-type ethics,"[44] which, he asserts, is also true of doctrine. Later in the work, he refers to a "church that believes—not due to its orthodoxy but because of its orthopraxis."[45]

Radical Particularity

De La Torre's ethics of place is helpful because it insists on the correspondence of social location to physical location, the idea that being physically present with the marginalized allows him "to radically be in solidarity with those on the margins."[46] But he takes this a step further to insist that ethics *requires* physical solidarity. If this definition were to become operative for ethics, and were extended to decision-making situations that are otherwise removed from those whom the decisions affect, it could be revolutionary for the Catholic Church. If we take De La Torre's ethics of place, with its emphasis on listening (in person) to the wisdom of those at the periphery, on respecting indigenous and organic peoples, cultures, and beliefs, and on identifying and challenging unjust structures, and join these to Raj's perspective of letting ritual unfold, cross boundaries, and develop organically, the impact on current practices could be significant.

A risk for even theologizing about these topics is that doing so might reinforce the notion that official stamps of approval by ordained magisterial leaders need to be in place for communal rituals and worship to be accomplished. Such a threat militates against part of what Raj is trying to accomplish: the recognition that the organic development of liturgies and identities, especially those at the peripheries, should itself be empowered. If the ritual scholars, the liturgists, the theologians, and the ordained hierarchical leaders—the rule-makers—spent time worshipping and living with the populations they study and to whom they dictate liturgical and other rules, it could help transform the power structure. In fact, it might even affect who gets to be a decision-maker.

Such an expansion of ethics of place could be termed "radical particularity." The requirement of presence not only prevents the claiming of social location minus actual presence, but it also helps enact decision-making at the most local level possible, a principle for which Raj, De La Torre, and many others advocate. According to De La Torre, this location or space does not just represent a context, but is an actual physical place where bodies are located. This would be the space where the decision-makers, whether discerning ritual and liturgical rules or economic impacts, should also be. In this respect, the processes that Raj discerns in the organic unfolding of ritual might provide valuable models for ethical and ecclesial decision-making more broadly, in the church and in the world.

Notes

[1]Karl Rahner, SJ, "Towards a Fundamental Theological Interpretation of Vatican II," *Theological Studies* 40 (1979): 716–27, esp. 720–24.

[2]Ibid., 723.

[3]See, for example, Declan Marmion, "Karl Rahner, Vatican II, and the Shape of the Church," *Theological Studies* 78 (2017): 25–48.

[4]Reid B. Locklin, ed., *Vernacular Catholicism, Vernacular Saints: Selva J. Raj on "Being Catholic the Tamil Way"* (Albany: State University of New York Press, 2017).

[5]Ibid., 127–28.

[6]Ibid., 29–44.

[7]Ibid., 131–32.

[8]Ibid., 147.

[9]Ibid., 190.

[10]Francis X. Clooney brought this point out effectively in his review of *Vernacular Catholicism* in *Horizons* 44 (2017): 538–40.

[11]Locklin, *Vernacular Catholicism*, xxii.

[12]Ibid., xvi.

[13]Emily Oster, "End the Plague of Secret Parenting," *Atlantic*, May 21, 2019, www.theatlantic.com.

[14]Locklin, *Vernacular Catholicism*, 1–2.

[15]Ibid., 2.

[16]Ibid.

[17]Ibid., 12.

[18]Ibid., 107–8.

[19]Ibid., 10.

[20]Ibid., 187.

[21]"Address of Pope Francis to Members of the International Theological Commission," December 6, 2013, w2.vatican.va.

[22]Sandra Marie Schneiders, *With Oil in Their Lamps: Faith, Feminism and the Future* (New York: Paulist Press, 2000), 96.

[23]On Thanksgiving as ritual, see Janet Siskind, "The Invention of Thanksgiving: A Ritual of American Nationality," *Critique of Anthropology* 12, no. 2 (1992): 167–91; and Elizabeth Pleck, "The Making of the Domestic Occasion: The History of Thanksgiving in the United States," *Journal of Social History* (1999): 773–89. See also the relatively more superficial survey analysis of Orrin E. Klapp, "Ritual and Family Solidarity," *Social Forces* 37, no. 3 (1959): 212–14.

[24]Victor Turner and Edith Turner, *Image and Pilgrimage in Christian Culture*, rev. ed. (1978; New York: Columbia University Press, 2011). See also Victor Turner, *The Ritual Process: Structure and Anti-Structure* (New York: Routledge, 1969); and Edith Turner, *Communitas: The Anthropology of Collective Joy* (New York: Palgrave Macmillan, 2012).

[25]Selva J. Raj, "Transgressing Boundaries, Transcending Turner," in Locklin, *Vernacular Catholicism*, 109.

[26]Ibid., 110.

[27]Ibid., 108.

[28]The political theology of William Cavanaugh is representative of both positions. See Cavanaugh, *Migrations of the Holy: God, State, and the Political Meaning of the Church* (Grand Rapids, MI: Eerdmans, 2011); *Torture and Eucharist: Theology, Politics, and the Body of Christ* (Malden, MA: Blackwell, 1998); and "Church," in *The Blackwell Companion to Political Theology* (Malden, MA: Blackwell, 2004), 393–406.

[29]Raj, "Dialogue 'On the Ground,'" in Locklin, *Vernacular Catholicism*, 177.

[30]Ibid.

[31]In this, I am compelled by the idea, elaborated by Adam Seligman et al., of ritual as subjunctive action, "the creation of an order as if it were truly the case." Adam Seligman, Robert P. Weller, Bennett Simon, and Michael J. Puett, *Ritual and Its Consequences: An Essay on the Limits of Sincerity* (New York: Oxford University Press, 2008), 20.

[32]Jean-Marie Roger Tillard, *Flesh of the Church, Flesh of Christ: At the*

Source of the Ecclesiology of Communion (Collegeville, MN: Liturgical Press, 2001), 68.

[33]There is, of course, a deeper tension to be identified in the implicit equation of equality with uniformity, the analysis of which lies beyond the scope of this essay.

[34]Written by Raj in an unpublished book proposal as quoted in Locklin, *Vernacular Catholicism*, xvii.

[35]Ibid., 33.

[36]Ibid. A more critical interrogation of Raj's assumptions about the collaboration of, and shared power between, academic theologians and ordained hierarchical leaders is beyond the scope of this essay. Suffice it to note here that Raj is not a theologian and that the assertion conveyed in this quotation, and elsewhere in his work, is at least arguable.

[37]See ibid., 186–87, for details.

[38]Ibid., 3.

[39]Ibid., 43.

[40]Ibid., 31.

[41]Ibid., 42.

[42]Ibid., 221.

[43]Miguel A. De La Torre, *The US Immigration Crisis: Toward an Ethics of Place* (Eugene, OR: Cascade Books, 2016), xx. A thorough treatment of De La Torre's approach cannot be adequately undertaken here, but I have raised several critical questions in a review for the American Academy of Religion's *Reading Religion* at http://readingreligion.org.

[44]De La Torre, *US Immigration Crisis*, xvii.

[45]Ibid., 111.

[46]Ibid., xx.

In Closing, Hope

You answer us with awesome deeds of justice,
O God our savior,
The hope of all the ends of the earth
and of those far off across the sea.
You are robed in power,
you set up the mountains by your might.
You still the roaring of the seas,
the roaring of their waves,
the tumult of the peoples.
Distant peoples stand in awe of your marvels;
the places of morning and evening you make resound
   with joy.
You visit the earth and water it,
make it abundantly fertile.
God's stream is filled with water;
you supply their grain.
Thus do you prepare it:
you drench its plowed furrows,
and level its ridges.
With showers you keep it soft,
blessing its young sprouts.
You adorn the year with your bounty;
your paths drip with fruitful rain.
The meadows of the wilderness also drip;
the hills are robed with joy.
The pastures are clothed with flocks,
the valleys blanketed with grain;
they cheer and sing for joy.
(Ps 65:6–14, NAB)

Contributors

Gregory Aabaa is a Dominican priest from Ghana. A young African scholar, he holds a master's degree in theology from Duquesne University. His research interests include African religious studies, history of Christian spirituality, environmental ethics, and ecological theology. He is currently an associate pastor of St. Mary's Catholic Church, Ejisu, Ghana.

Maria Clara Lucchetti Bingemer, a noted Brazilian theologian and full professor at the Pontifical Catholic University of Rio de Janeiro, completed her PhD in systematic theology at the Pontifical Gregorian University in Rome, and later spent a year in postdoctoral work at the Catholic University of Leuven, Belgium. The former dean of the Center of Theology and Human Sciences at her university, she now holds the Brazilian Fulbright Distinguished Chair in Democracy and Human Development in the department of theology. She has published widely and in many languages, on systematic theology, faith and culture, mysticism, and in particular on Latin American and liberation theology.

James Dechant is a doctoral candidate in systematic theology at Fordham University. His research interests lie primarily in ecological theology and hermeneutics. Recently, his reading has focused on how doctrines of creation shape our relationship with the earth. With a background in teaching, he is also dedicated to theological pedagogy.

Wilson Angelo Espiritu is a faculty member of the Ateneo de Manila University. He is a doctoral candidate in theology at the Katholieke Universiteit (KU) Leuven, where he is a recipient of the Global Minds Scholarship and a member of the research group Fundamental and Political Theology and the Center for Liberation Theology.

Michael L. Hahn received a PhD in theology and education from Boston College in 2019. His research focuses on the intersection of ecclesiology and pastoral theology, including the ecclesial practice of synodality as it has emerged in the teaching of Pope Francis.

Stewart L. Heatwole, who holds a master of theological studies degree from Boston College School of Theology and Ministry, is a high school theology teacher at St. Agnes Academy in Houston, Texas. He is interested in the shaping of the secondary theological curriculum with a particular focus on issues of race, gender, and wealth inequality.

Stan Chu Ilo is a research professor of world Christianity and African studies at the Center for World Catholicism and Intercultural Theology, DePaul University, Chicago, where he coordinates the African Catholicism Project. He is the 2019/2020 Alan Richardson Fellow at the Department of Theology and Religion, Durham University, UK. He is the author of *A Poor and Merciful Church: The Illuminative Ecclesiology of Pope Francis* (Orbis), and the editor of the *Handbook of African Catholicism*, forthcoming from University of Notre Dame Press.

Tracey Lamont is an assistant professor of religious education at the Loyola Institute for Ministry at Loyola University, New Orleans. She earned her MA and PhD in religion and religious education from Fordham University and specializes in youth and young adult ministry and religious education, shaped by her vision of education as a prophetic act aimed at the transformation of society.

Linda Land-Closson is an assistant professor in the Peace and Justice Studies Department at Regis University in Denver, CO. She received her PhD from the Joint PhD Program of the University of Denver and Iliff School of Theology in religious and psychological studies.

Jane E. Linahan holds a PhD in religious studies from Marquette University. She is an associate professor and Director of Religious Studies and Philosophy and of the Master of Arts in Pastoral Ministry Program at Madonna University in Livonia, Michigan. She has contributed articles on the theology of kenosis and the Holy Spirit to past CTS annual volumes.

Reid B. Locklin is an associate professor of Christianity and the Intellectual Tradition at the University of Toronto, a joint appointment with St. Michael's College and the Department for the Study of Religion. His research focuses on issues in comparative theology and Hindu-Christian studies, particularly the engagement between Christian thought and Advaita Vedānta.

Shalini Mulackal, PBVM, is a Presentation Sister and professor of systematic theology at Vidyajyoti College of Theology, Delhi. She is a member of the Indian Theological Association (ITA) and was its first woman president. She is also a member of the Indian Women Theologians Forum (IWTF), Ecclesia of Women of Asia (EWA), and Indian Christian Women's Movement (ICWM). She has published many articles and contributed essays to many books with special emphasis on women's empowerment.

Maureen R. O'Brien is an associate professor of theology at Duquesne University in Pittsburgh, PA. Her research interests focus on practical theology, mission-oriented pedagogy, religious education, and the education of lay ecclesial ministers. In 2014 she co-edited with Susan Yanos *Emerging from the Vineyard* (Fortuity Press), the fruit of collaborative theological reflection and writing by lay ecclesial ministers.

Cyril Orji is a professor of theology at the University of Dayton, Ohio. He specializes in systematic and fundamental theology with particular emphases on Bernard Lonergan, whom he brings into conversation with the American pragmatist and semiotician Charles Sanders Peirce and the German Lutheran theologian Wolfhart Pannenberg. Professor Orji also researches interreligious dialogue and inculturation. His most recent books include *A Science-Theology Rapprochement* (Cambridge Scholars) and *A Semiotic Approach to the Theology of Inculturation* (Pickwick).

Susan Bigelow Reynolds is an assistant professor of Catholic studies at Emory University Candler School of Theology. She holds a PhD and MTS from Boston College and an MEd and BA from the University of Notre Dame. Her work examines lived Catholicism and ecclesiology in contexts of diversity, marginality, and suffering, and has appeared in *New Theology Review,* the 2016 CTS annual volume *Liturgy and Power*, *The Atlantic,* and *America* magazine, among others.

Daniel A. Rober is an advanced lecturer in Catholic studies at Sacred Heart University. He holds a PhD in systematic theology from Fordham University. His first book, *Recognizing the Gift: Toward a Renewed Theology of Nature and Grace*, was published by Fortress Press in 2016.

Paul J. Schutz is an assistant professor of religious studies at Santa Clara University. His research focuses on the relationship between religion and ecology, with an emphasis on how contemporary scientific knowledge grounds and informs humanity's relationship with the natural world and other-than-human creatures. His dissertation offers the first synthesis of the theological writings of Jesuit astronomer William R. Stoeger.

Annie Selak is a doctoral candidate in systematic theology at Boston College. Her research focuses on ecclesiology, practical theology, feminist theology, race and whiteness, Karl Rahner, and interdisciplinary trauma studies. Her dissertation, titled "Towards an Ecclesial Vision in the Shadow of Wounds," is in the area of ecclesiology. Her background is in ministry, particularly with young women and vocational discernment.

John Sniegocki is an associate professor of religious ethics and director of the Peace and Justice Studies program at Xavier University in Cincinnati, Ohio. He is the author of *Catholic Social Teaching and Economic Globalization: The Quest for*

Alternatives (Marquette University Press), as well as numerous journal articles and book chapters on Catholic social teaching, economic justice, food ethics, ecology, the Catholic Worker movement, and Buddhist-Christian dialogue.

Mary Beth Yount is an associate professor of theological studies and director of the PhD in Counselor Education and Supervision with Spiritual and Pastoral Integration at Neumann University. A two-time Catholic Press Association awardee and recipient of a medal from Pope Francis, her work is in media outlets from *Time* magazine to *Rome Reports*. She has published widely in several areas of applied theology and ethics.